C++ Network Programming
Volume 1

The C++ In-Depth Series

Bjarne Stroustrup, Editor

"I have made this letter longer than usual, because I lack the time to make it short."
—BLAISE PASCAL

The advent of the ISO/ANSI C++ standard marked the beginning of a new era for C++ programmers. The standard offers many new facilities and opportunities, but how can a real-world programmer find the time to discover the key nuggets of wisdom within this mass of information? **The C++ In-Depth Series** minimizes learning time and confusion by giving programmers concise, focused guides to specific topics.

Each book in this series presents a single topic, at a technical level appropriate to that topic. The Series' practical approach is designed to lift professionals to their next level of programming skills. Written by experts in the field, these short, in-depth monographs can be read and referenced without the distraction of unrelated material. The books are cross-referenced within the Series, and also reference *The C++ Programming Language* by Bjarne Stroustrup.

As you develop your skills in C++, it becomes increasingly important to separate essential information from hype and glitz, and to find the in-depth content you need in order to grow. The C++ In-Depth Series provides the tools, concepts, techniques, and new approaches to C++ that will give you a critical edge.

Titles in the Series

Accelerated C++: Practical Programming by Example, Andrew Koenig and Barbara E. Moo

Applied C++: Practical Techniques for Building Better Software, Philip Romanik and Amy Muntz

The Boost Graph Library: User Guide and Reference Manual, Jeremy G. Siek, Lie-Quan Lee, and Andrew Lumsdaine

C++ In-Depth Box Set, Bjarne Stroustrup, Andrei Alexandrescu, Andrew Koenig, Barbara E. Moo, Stanley B. Lippman, and Herb Sutter

C++ Network Programming, Volume 1: Mastering Complexity Using ACE and Patterns, Douglas C. Schmidt and Stephen D. Huston

C++ Network Programming, Volume 2: Systematic Reuse with ACE and Frameworks, Douglas C. Schmidt and Stephen D. Huston

Essential C++, Stanley B. Lippman

Exceptional C++: 47 Engineering Puzzles, Programming Problems, and Solutions, Herb Sutter

Modern C++ Design: Generic Programming and Design Patterns Applied, Andrei Alexandrescu

More Exceptional C++: 40 New Engineering Puzzles, Programming Problems, and Solutions, Herb Sutter

C++ Network Programming
Volume 1

Mastering Complexity with ACE and Patterns

Douglas C. Schmidt
Stephen D. Huston

✦✦Addison-Wesley

Boston • San Francisco • New York • Toronto • Montreal
London • Munich • Paris • Madrid
Capetown • Sydney • Tokyo • Singapore • Mexico City

The publisher offers discounts on this book when ordered in quantity for bulk purchases and special sales. For more information, please contact:

U.S. Corporate and Government Sales
(800) 382-3419
corpsales@pearsontechgroup.com

For sales outside of the U.S., please contact:

International Sales
international@pearsontechgroup.com

Visit Addison-Wesley on the Web at www.awprofessional.com

Library of Congress Cataloging-in-Publication Data

Schmidt, Douglas C.
   C++ network programming / Douglas C. Schmidt, Stephen D. Huston.
      p. cm.
   Includes bibliographical references and index.
   Contents: Vol. 1. Mastering complexity with ACE and patterns.
   ISBN 0-201-60464-7 (v. 1 : pbk.)
   1. C++ (Computer program language) 2. Object-oriented programming (Computer
science) 3. Computer networks. I. Huston, Stephen D. II. Title.

QA 76.73.C153 S368 2002
005.2'762-dc21

                                                            2001053345

ISBN 0201604647

Text printed in the United States at Offset Paperback Manufacturers in Laflin, Pennsylvania.

Printing 7 August, 2006.

Contents

List of Figures

Foreword

As I write this foreword I'm traveling through Europe, relying on the excellent European public transportation infrastructure. Being an American, I'm fascinated and amazed by this infrastructure. Wherever I land at an airport I have easy access to trains and buses that are fast, clean, reliable, on time, and perhaps most importantly, going directly to my destination. Departure and arrival announcements are available in multiple languages. Signs and directions are easy to follow, even for non-native speakers like me.

I live and work in the Boston area, and like most Americans I rely almost entirely on my automobile to get from one place to the next. Except for an occasional use of the Boston subway system, I use my car to get around because the public transportation infrastructure is too limited to get me to my destination. Since millions of others in Boston and elsewhere are in the same predicament, our highway infrastructure is now well past the point of coping with the traffic volume. I know I'd be appalled if I knew exactly how much of my life I've wasted sitting in traffic jams.

There are some interesting similarities between networked computing systems and transportation systems, the most significant of these being that the success of both depends on scalable infrastructure. Scalable transportation systems comprise not just obvious infrastructure elements, such as trains and rails or airplanes and airports. They also require scheduling, routing, maintenance, ticketing, and monitoring, for example, all of which must scale along with the physical transportation system itself. Similarly, networked computing requires not only host machines and networks—the physical computing and communication infrastructure—

but also software-based scheduling, routing, dispatching, configuration, versioning, authentication, authorization, and monitoring that allows the networked system to scale as necessary.

An ironic fact about infrastructure is that it's extremely difficult to do well, and yet the more transparent to the user it is, the more successful we consider it to be. Despite the rugged terrain of the Swiss Alps, for example, a few architects, engineers, and builders have applied their expertise to provide an efficient transportation system that millions of people in Switzerland use daily with ease. In fact, the system is so reliable and easy to use that you quickly take it for granted, and it becomes transparent to you. For example, when boarding the Swiss railway your focus is simply on getting from one point to another, not on the machinery used to get you there. Unless you're a tourist, you probably miss the fact that you're traversing a tunnel that took years to design and build, or ascending an incline so steep that the railway includes a cog rail to help the train climb. The rail infrastructure does flawlessly what it's supposed to do, and as a result, you don't even notice it.

This book is about infrastructure software, normally called *middleware*, for networked computing systems. It's called middleware because it's the "waist in the hourglass" that resides above the operating system and networks, but underneath the application. Middleware comes in a wide variety of shapes, sizes, and capabilities, ranging from J2EE application servers, asynchronous messaging systems, and CORBA ORBs to software that monitors sockets for small embedded systems. Middleware must support an ever-wider variety of applications, operating systems, networking protocols, programming languages, and data formats. Without middleware, taming the ever-increasing diversity and heterogeneity in networked computing systems would be tedious, error prone, and expensive.

Despite the variety of types of middleware, and the variety of issues that middleware addresses, different types of middleware tend to use the same patterns and common abstractions to master complexity. If you were to peek inside a scalable and flexible application server, messaging system, or CORBA ORB, for example, you would likely find that they employ similar techniques for tasks such as connection management, concurrency, synchronization, event demultiplexing, event handler dispatching, error logging, and monitoring. Just as the users of the Swiss railways far outnumber those who designed and built it, the number of users of successful middleware far exceeds the number of people who designed and built it. If you design, build, or use middleware, your success depends on knowing, understanding, and applying these common patterns and abstractions.

While many understand the need for scalability and flexibility in middleware, few can provide it as effectively as the ADAPTIVE Communication Environment (ACE) that Doug Schmidt and Steve Huston describe in this book. ACE is a widely used C++ toolkit that captures common patterns and abstractions used in a variety of highly successful middleware and networked applications. ACE has become the basis for many networked computing systems, ranging from real-time avionics applications to CORBA ORBs to mainframe peer-to-peer communication support.

Like all good middleware, ACE hides the complexity of the diverse and heterogeneous environments beneath it. What sets ACE apart from most other infrastructure middleware, however, is that even though it allows for maximum flexibility wherever needed by the application, it doesn't degrade the performance or scalability of the system. Being a long-time middleware architect myself, I know all too well that achieving both performance and flexibility in the same package is hard.

In a way, though, the flexibility and performance aspects of ACE don't surprise me. Due to my long-time association with Doug, I'm well aware that he is a pioneer in this area. The wide variety of scalable, high-performing, and flexible middleware that exists today clearly bears his mark and influence. His teaming with Steve, who's a gifted C++ developer and author whose work on ACE has led to many improvements over the years, has yielded a work that's a "must read" for anyone involved in designing, building, or even using middleware. The increasing pervasiveness of the World Wide Web and of interconnected embedded systems means that the number, scale, and importance of networked computing systems will continue to grow. It's only through understanding the key patterns, techniques, classes, and lessons that Doug and Steve describe in this book that we can hope to supply the middleware infrastructure to make it all transparent, efficient, and reliable.

Steve Vinoski
Chief Architect & Vice President, Platform Technologies
IONA Technologies
September 2001

About This Book

Over the past decade, concurrent object-oriented network programming has emerged as an effective paradigm for developing software applications whose collaborating objects can either be

1. Collocated within one process or computer or
2. Distributed across a set of computers connected by a network, such as an embedded system interconnect, a local area network (LAN), an enterprise intranet, or the Internet.

When objects are distributed, the various entities that constitute these objects must communicate and coordinate with each other effectively. Moreover, they must continue to do so as applications change over their lifetimes. The placement of objects, the available networking infrastructure, and platform concurrency options allow for a level of freedom that's powerful, yet challenging.

When designed properly, concurrent object-oriented network programming capabilities can add a great deal of flexibility to your application options. For instance, in accordance with the requirements and resources available to your projects, you can use

- Real-time, embedded, or handheld systems
- Personal or laptop computers
- An assortment of various-sized UNIX or Linux systems
- "Big iron" mainframes and even supercomputers

You'll likely encounter complex challenges, however, when developing and porting networked applications on multiple operating system (OS) platforms. These complexities appear in the form of incompatible networking protocols or component libraries that have different APIs and semantics on different hardware and software *platforms*, as well as *accidental complexities* introduced by limitations with the native OS interprocess communication (IPC) and concurrency mechanisms themselves. To alleviate these problems, the *ADAPTIVE Communication Environment* (ACE) provides an object-oriented toolkit that runs portably on dozens of hardware and OS platforms, including most versions of Win32 and UNIX, as well as many real-time and embedded operating systems.

Some would have you believe that *de facto* or *de jure* OS standards, such as POSIX, UNIX98, or Win32, are all programmers need to shield their applications from portability challenges. Unfortunately, the adage that "the nice thing about standards is that there are so many to choose from" [Tan96] is even more applicable today than it was a decade ago. There are now dozens of different OS platforms used in commercial, academic, and governmental projects, and the number of permutations grows with each new version and variant.

We've developed many multiplatform, concurrent, and networked systems for the past two decades. We can therefore assure you that OS vendors often choose to implement different standards at different times. Moreover, standards change and evolve. It's likely that you'll work on multiple platforms that implement different standards in different ways at different times. Programming directly to OS APIs therefore yields the following two problems:

1. **It's error-prone** since native OS APIs written in C often lack type-safe, portable, reentrant, and extensible system function interfaces and function libraries. For example, endpoints of communication in the widely used Sockets API (discussed in Chapter 2) are identified via weakly typed integer or pointer I/O handles, which increase the likelihood of subtle programming errors at run-time.

2. **It encourages inadequate design techniques** since many networked applications written using OS APIs are based upon algorithmic design, rather than object-oriented design. Algorithmic design decomposes the structure of an application according to specific functional requirements, which are volatile and likely to evolve over time. This design paradigm therefore yields nonextensible software architectures that can't be customized rapidly to meet changing application requirements [Boo94].

In this age of economic upheaval, deregulation, and stiff global competition, it's becoming prohibitively expensive and time consuming to develop applications entirely from scratch using native OS APIs and algorithmic design techniques.

If you've been developing networked software systems for many years, you may have learned to accept some of these problems as a fact of life. There is a better way, however. In this book, we show how C++ and ACE provide object-oriented capabilities that allow you to avoid many traps and pitfalls, while still leveraging standards—and even certain platform-specific features—whenever possible. Object-oriented designs exhibit greater stability over time than algorithmic designs, which makes them the preferred basis for developing many types of networked applications.

Not surprisingly, there's a price for all this flexibility: you may need to learn some new concepts, methods, patterns, tools, and development techniques. Depending on your background, this learning curve may be trivial or it may initially seem steep. The bottom line, however, is that the object-oriented paradigm can offer you a mature set of techniques that alleviates many challenges of networked application development. This book presents a series of concrete examples to illustrate the object-oriented techniques used to develop and apply the classes in the ACE toolkit. You can use the same techniques and ACE classes to simplify your own applications.

Intended Audience

This book is intended for "hands-on" developers or advanced students interested in understanding the strategies and tactics of concurrent network programming using C++ and object-oriented design. We describe the key design dimensions, patterns, and principles needed to develop flexible and efficient concurrent networked applications quickly and easily. Our numerous C++ code examples reinforce the design concepts and illustrate concretely how to use the core classes in ACE right away. We also take you "behind the scenes" to understand how and why the IPC and concurrency mechanisms in the ACE toolkit are designed the way they are. This material will help to enhance your design skills and to apply C++ and *patterns* more effectively in your own object-oriented networked applications.

This book is not a comprehensive tutorial on object-oriented development, patterns, UML, C++, systems programming, or networking. We therefore assume readers of this book have some familiarity with the following topics:

- **Object-oriented design and programming techniques,** for example, frameworks [Joh97, FJS99b, FJS99a], patterns [GHJV95, BMR+96, SSRB00], modularity [Mey97], information hiding [Par72], and modeling [Boo94]

- **Object-oriented notations and processes,** such as the Unified Modeling Language (UML) [RJB98], eXtreme Programming [Bec00], and the Rational Unified Process (RUP) [JBR99]

- **Fundamental C++ language features,** such as classes, *inheritance, dynamic binding,* and *parameterized types* [Bja00]

- **Core systems programming mechanisms,** such as event demultiplexing, process and thread management, virtual memory, and IPC mechanisms and APIs commonly available on UNIX [Ste98, Ste99, Ste92, Lew95, KSS96, But97] and Win32 [Ric97, Sol98, JO99] platforms

- **Networking terminology and concepts,** such as TCP/IP [Ste93], remote operation invocations [Obj01], and client/server architectures [CS92]

We encourage you to use the extensive bibliography to locate sources of information on topics about which you want to learn more.

This book is also not an ACE programmer's manual; that is, we don't explain every method of every class in ACE. For that level of detail we refer you to the extensive online ACE documentation, generated by Doxygen [Dim01], at `http://ace.ece.uci.edu/Doxygen/` and `http://www.riverace.com/docs/`. Instead, this book focuses on

- The key concepts, patterns, and C++ features that shape the design of successful object-oriented networked applications and middleware and

- The motivation behind, and basic usage of, the most commonly used ACE TCP/IP and concurrency wrapper facade classes

Structure and Content

This book describes how C++ and middleware help address key challenges associated with developing networked applications. We review the core native OS mechanisms available on popular OS platforms and illustrate how C++ and patterns are applied in ACE to encapsulate these mechanisms in class library wrapper facades that improve application portability and robustness. The book's primary application example is a networked logging service that transfers log records from client applications to a logging server over TCP/IP. We use this service as a running example throughout the book to

- Show concretely how C++ and ACE can help achieve efficient, predictable, and scalable networked applications and
- Demonstrate key design and implementation considerations and solutions that will arise when you develop your own concurrent object-oriented networked applications

The book is organized into 11 chapters as follows:

- **Introduction**—Chapter 0 presents an introduction to C++ network programming. It starts by outlining the problem space and presenting the challenges that can arise when applications extend beyond a single thread in a single process. We then introduce a taxonomy of middleware layers and describe how host infrastructure middleware and the ACE toolkit can be applied to address common network programming challenges.
- **Part I**—Chapters 1 through 4 outline communication design alternatives and describe the object-oriented techniques used in ACE to program OS IPC mechanisms effectively. The resulting classes form the basis of the first version of the book's running example, a networked logging service.
- **Part II**—Chapters 5 through 10 outline concurrency design alternatives and describe the object-oriented techniques used in ACE to program OS concurrency mechanisms effectively.

Throughout Parts I and II we present a series of increasingly sophisticated implementations of our networked logging service to illustrate how the ACE IPC and concurrency wrapper facades can be applied in practice.

Appendix A summarizes the class design and implementation principles that underlie the ACE IPC and concurrency wrapper facades. Appendix B explains the inception and open-source evolution of ACE over the past decade and outlines where it's heading in the future. The book concludes with a glossary of technical terms (including the *italicized* terms in this book), an extensive list of references for further research, and a general subject index.

Related Material

This book focuses on resolving complexity using specific C++ features, patterns, and ACE. The second volume in this series—*C++ Network Programming: Systematic Reuse with ACE and Frameworks* [SH]—extends our coverage to include object-oriented network programming frameworks provided by ACE. These frameworks reify common usage patterns of the ACE wrapper facade classes presented in this book to support broader, more extensible levels of systematic reuse. A distinguishing factor between the ACE wrapper facade classes covered in this book and the ACE framework classes covered in Volume 2 is that the ACE wrapper facade classes have few virtual methods, whereas the ACE framework classes have mostly virtual methods.

This book is based on ACE version 5.2, released in October 2001. The ACE software and all the sample applications described in our books are open-source and can be downloaded at `http://ace.ece.uci.edu` and `http://www.riverace.com`. These sites also contain a wealth of other material on ACE, such as tutorials, technical papers, and an overview of other ACE wrapper facades for IPC and synchronization mechanisms that aren't covered in this book. We encourage you to obtain a copy of ACE so you can follow along, see the actual ACE classes and frameworks in complete detail, and run the code examples interactively as you read through the book. Precompiled versions of ACE can also be purchased at a nominal cost from `http://www.riverace.com`.

To learn more about ACE, or to report any errors you find in the book, we recommend you subscribe to the ACE mailing list, `ace-users@cs.wustl.edu`. You can subscribe by sending e-mail to the Majordomo list server at `ace-users-request@cs.wustl.edu`. Include the following command in the body of the e-mail (the subject line is ignored):

```
subscribe ace-users [emailaddress@domain]
```

You must supply `emailaddress@domain` only if your message's `From` address is not the address you wish to subscribe.

Postings to the ACE mailing list are also forwarded to the USENET newsgroup `comp.soft-sys.ace`. Archives of postings to the ACE mailing list are available at `http://groups.yahoo.com/group/ace-users`.

Acknowledgments

Champion reviewing honors go to Christopher Allen, Tomer Amiaz, Alain Decamps, Eric Eide, Don Hinton, Alexander Holler, Susan Liebeskind, Dennis Mancl, Craig Perras, Patrick Rabau, Eamonn Saunders, and Johnny Willemsen, who reviewed the entire book and provided extensive comments that improved its form and content substantially.

Many ACE users worldwide provided feedback on drafts of this book, including Mark Appel, Shahzad Aslam-Mir, Kevin Bailey, Barry Benowitz, Fang Chow, Emmanuel Croze, Yasir Faiz, Gillmer Derge, Iain Hanson, Brad Hoskins, Bob Huston, Christopher Kohlhoff, Serge Kolgan, Daire Lynch, Andy Marchewka, Jeff McNiel, Simon McQueen, Phil Mesnier, Arturo Montes, Vince Mounts, Aaron Nielsen, Jeff Parsons, Pim Philipse, Yaron Pinto, Stephane Pion, Nick Pratt, Paul Rubel, Val Salamakha, Shourya Sarcar, Chris Smith, Leo Stutzmann, Tommy Svensson, Alain Totouom, Roger Tragin, Bruce Trask, Chris Uzdavinis, and Reuven Yagel.

We are indebted to all the members, past and present, of the DOC groups at Washington University, St. Louis and the University of California, Irvine, and the team members at Object Computing Inc. and Riverace Corporation, who developed, refined, and optimized many of the ACE capabilities presented in this book. This group includes Everett Anderson, Alex Arulanthu, Shawn Atkins, John Aughey, Luther Baker, Darrell Brunsch, Don Busch, Chris Cleeland, Angelo Corsaro, Chad Elliot, Sergio Flores-Gaitan, Chris Gill, Pradeep Gore, Andy Gokhale, Priyanka Gontla, Myrna Harbibson, Tim Harrison, Shawn Hannan, John Heitmann, Joe Hoffert, James Hu, Frank Hunleth, Prashant Jain, Vishal Kachroo, Ray Klefstad, Kitty Krishnakumar, Yamuna Krishnamurthy, Michael Kircher, Fred Kuhns, David Levine, Chanaka Liyanaarachchi, Michael Moran, Ebrahim Moshiri, Sumedh Mungee, Bala Natarajan, Ossama Othman, Jeff Parsons, Kirthika Parameswaran, Krish Pathayapura, Irfan Pyarali, Sumita Rao, Carlos O'Ryan, Rich Siebel, Malcolm Spence, Marina Spivak, Naga Surendran, Steve Totten, Bruce Trask, Nanbor Wang, and Seth Widoff.

We also want to thank the thousands of C++ developers from over fifty countries who've contributed to ACE during the past decade. ACE's excellence and success is a testament to the skills and generosity of many talented developers and the forward-looking companies that have had the vision to contribute their work to ACE's open-source code base. Without their support, constant feedback, and encouragement, we never would have written this book. In recognition of the efforts of the ACE open-source community, we maintain a list of all contributors, which is available at http://ace.ece.uci.edu/ACE-members.html.

We are also grateful for the support from colleagues and sponsors of our research on patterns and development of the ACE toolkit, notably the contributions of Ron Akers (Motorola), Steve Bachinsky (SAIC), John Bay (DARPA), Detlef Becker (Siemens), Dave Busigo (DARPA), John Buttitto (Sun), Becky Callison (Boeing), Wei Chiang (Nokia), Joe Cross (Lockheed Martin), Lou DiPalma (Raytheon), Bryan Doerr (Boeing), Karlheinz Dorn (Siemens), Matt Emerson (Escient Convergence Group, Inc.), Sylvester Fernandez (Lockheed Martin), Nikki Ford (DARPA), Andreas Geisler (Siemens), Helen Gill (NSF), Bob Groschadl (Pivotech Systems, Inc.), Jody Hagins (ATD), Andy Harvey (Cisco), Sue Kelly (Sandia National Labs), Gary Koob (DARPA), Petri Koskelainen (Nokia Inc), Sean Landis (Motorola), Patrick Lardieri (Lockheed Martin), Doug Lea (SUNY Oswego), Hikyu Lee (SoftLinx), Joe Loyall (BBN), Mike Masters (NSWC), Ed Mays (U.S. Marine Corps), John Mellby (Raytheon), Jeanette Milos (DARPA), Stan Moyer (Telcordia), Russ Noseworthy (Object Sciences), Dieter Quehl (Siemens), Vijay Raghavan (Vanderbilt U.), Lucie Robillard (U.S. Air Force), Craig Rodrigues (BBN), Rick Schantz (BBN), Steve Shaffer (Kodak), Tom Shields (Raytheon), Dave Sharp (Boeing), Naval Sodha (Ericsson), Paul Stephenson (Ericsson), Tatsuya Suda (UCI), Umar Syyid (Hughes), Janos Sztipanovits (Vanderbilt U.), Gautam Thaker (Lockheed Martin), Lothar Werzinger (Krones), and Don Winter (Boeing).

Very special thanks go to Susan Cooper, our copy editor, for enhancing our written material. In addition, we are grateful for the encouragement and patience of our editor, Debbie Lafferty, our production coordinator, Elizabeth Ryan, the series editor and inventor of C++, Bjarne Stroustrup, and everyone else at Addison-Wesley who made it possible to publish this book.

Finally, we would also like to express our gratitude and indebtedness to the late W. Richard Stevens, the father of network programming literature.

His books brought a previously unknown level of clarity to the art and science of network programming. We endeavor to stand on his virtual shoulders, and extend the understanding that Richard's books brought into the world of object-oriented design and C++ programming.

Steve's Acknowledgments

I would like to thank God, who gave me an enjoyment of computers and networking. I hope He's pleased. To Jane, my wife of 20 years, thank you for loving me and cheering me on every day. I would not have completed this work without your support—you are a blessing. Thank you to the late David N. Drummond, who took a chance on a kid without a degree. And thank you to Doug Schmidt, a scholar and a gentleman, whose insight, enthusiasm, and creativity impress and challenge me daily.

Doug's Acknowledgments

I've been writing this book for over a decade, so it's an enormous thrill (and relief) to see it in print at last! For this, I'm grateful to Steve Huston, Debbie Lafferty, and Bjarne Stroustrup for their immense help and patience in seeing this project through to fruition. I'd also like to thank my wife Sonja for her love and support during the writing of this book—now that it's finished we'll have more time for ballroom dancing! Finally, thanks to my many friends and colleagues at the College of William and Mary; Washington University, St. Louis; University of California, Irvine; DARPA; and Siemens—as well as the thousands of ACE and TAO developers and users worldwide—who have greatly enriched my intellectual and interpersonal life over the past two decades.

Design Challenges, Middleware Solutions, and ACE

CHAPTER SYNOPSIS

This chapter describes the paradigm shift that occurs when transitioning from *stand-alone application architectures* to *networked application architectures*. This shift yields new challenges in two categories: those in the problem space that are oriented to software architecture and design and those in the solution space that are related to software tools and techniques used to implement networked applications. This chapter first presents a domain analysis of design dimensions affecting the former category, and the middleware that is motivated by and applied to the latter category. The chapter then introduces the ACE toolkit and the example networked application that's used to illustrate the solutions throughout this book.

0.1 Challenges of Networked Applications

Most software developers are familiar with stand-alone application architectures, in which a single computer contains all the software components related to the graphical user interface (GUI), application service processing, and persistent data resources. For example, the stand-alone application architecture illustrated in Figure 0.1 consolidates the GUI, service processing, and persistent data resources within a single computer, with all peripherals attached directly. The flow of control in a stand-alone application resides solely on the computer where execution begins.

1

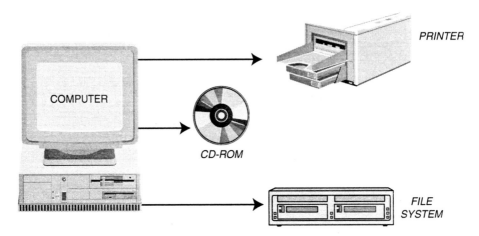

Figure 0.1: **A Stand-alone Application Architecture**

In contrast, networked application architectures divide the application system into *services* that can be shared and reused by multiple applications. To maximize effectiveness and usefulness, services are distributed among multiple computing devices connected by a network, as shown in Figure 0.2. Common network services provided to *clients* in such environments include distributed naming, network file systems, routing table management, logging, printing, e-mail, remote login, file transfer, Web-based e-commerce services, payment processing, customer relationship management, help desk systems, MP3 exchange, streaming media, instant messaging, and community chat rooms.

The networked application architecture shown in Figure 0.2 partitions the interactive GUI, instruction processing, and persistent data resources among a number of independent *hosts* in a network. At run time, the flow of control in a networked application resides on one or more of the hosts. All the system components communicate cooperatively, transferring data and execution control between them as needed. Interoperability between separate components can be achieved as long as compatible communication protocols are used, even if the underlying networks, operating systems, hardware, and programming languages are heterogeneous [HV99]. This delegation of networked application service responsibilities across multiple hosts can yield the following benefits:

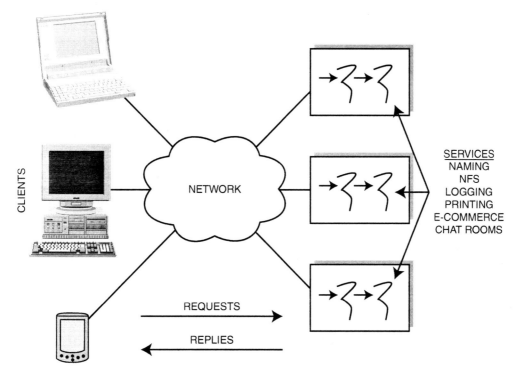

Figure 0.2: **A Common Networked Application Environment**

1. **Enhanced connectivity and collaboration** disseminates information rapidly to more potential users. This connectivity avoids the need for manual information transfer and duplicate entry.
2. **Improved performance and scalability** allows system configurations to be changed readily and robustly to align computing resources with current and forecasted system demand.
3. **Reduced costs** by allowing users and applications to share expensive peripherals and software, such as sophisticated database management systems.

Your job as a developer of networked applications is to understand the services that your applications will provide and the environment(s) available to provide them, and then

1. Design mechanisms that services will use to communicate, both between themselves and with clients.

2. Decide which architectures and service arrangements will make the most effective use of available environments.
3. Implement these solutions using techniques and tools that eliminate complexity and yield correct, extensible, high-performance, low-maintenance software to achieve your business's goals.

This book provides the information and tools you need to excel at these tasks.

Your job will not be easy. Networked applications are often much harder to design, implement, debug, optimize, and monitor than their stand-alone counterparts. You must learn how to resolve the inherent and accidental complexities [Bro87] associated with developing and configuring networked applications. *Inherent complexities* arise from key *domain* challenges that complicate networked application development, including

- Selecting suitable communication mechanisms and designing protocols to use them effectively
- Designing network services that utilize the available computing resources efficiently and reduce future maintenance costs
- Using *concurrency* effectively to achieve predictable, reliable, high performance in your system
- Arranging and configuring services to maximize system availability and flexibility.

Dealing with inherent complexity requires experience and a thorough understanding of the domain itself. There are many design tradeoffs related to these inherent complexity issues that we will investigate in Chapters 1 and 5.

Accidental complexities arise from limitations with tools and techniques used to develop networked application software, including

- The lack of type-safe, portable, and extensible native OS *APIs*
- The widespread use of *algorithmic decomposition*, which makes it unnecessarily hard to maintain and extend networked applications
- The continual rediscovery and reinvention of core networked application concepts and capabilities, which keeps software life-cycle costs unnecessarily high

Networked application developers must understand these challenges and apply techniques to deal with them effectively. Throughout this book we illustrate by example how ACE uses object-oriented techniques and C++ language features to address the accidental complexities outlined above.

0.2 Networked Application Design Dimensions

It's possible to learn programming APIs and interfaces without appreciating the key design dimensions in a domain. In our experience, however, developers with deeper knowledge of networked application domain fundamentals are much better prepared to solve key design, implementation, and performance challenges effectively. We therefore explore the core architectural design dimensions for networked application development first. We focus on servers that support multiple services, or multiple instances of a service, and that collaborate with many clients simultaneously, similar to the networked application environment shown in Figure 0.2.

The design dimensions discussed in this book were identified by a thorough *domain analysis* based on hands-on design and implementation experience with hundreds of production networked applications and systems developed over the past decade. A domain analysis is an inductive, feedback-driven process that examines an application domain systematically to identify its core challenges and design dimensions in order to map them onto effective solution techniques. This process yields the following benefits:

• **It defines a common vocabulary of domain abstractions,** which enables developers to communicate more effectively with each other [Fow97]. In turn, clarifying the vocabulary of the problem space simplifies the mapping onto a suitable set of patterns and software abstractions in the solution space. For example, a common understanding of network protocols, *event* demultiplexing strategies, and concurrency architectures allows us to apply these concepts to our discussions of wrapper facades, as well as to our discussions of ACE frameworks in [SH].

• **It enhances reuse** by separating design considerations into two categories:

1. Those that are specific to particular types of applications and
2. Those that are common to all applications in the domain.

By focusing on common design concerns in a domain, application and *middleware* developers can recognize opportunities for adapting or building reusable software class libraries. When the canonical control flows between these class libraries are factored out and reintegrated, they can form middleware frameworks, such as those in ACE, that can reduce subsequent application development effort significantly. In a mature domain,

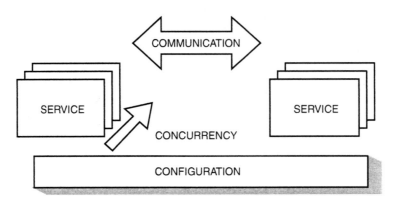

Figure 0.3: **Networked Application Design Dimensions**

application-specific design considerations can be addressed systematically by extending and customizing existing middleware frameworks via object-oriented language features, such as inheritance, dynamic binding, parameterized types, and exceptions.

Within the domain of networked applications, developers are faced with design decisions in each of the four dimensions depicted in Figure 0.3. These design dimensions are concerned mainly with managing inherent complexities. They are therefore largely independent of particular life-cycle processes, design methods and notations, programming languages, operating system platforms, and networking hardware. Each of these design dimensions is composed of a set of relatively independent alternatives. Although mostly orthogonal to each other, changes to one or more dimensions of your networked application can change its "shape" accordingly. Design changes therefore don't occur in isolation. Keep this in mind as you consider the following design dimensions:

1. **Communication dimensions** address the rules, form, and level of abstraction that networked applications use to interact.

2. **Concurrency dimensions** address the policies and mechanisms governing the proper use of processes and threads to represent multiple service instances, as well as how each service instance may use multiple threads internally.

3. **Service dimensions** address key properties of a networked application service, such as the duration and structure of each service instance.

4. **Configuration dimensions** address how networked services are identified and the time at which they are bound together to form complete applications. Configuration dimensions often affect more than one service, as well as the relationships between services.

We examine the first two dimensions in more depth in Chapters 1 and 5, respectively, while the third and fourth are discussed in [SH]. We illustrate the key vocabulary, design trade-offs, and solution abstractions first, followed by the platform capabilities related to each dimension, its associated accidental complexities, and the solutions provided by ACE, which evolved over the past decade in response to these design dimensions. As you'll see, the ACE toolkit uses time-proven object-oriented partitioning, *interface* design, data encapsulation patterns, and C++ features to enable the design dimensions of your networked applications to vary as independently and portably as possible.

0.3 Object-Oriented Middleware Solutions

Some of the most successful techniques and tools devised to address accidental and inherent complexities of networked applications have centered on object-oriented middleware, which helps manage the complexity and heterogeneity in networked applications. Object-oriented middleware provides reusable service/protocol component and framework software that functionally bridges the gap between

1. End-to-end application functional requirements and
2. The lower-level operating systems, networking *protocol stacks*, and hardware devices.

Object-oriented middleware provides capabilities whose qualities are critical to help simplify and coordinate how networked applications are connected and how they interoperate.

0.3.1 Object-Oriented Middleware Layers

Networking protocol stacks, such as TCP/IP [Ste93], can be decomposed into multiple layers, such as the physical, data-link, network, transport, session, presentation, and application layers defined in the OSI reference model [Bla91]. Likewise, object-oriented middleware can be decomposed

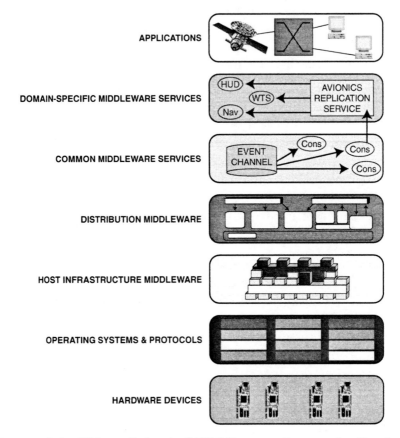

APPLICATIONS

DOMAIN-SPECIFIC MIDDLEWARE SERVICES

COMMON MIDDLEWARE SERVICES

DISTRIBUTION MIDDLEWARE

HOST INFRASTRUCTURE MIDDLEWARE

OPERATING SYSTEMS & PROTOCOLS

HARDWARE DEVICES

Figure 0.4: **Object-Oriented Middleware Layers in Context**

into multiple layers [SS01], as shown in Figure 0.4. A common hierarchy of object-oriented middleware includes the layers described below:

Host infrastructure middleware encapsulates OS concurrency and inter-process communication (IPC) mechanisms to create object-oriented network programming capabilities. These capabilities eliminate many tedious, error-prone, and nonportable activities associated with developing networked applications via native OS APIs, such as Sockets or POSIX threads (Pthreads). Widely used examples of host infrastructure middleware include Java Packages [AGH00] and ACE.

Distribution middleware uses and extends host infrastructure middleware in order to automate common network programming tasks, such as connection and memory management, *marshaling* and *demarshaling*, end-point and request *demultiplexing*, synchronization, and multithreading. Developers who use distribution middleware can program distributed applications much like stand-alone applications, that is, by invoking operations on target objects without concern for their location, language, OS, or hardware [HV99]. At the heart of distribution middleware are *Object Request Brokers* (ORBs), such as COM+ [Box97], Java RMI [Sun98], and *CORBA* [Obj01].

Common middleware services augment distribution middleware by defining higher-level domain-independent services, such as event notification, logging, persistence, security, and recoverable transactions. Whereas distribution middleware focuses largely on managing end-system resources in support of an object-oriented distributed programming model, common middleware services focus on allocating, scheduling, and coordinating various resources throughout a distributed system. Without common middleware services, these end-to-end capabilities would have to be implemented *ad hoc* by each networked application.

Domain-specific middleware services satisfy specific requirements of particular domains, such as telecommunications, e-commerce, health care, process automation, or avionics. Whereas the other object-oriented middleware layers provide broadly reusable "horizontal" mechanisms and services, domain-specific services target vertical markets. From a "commercial off-the-shelf" (COTS) perspective, domain-specific services are the least mature of the middleware layers today. This is due in part to the historical lack of middleware standards needed to provide a stable base upon which to create domain-specific services.

Object-oriented middleware is an important tool for developing networked applications. It provides the following three broad areas of improvement for developing and evolving networked applications:

1. **Strategic focus,** which elevates application developer focus beyond a preoccupation with low-level OS concurrency and networking APIs. A solid grasp of the concepts and capabilities underlying these APIs is foundational to all networked application development. However, middleware helps abstract the details away into higher-level, more easily used artifacts. Without needing to worry as much about low-

level details, developers can focus on more strategic, application-centric concerns.

2. **Effective reuse,** which amortizes software life-cycle effort by leveraging previous development expertise and reifying implementations of key patterns [SSRB00, GHJV95] into reusable middleware frameworks. In the future, most networked applications will be assembled by integrating and scripting domain-specific and common "pluggable" middleware service components, rather than being programmed entirely from scratch [Joh97].

3. **Open standards,** which provide a portable and interoperable set of software artifacts. These artifacts help to direct the focus of developers toward higher-level software application architecture and design concerns, such as interoperable security, layered distributed resource management, and fault tolerance services. An increasingly important role is being played by open and/or standard COTS object-oriented middleware, such as CORBA, Java virtual machines, and ACE, which can be purchased or acquired via open-source means. COTS middleware is particularly important for organizations facing time-to-market pressures and limited software development resources.

Although distribution middleware, common middleware services, and domain-specific middleware services are important topics, they are not treated further in this book for the reasons we explore in the next section. For further coverage of these topics, please see either `http://ace.ece.uci.edu/middleware.html` or *Advanced CORBA Programming with C++* [HV99].

0.3.2   The Benefits of Host Infrastructure Middleware

Host infrastructure middleware is preferred over the higher middleware layers when developers are driven by stringent *quality of service (QoS)* requirements and/or cost containment. It's also a foundational area for advancing the state-of-the-art of middleware. These areas and their rationale are discussed below.

Meeting stringent QoS requirements.   Certain types of applications need access to native OS IPC mechanisms and protocols to meet stringent efficiency and predictability QoS requirements. For example, multimedia applications that require long-duration, bidirectional bytestream communication services are poorly suited to the synchronous request/response paradigm provided by some distribution middleware [NGSY00]. Despite major advances [GS99, POS+00] in optimization technology, many conventional distribution middleware implementations still incur significant throughput and *latency* overhead and lack sufficient hooks to manipulate other QoS-related properties, such as *jitter* and dependability.

In contrast, host infrastructure middleware is often better suited to ensure end-to-end QoS because it allows applications to

- Omit functionality that may not be necessary, such as omitting marshaling and demarshaling in homogeneous environments
- Exert fine-grained control over communication behavior, such as supporting IP multicast transmission and asynchronous I/O and
- Customize networking protocols to optimize network *bandwidth* usage or to substitute shared memory communication in place of loopback network communication

By the end of the decade, we expect research and development (R&D) on distribution middleware and common services will reach a point where its QoS levels rival or exceed that of handwritten host infrastructure middleware and networked applications. In the meantime, however, much production software must be written and deployed. It's within this context that host infrastructure middleware plays such an important role by elevating the level of abstraction at which networked applications are developed without unduly affecting their QoS.

Cost containment. To survive in a globally competitive environment, many organizations are transitioning to object-oriented development processes and methods. In this context, host infrastructure middleware offers powerful and time-proven solutions to help contain the costs of the inherent and accidental complexities outlined in Section 0.1, page 4.

For example, adopting new compilers, development environments, debuggers, and toolkits can be expensive. Training software engineers can be even more expensive due to steep learning curves needed to become proficient with new technologies. Containing these costs is important when embarking on software projects in which new technologies are being evaluated or employed. Host infrastructure middleware can be an effective tool for leveraging existing OS and networking experience, knowledge, and skills while expanding development to new platforms and climbing the learning curve toward more advanced, cost-saving software technologies.

Advancing the state-of-the-practice by improving core knowledge. A solid understanding of host infrastructure middleware helps developers identify higher-level patterns and services so they can become more productive in their own application domains. There are many new technology challenges to be conquered beyond today's method- and message-oriented middleware technologies. Infrastructure middleware provides an important building block for future R&D for the following reasons:

- Developers with a solid grasp of the design challenges and patterns underlying host infrastructure middleware can become proficient with software technology advances more rapidly. They can then catalyze the adoption of more sophisticated middleware capabilities within a team or organization.
- Developers with a thorough understanding of what happens "under the covers" of middleware are better suited to identify new ways of improving their networked applications.

0.4   An Overview of the ACE Toolkit

The *ADAPTIVE Communication Environment* (ACE) is a widely used example of host infrastructure middleware. The ACE library contains ~240,000 lines of C++ code and ~500 classes. The ACE software distribution also contains hundreds of automated regression tests and example applications. ACE is freely available as open-source software and can be downloaded from http://ace.ece.uci.edu/ or http://www.riverace.com.

To separate concerns, reduce complexity, and permit functional subsetting, ACE is designed using a layered architecture [BMR+96], shown in Figure 0.5. The foundation of the ACE toolkit is its combination of OS adaptation *layer* and C++ wrapper facades [SSRB00], which encapsulate core OS concurrent network programming mechanisms. The higher layers of ACE build upon this foundation to provide reusable *frameworks*, networked service components, and standards-based middleware. Together, these middleware layers simplify the creation, composition, configuration, and porting of networked applications without incurring significant performance overhead.

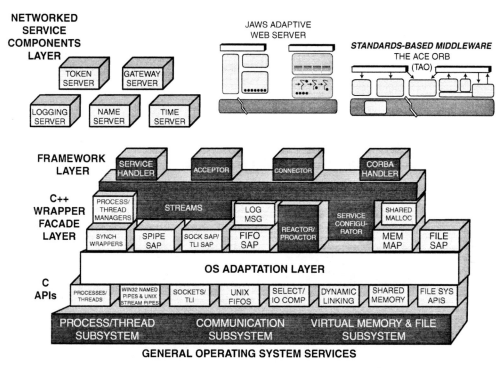

Figure 0.5: **The Layered Architecture of ACE**

This book focuses on the ACE wrapper facades for native OS IPC and concurrency mechanisms. The additional benefits of frameworks and a comprehensive description of the ACE frameworks are described in the second volume of *C++ Network Programming* [SH]. The remainder of this chapter outlines the structure and functionality of the various layers in ACE. Section B.1.4 on page 263 describes the standards-based middleware (TAO [SLM98] and JAWS [HS99]) that's based upon and bundled with ACE.

0.4.1 The ACE OS Adaptation Layer

The ACE OS adaptation layer constitutes approximately 10 percent of ACE (about 27,000 lines of code). It consists of a class called ACE_OS that contains over 500 C++ static methods. These methods encapsulate the native, C-oriented OS APIs that hide platform-specific details and expose a uniform interface to OS mechanisms used by higher ACE layers. The ACE_OS adaptation layer simplifies the portability and maintainability of ACE and ensures that only ACE developers—not applications developers—must understand the arcane platform-specific knowledge underlying the ACE wrapper facades. The abstraction provided by the ACE_OS class enables the use of a single source tree for all the OS platforms shown in Sidebar 1.

Sidebar 1: OS Platforms Supported by ACE

ACE runs on a wide range of operating systems, including:

- PCs, for example, Windows (all 32/64-bit versions), WinCE; Redhat, Debian, and SuSE Linux; and Macintosh OS X;
- Most versions of UNIX, for example, SunOS 4.x and Solaris, SGI IRIX, HP-UX, Digital UNIX (Compaq Tru64), AIX, DG/UX, SCO OpenServer, UnixWare, NetBSD, and FreeBSD;
- Real-time operating systems, for example, VxWorks, OS/9, Chorus, LynxOS, Pharlap TNT, QNX Neutrino and RTP, RTEMS, and pSoS;
- Large enterprise systems, for example, OpenVMS, MVS OpenEdition, Tandem NonStop-UX, and Cray UNICOS.

ACE can be used with all of the major C++ compilers on these platforms. The ACE Web site at http://ace.ece.uci.edu contains a complete, up-to-date list of platforms, along with instructions for downloading and building ACE.

0.4.2 The ACE C++ Wrapper Facade Layer

A wrapper facade consists of one or more classes that encapsulate functions and data within a type-safe object-oriented interface [SSRB00]. The ACE C++ wrapper facade layer resides atop its OS adaptation layer and provides largely the same functionality, as shown in Figure 0.5. Packaging this functionality as C++ classes, rather than stand-alone C functions, significantly reduces the effort required to learn and use ACE correctly. The ACE wrapper facades are designed carefully to minimize or eliminate performance overhead resulting from its increased usability and safety. The principles that guide ACE's design are discussed in Appendix A.

ACE provides an extensive set of wrapper facades, constituting nearly 50 percent of its total source base. Applications combine and refine these wrapper facades by selectively inheriting, aggregating, and/or instantiating them. In this book we show how the socket, file, concurrency, and synchronization wrapper facades are used to develop efficient, portable networked applications.

0.4.3 The ACE Framework Layer

The remaining ~40 percent of ACE consists of *object-oriented frameworks*, which are integrated sets of classes that collaborate to provide a reusable software architecture for a family of related applications [FS97]. Object-oriented frameworks are a key to successful systematic reuse because they complement and amplify other reuse techniques, such as class libraries, components, and patterns [Joh97]. By emphasizing the integration and collaboration of application-specific and application-independent classes, for example, the ACE frameworks enable larger-scale reuse of software than is possible by reusing individual classes or stand-alone functions. The frameworks in ACE integrate and augment its C++ wrapper facade classes by applying advanced concurrency and network programming patterns [BMR$^+$96, SSRB00] to *reify* the canonical control flow and collaboration among families of related classes in ACE.

The following ACE frameworks support the efficient, robust, and flexible development and configuration of concurrent networked applications and services:

Event demultiplexing and dispatching frameworks. The ACE Reactor and Proactor frameworks implement the Reactor and Proactor patterns [SSRB00], respectively. The Reactor and Proactor frameworks automate the demultiplexing and dispatching of application-specific handlers in response to various types of I/O-based, timer-based, signal-based, and synchronization-based events.

Connection establishment and service initialization framework. The ACE Acceptor-Connector framework implements the *Acceptor-Connector pattern* [SSRB00]. This framework decouples the active and passive initialization roles from application processing performed by communicating peer services after initialization is complete.

Concurrency framework. ACE provides the Task framework that can be used to implement key concurrency patterns [SSRB00, Lea99], such as Active Object and Half-Sync/Half-Async, which simplify concurrent programming by decoupling method execution from method invocation and decoupling asynchronous and synchronous processing, respectively.

Service configurator framework. This framework implements the *Component Configurator pattern* [SSRB00] to support the configuration of applications whose services can be assembled dynamically late in their design cycle, for example, at installation time. It also supports the dynamic reconfiguration of services in an application at run time.

Streams framework. This framework implements the *Pipes and Filters pattern* [BMR+96], wherein each processing step is encapsulated in a filtering module that can access and manipulate data flowing through the stream of modules. The ACE Streams framework simplifies the development of hierarchically layered services that can be composed flexibly to create certain types of networked applications, such as user-level protocol stacks and network management agents [SS94].

An in-depth discussion of the motivation, design, and use of the frameworks in ACE appears in *C++ Network Programming: Systematic Reuse with ACE and Frameworks* [SH]. Additional information on the ACE wrapper facades and frameworks is also available in *The ACE Programmer's Guide* [HJS].

0.4.4 The ACE Networked Service Components Layer

In addition to its host infrastructure middleware wrapper facades and frameworks previously described, ACE also provides a library of networked services that are packaged as components. A *component* is an encapsulated part of a software system that implements a specific service or set of services [Szy98]. Although these components aren't included in the ACE library itself, they are bundled with the ACE software distribution to provide the following capabilities:

- **Demonstrate common uses of ACE capabilities**—The components demonstrate how key ACE frameworks and classes can be used to develop flexible, efficient, and robust networked services.

- **Factor out reusable networked application building blocks**—These components provide reusable implementations of common networked application services, such as naming, event routing [Sch00], logging, time synchronization [SSRB00], and network locking.

0.5 Example: A Networked Logging Service

Throughout this book we use a running example of a networked logging service to help illustrate key points and ACE capabilities. This service collects and records diagnostic information sent from one or more client applications. It's a departure from the usual way of logging to a Windows NT/2000 event log, which is not available on Windows 95 or 98. If you're an experienced UNIX programmer, however, you may be thinking this is a waste of time since SYSLOGD provides this type of service already. Yet this underscores a key benefit of the logging service: it's portable, so applications can log messages on all platforms that ACE supports.

The logging service example is a microcosm of the actual Logging Service in ACE. ACE's logging service can be configured dynamically via the Component Configurator pattern [SSRB00] and ACE Service Configurator framework [SH]. By applying the Adapter pattern [GHJV95], records can be redirected to a UNIX SYSLOGD or to the Windows NT/2000 event log, or both—even if the initiating application is on another type of OS platform. This book's logging service example is purposely scaled back so we can focus on mastering complexity. Figure 0.6 illustrates the application processes and server in our networked logging service. Below, we outline the key entities shown in Figure 0.6.

Client application processes run on client hosts and generate log records ranging from debugging messages to critical error messages. The logging information sent by a client application indicates the following:

1. The time the log record was created

2. The process identifier of the application

3. The priority level of the log record and

4. A string containing the logging message text, which can vary in size from 0 to a configurable maximum length, such as 4K bytes.

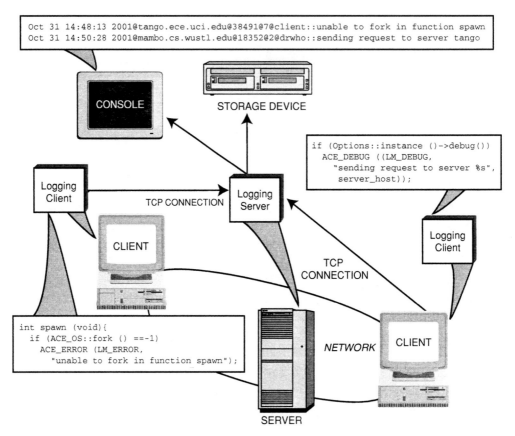

```
Oct 31 14:48:13 2001@tango.ece.uci.edu@38491@7@client::unable to fork in function spawn
Oct 31 14:50:28 2001@mambo.cs.wustl.edu@18352@2@drwho::sending request to server tango
```

```
if (Options::instance ()->debug())
   ACE_DEBUG ((LM_DEBUG,
      "sending request to server %s",
      server_host));
```

```
int spawn (void){
  if (ACE_OS::fork () ==-1)
    ACE_ERROR (LM_ERROR,
       "unable to fork in function spawn");
```

Figure 0.6: **Participants in the Networked Logging Service**

Logging servers collect and output log records received from client applications. A logging server can determine which client host sent each
message by using addressing information it obtains from the Socket API.
There's generally one logging server per system configuration, though they
can be replicated to enhance fault tolerance.

Throughout the book, we refer to the networked logging service to make
our discussion of domain analysis dimensions for networked applications
more concrete. The architecture of our logging service is driven by this
domain analysis. Just as real products change in scope as they progress
through their life cycles, the logging service's design, functionality, scalability, and robustness will evolve as we progress through this book and
[SH]. We'll continue developing this service incrementally to show solu-

tions to common design challenges using many key patterns implemented by classes in ACE. Sidebar 2 describes how to build the ACE library so that you can experiment with the examples we present in this book.

Sidebar 2: Building ACE and Programs that Use ACE

ACE is open-source software, so you can download it from `http://ace.ece.uci.edu` and build it yourself. Here are some tips to help you understand the source examples we show, and how to build ACE, the examples, and your own applications:

- Install ACE in an empty directory. The top-level directory in the distribution is named `ACE_wrappers`. We refer to this top-level directory as `$ACE_ROOT`. Create an environment variable by that name containing the full path to the top-level ACE directory.
- The ACE source and header files reside in `$ACE_ROOT/ace`.
- The source and header files for this book's networked logging service examples reside in `$ACE_ROOT/examples/C++NPv1`.
- When compiling your programs, the `$ACE_ROOT` directory must be added to your compiler's file include path, which is often designated by the `-I` or `/I` compiler option.
- The `$ACE_ROOT/ACE-INSTALL.html` file contains complete instructions on building and installing ACE and programs that use ACE.

You can also purchase a prebuilt version of ACE from Riverace at a nominal cost. A list of the prebuilt compiler and OS platforms supported by Riverace is available at `http://www.riverace.com`.

0.6 Summary

This chapter described the challenges of developing networked applications and middleware that can run effectively in distributed computing environments. We introduced the inherent and accidental complexities encountered when developing software ranging from tightly constrained real-time and embedded systems [SLM98] to newly evolving middleware abstractions [MSKS00] and next-generation networked applications [SKKK00] with stringent QoS requirements. We presented a taxonomy of middleware layering, emphasizing the benefits of host infrastructure middleware, which is the focus of this book.

This chapter also introduced the results of a domain analysis of the key design dimensions for networked application architectures. These were grouped into four categories:

1. Communication protocols and mechanisms
2. Concurrency architectures
3. Service architectures and
4. Service configuration strategies.

This domain analysis has been refined while developing hundreds of networked applications and middleware components during the past decade. This analysis also guided the development of the ACE concurrent network programming toolkit. ACE exemplifies the principles and benefits gained through *refactoring* [FBB+99] the recurring structure and behavior of networked applications into host infrastructure middleware. ACE's pattern-oriented software architecture constitutes an industrial-strength example of how proper object-oriented design and C++ usage can yield significant improvements in your development schedules and the quality, flexibility, and performance of your networked applications and middleware.

Finally, we introduced the networked logging service, which stores diagnostic information sent from one or more client applications. We use this example throughout the book to illustrate common design problems and their effective solutions using ACE. The next two parts of the book are organized as follows:

- **Part I**—Chapters 1 through 4 outline communication design alternatives and describe the object-oriented techniques used in ACE to programming OS IPC mechanisms effectively.
- **Part II**—Chapters 5 through 10 outline concurrency design alternatives and describe the object-oriented techniques used in ACE to program OS concurrency mechanisms effectively.

Throughout both parts of the book, we illustrate common problems that arise when developers design networked applications and when they program them using native OS IPC and concurrency APIs directly. We also show how ACE applies object-oriented design techniques, C++ features, and patterns to resolve these problems.

Part I

Object-Oriented Network Programming

## CHAPTER 1

Communication Design Dimensions

CHAPTER SYNOPSIS

Communication is fundamental to networked application design. This chapter presents a domain analysis of communication design dimensions, which address the rules, form, and levels of abstraction that networked applications use to interact with each other. We cover the following design dimensions in this chapter:

- Connectionless versus connection-oriented protocols
- Synchronous versus asynchronous *message* exchange
- Message-passing versus shared memory

1.1 Connectionless versus Connection-Oriented Protocols

A *protocol* is a set of rules that specify how control and data information is exchanged between communicating entities, such as application processes interacting within a networked computing environment. Protocols can be generally classified as connectionless or connection-oriented. The primary trade-offs in this dimension involve latency, scalability, and reliability.

Connectionless protocols provide a message-oriented service in which each message can be routed and delivered independently. Connectionless protocols often use "best-effort" delivery semantics. These semantics don't guarantee that a series of messages will arrive in a particular order at their destination, or even that they'll ever arrive at all!

Widely used examples of connectionless protocols are the User Datagram Protocol (UDP) and Internet Protocol (IP). These protocols can be used directly by multimedia applications, such as voice-over-IP or streaming video [MSKS00], that can tolerate some degree of data loss. UDP/IP also supports unreliable multicast [DC90] and broadcast capabilities that enable a sender to communicate with a group of receivers.

Connection-oriented protocols provide a reliable, sequenced, nonduplicated delivery service, which is useful for applications that can't tolerate data loss. To enhance performance and ensure reliability, connection-oriented protocols exchange and maintain state information at the sender and/or receiver(s). The Transmission Control Protocol (TCP) is a connection-oriented protocol used in many session-oriented Internet applications, such as Web services and e-mail.

When connection-oriented protocols are used, application and middleware developers must also select from the following design alternatives:

• **Data framing strategies.** Connection-oriented protocols offer different types of data framing strategies. For example, message-oriented delivery strategies are supported by certain connection-oriented protocols, such as TP4 and XTP. In contrast, TCP is a bytestream protocol that doesn't preserve application message boundaries. Thus, if an application makes four `send()` calls to transmit four distinct messages over TCP, there will be one or more (and possibly greater than 4) TCP segments transmitted to the receiver. If an application requires message-oriented delivery therefore, the sender and receiver must perform extra processing to frame the four messages exchanged via TCP. If messages are always equal lengths and network errors never occur, framing is relatively simple; otherwise, it can be a nontrivial problem.

• **Connection multiplexing strategies.** The two general strategies for transmitting data over a connection-oriented protocol are shown in Figure 1.1 and described below:

  1. **Multiplexed,** wherein all client requests emanating from threads in a single process pass through one TCP *connection* to a server process,

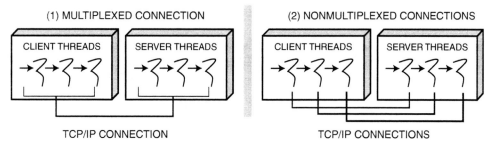

Figure 1.1: **Alternative Connection Multiplexing Strategies**

as shown in Figure 1.1 (1). An advantage of connection multiplexing is that it conserves OS communication resources, such as socket handles and connection control blocks. The disadvantages of this strategy are that it's harder to program [AOS+00], less efficient [CB01], and less deterministic [SMFGG01]. These problems stem from the synchronization and context switching mechanisms required to associate requests with responses over a multiplexed connection.

2. **Nonmultiplexed,** wherein each client uses a different connection to communicate with a peer service, as shown in Figure 1.1 (2). The primary advantage of nonmultiplexed connections is finer control of communication priorities. In the nonmultiplexed connection design, each connection's priority can be set individually, so that high-priority communication will be transmitted quickly, even if there's a large volume of low-priority communications traffic between other threads. This design avoids *priority inversion*, wherein low-priority threads monopolize a single multiplexed connection. In addition, since connections aren't shared, this strategy incurs low synchronization overhead because additional locks aren't needed to send and receive two-way requests. Compared with multiplexed connection strategies, nonmultiplexed strategies use more OS resources, and therefore may not scale well in certain environments, such as high-volume Internet e-commerce servers.

Additional information on the design and trade-offs of connection multiplexing strategies is available in [SMFGG01, SSRB00].

Logging service ⇒ Our networked logging service implementations use the connection-oriented TCP/IP protocol to transmit log records from client applications to a logging server. Connection setup overhead is amortized by establishing a connection once and caching it for the duration of the client/server conversations. The connections are nonmultiplexed, with each logging client application opening a separate TCP connection to the logging server.

The choice of TCP does require us to implement a data framing mechanism atop TCP bytestreams (which we show in Sidebar 9 on page 86). The ubiquity of TCP makes this effort pay off, however, in terms of interoperability and portability across OS platforms and data link layer networks. Moreover, the transport layer, not the application, is responsible for flow and congestion control, retransmitting lost packets, and ensuring the data is delivered in the proper order. These capabilities are important for networked applications that can't afford to lose log records.

1.2 Synchronous versus Asynchronous Message Exchange

In many networked applications, a client sends a request to a server, which processes the request and then sends back a response. These request/response protocols can be implemented over either connectionless or connection-oriented protocols. Two alternative strategies for arranging request/response protocol exchanges are synchronous and asynchronous, as shown in Figure 1.2. The two factors that affect whether to use syn-

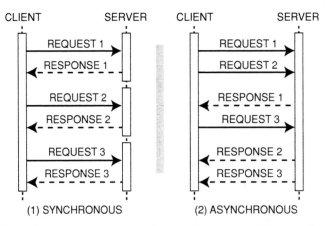

Figure 1.2: **Synchronous versus Asynchronous Messaging Strategies**

chronous or asynchronous message exchange strategies are

1. The interrelatedness of requests and
2. The latency of the underlying protocol or communication media.

We examine how these factors affect the choice of strategy below.

Synchronous request/response protocols are the simplest form to implement. In these protocols, requests and responses are exchanged in a *lock-step* sequence. Each request must receive a response synchronously before the next is sent, as shown in Figure 1.2 (1). Synchronous request/response protocols are appropriate in the following contexts:

- When the result of a request determines subsequent requests, for example, an application that requires an authentication exchange won't send sensitive information requests until the security certificate exchange completes successfully
- When applications exchange messages requiring short-duration processing in low-latency networks, such as NFS read() and write() operations in high-speed LANs
- When simplicity of implementation or a small number of protocol exchanges overrides any possible performance improvement that may be gained by the asynchronous request/response protocols described next.

Asynchronous request/response protocols stream requests from client to server without waiting for responses synchronously [AOS+00]. Multiple client requests can be transmitted before any responses arrive from a server, as shown in Figure 1.2 (2). Asynchronous request/response protocols therefore often require a strategy for detecting lost or failed requests and resending them later. Asynchronous request/response protocols are appropriate in the following contexts:

- When a response is not required before deciding on subsequent requests. For example, Web browsers can use asynchronous strategies to fetch multiple embedded images from the same server. Since each request is independent, they can all be sent asynchronously without waiting for the intervening responses. Each response includes information the browser can use to match it to the corresponding request even when the order of responses is different from the order the requests were sent.

- When communication latency is high relative to the processing time
  required for the request. Asynchronous request strategies help to
  make efficient use of the network, reducing the effects of high latency. The resulting performance improvement greatly outweighs the
  extra complexity of associating responses with requests and correctly
  implementing retry strategies.

Logging service ⇒ Our networked logging server uses a one-way variant
of an asynchronous request/response protocol that doesn't require application-level responses. Log records are just transferred from client applications to the logging server; that is, there's no need for application-level
acknowledgments from the server. The logging server itself writes each log
record to disk immediately after receiving it, with the assumption that each
log record sent is recorded reliably. This design suffices as long as client
applications don't require the networked logging service to take heroic mea-
sures to guarantee that all log records are stored persistently, even when
catastrophic failures occur. If this became a requirement, we'd need to develop a transaction-based logging service, which is much more complicated
and incurs significantly higher time/space overhead.

1.3   Message Passing versus Shared Memory

Our discussion of protocols has so far assumed information is transferred
between peers that reside on different computers. This type of exchange is
referred to as message passing. A different type of information exchange
can occur when communicating peers have access to a region of shared
memory. This section describes these two mechanisms and their trade-
offs.

Message passing exchanges bytestream and record-oriented data explicitly
via the IPC mechanisms that we'll explore in Chapter 2. Application developers generally define the format and content of these messages, as well
as the application protocol that participants must follow to exchange messages. This protocol also defines the number of possible participants in
each exchange (e.g., point-to-point (*unicast*), *multicast*, or *broadcast*) and
how participants begin, conduct, and end a message-passing session.

   The message-passing IPC mechanisms transfer data from one process
or thread to another in messages across an IPC channel, as shown in

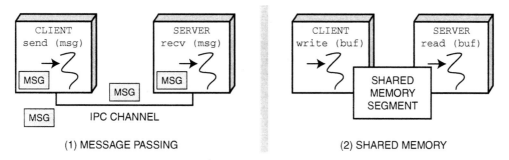

Figure 1.3: **Message Passing versus Shared Memory**

Figure 1.3 (1). If a large amount of data is transferred, it may be fragmented and sent in a sequence of messages. If there's more than one process receiving the data, each message may be sent multiple times, once for each recipient. Many popular middleware architectures, such as RPC, CORBA, and message-oriented middleware (MOM), are based on a message-passing communication model internally.

Shared memory allows multiple processes on the same or different hosts to access and exchange data as though it were local to the address space of each process. When networked applications have data that must be viewed and/or manipulated by multiple processes, shared memory facilities may be a more efficient communication mechanism than message passing. Rather than define the method for transmitting information between entities, applications using native OS shared memory mechanisms must define how to locate and map the shared memory region(s) and the data structures that are placed in shared memory.

Shared memory can be divided into local and distributed variants, as described next.

• **Local shared memory** allows processes on the same computer to have one or more shared memory regions mapped to different virtual address ranges. Two common shared memory mechanisms include

1. **System V UNIX shared memory,** wherein the `shmget()` system function creates a new region of shared memory or returns an existing one. A process attaches a shared memory region to its virtual address space with the `shmat()` system function.

2. **Memory-mapped files,** wherein all or part of a file can be mapped to an area of virtual memory that's shared across multiple processes.

The contents of memory-mapped files can be flushed to persistent storage, which provides a convenient way to save and restore information across program execution.

In both mechanisms, the OS enables multiple processes to map shared memory regions into their address spaces, as shown in Figure 1.3 (2). All processes that map the shared memory region(s) can read from and write to the shared memory's contents directly.

Despite its flexibility, communicating between multiple processes via shared memory requires careful programming. For example, application developers must ensure that data being shared aren't corrupted by race conditions. The system-scope synchronization mechanisms described in Chapter 10 can enforce *serialization* to a shared memory region so that shared information is accessed in an orderly manner. Likewise, applications must be designed carefully if they store C++ objects in shared memory, as described in Sidebar 3.

Sidebar 3: C++ Objects and Shared Memory

The C++ placement `new` operator can initialize C++ objects in shared memory. This feature works for concrete classes (Bja00) because each contains all operations necessary for its support. All methods in a *concrete class* are nonvirtual; that is, they are called directly rather than indirectly through a pointer-to-function. Many ACE wrapper facades are concrete types, for the reasons described in Section A.6 on page 255.

In contrast, *abstract* types that contain virtual methods are hard to program portably when placed in shared memory. Virtual methods are usually invoked using an indirect call through a table of function pointers (a vtable) located in the object's memory. A shared memory region may reside at a different virtual memory location in each process that maps it (BC94, Jor91). Moreover, a C++ compiler/linker needn't locate vtables at the same address in separate processes. The vtable, as well as the functions it refers to, may therefore be mapped at different virtual addresses in each process, which guarantees problems at run time.

- **Distributed shared memory (DSM)** is a programming abstraction that provides applications with an extension to OS virtual memory mechanisms [JM98]. Virtual memory provides a set of policies for fetching, placing, and replacing a set of pages on demand to give programs the illusion that they have a much larger address space than actually exists in physical memory. DSM extends the virtual memory concept across a network to enable transparent interprocess communication via data in global/shared memory. It represents a hybrid of two computing paradigms: shared memory multiprocessors and distributed systems [PTM97].

For example, there are hardware/software platforms that cluster multiple computers into one logical system in which memory is shared across the cluster. Participating applications communicate via distributed shared memory managed across the networked computers. DSM systems provide mechanisms for coordinating updates across processes and network nodes. This communication model often employs message-passing mechanisms in its lower layers to coordinate the exchange of data and to synchronize readers and writers.

Logging service ⇒ Our networked logging service uses a message-passing IPC model implemented over TCP/IP. Message-passing IPC is usually more practical than developing a DSM mechanism and managing it via complex distributed cache coherency protocols. Since DSM is an advanced research topic that's not commonly used in practice, we don't consider it further in this book. Good overviews of DSM research appear in [NL91, PTM97].

1.4 Summary

Separate entities within the single address space of a stand-alone application often interact by passing parameters via function calls and/or by accessing global variables. Entities located in different address spaces in networked applications, however, require different interprocess communication mechanisms. This chapter described how IPC mechanisms yield a number of communication dimensions to consider when designing networked applications. We described connection modes, request/response protocols, and information exchange alternatives, as well as factors and tradeoffs to guide your choices.

The next chapter discusses the Socket API. It's the most common IPC facility you'll encounter when implementing your designs, so it's important to understand its capabilities and shortcomings, as well as ACE's solutions. The ACE toolkit provides a range of classes that help guide your communication choices in accordance with the design dimensions discussed in this chapter. For example,

- The ACE wrapper facades that encapsulate connection-oriented and synchronous message-passing functionality are presented in Chapter 3.
- Asynchronous connection-establishment and data transfer is illustrated in [SH].
- The ACE memory-mapped file mechanism is described in Sidebar 7 on page 68 and its shared memory mechanisms are shown in [HJS].

Using these ACE capabilities in your networked applications can help to reduce inherent and accidental complexities.

## CHAPTER 2

An Overview of the Socket API

CHAPTER SYNOPSIS

The previous chapter focused on modeling the design space of networked application communication, which provides many opportunities to address inherent complexities. This chapter starts delving into the solution space, beginning with the most common interprocess communication (IPC) mechanism: *sockets*. We describe the Socket API and its use with TCP/IP, followed by an analysis of common accidental complexities encountered when developers program their networked applications using native OS APIs.

2.1 An Overview of Operating System IPC Mechanisms

Networked applications require interprocess communication (IPC) mechanisms to enable clients and servers to exchange information. The IPC mechanisms provided by operating systems can be classified into two general categories:

- **Local IPC**—Certain IPC mechanisms, such as shared memory, pipes, UNIX-domain sockets, doors, or signals, enable communication only between entities that are collocated on the same computer [Ste99].

- **Remote IPC**—Other IPC mechanisms, such as Internet-domain sockets [Ste98], X.25 circuits, and Win32 Named Pipes, support communication between entities that can be collocated or distributed across a network.

Although networked applications are largely concerned with remote IPC mechanisms, the patterns and ACE wrapper facades we present also apply to most local IPC mechanisms.

A complete discussion of OS IPC mechanisms and their APIs is beyond the scope of this book. We recommend that you consult [Rag93, MBKQ96, Ric97, Sol98, Ste98, Ste99] for complete coverage. This chapter focuses on the Socket API and TCP/IP since they are the most common IPC API and networking protocol, respectively. We show how hard it is to rely on the Socket API when writing portable and robust programs for heterogeneous platforms. Chapters 3 and 4 then illustrate how ACE uses C++ and patterns to resolve these problems.

2.2 The Socket API

The Socket API was developed in BSD UNIX [MBKQ96] to provide an application-level interface to the TCP/IP protocol suite. This API has since been ported to most operating systems, including all those supported by ACE. It's now the *de facto* standard for programming interprocess communication over TCP/IP.

Applications can use the C functions in the Socket API to create and manage local *endpoints* of communication, which are called sockets. Each socket is accessed via a *handle*, which is also referred to as a descriptor in the UNIX literature. A socket handle identifies a single communication endpoint maintained by the OS, while shielding applications from differences between, and dependencies on, low-level OS kernel implementation details, such as the following:

- In UNIX, socket handles and other I/O handles, such as file, pipe, and terminal device handles, can be used interchangeably for most operations.

- In Microsoft Windows, socket handles can't be used interchangeably with I/O handles for most operations, though they serve similar purposes.

Each socket can be bound to a local and a remote address. These addresses define the association between two or more peers that communicate via the socket.

The Socket API contains approximately two dozen system functions that can be classified into the following five categories:

1. **Local context management.** The Socket API provides functions to manage local context information, which is normally stored within the OS kernel or in system libraries:

Function	Description
`socket()`	A factory function that allocates a socket handle and returns it to the caller.
`bind()`	Associates a socket handle with a local or remote address.
`getsockname()`	Returns the local address to which a socket is bound.
`getpeername()`	Returns the remote address to which a socket is bound.
`close()`	Deallocates a socket handle, making it available for reuse.

2. **Connection establishment and connection termination.** The Socket API provides functions to establish and terminate connections:

Function	Description
`connect()`	Establishes a connection *actively* on a socket handle.
`listen()`	Indicates its willingness to listen *passively* for incoming client connection requests.
`accept()`	A *factory* function that creates a new communication endpoint to service client requests.
`shutdown()`	Selectively terminates the read-side and/or write-side stream of a bidirectional connection.

3. **Data transfer mechanisms.** The Socket API provides functions to send and receive data via socket handles:

Function	Description
`send()` `recv()`	Transmit and receive buffers of data via a particular I/O handle.
`sendto()` `recvfrom()`	Exchanges connectionless datagrams, where each `sendto()` call provides the networking address of the recipient.

On UNIX, these functions can also be used for other types of I/O handles, such as files and terminal devices. UNIX platforms also provide the following data transfer mechanisms:

Function	Description
`read()` `write()`	Receive and transmit buffers of data via a particular handle.
`readv()` `writev()`	Supports *scatter-read* and *gather-write* semantics, respectively, to optimize mode switching and simplify memory management.
`sendmsg()` `recvmsg()`	General-purpose functions that subsume the behavior of the other data transfer functions.

4. **Options management.**   The Socket API defines functions that allow programmers to alter default socket behavior to enable multicasting, broadcasting, and modifying/querying the size of transport buffers:

Function	Description
setsockopt()	Modifies options in different protocol stack layers.
getsockopt()	Queries options in different protocol stack layers.

5. **Network addressing.**   In addition to the functions described above, networked applications often use functions to resolve humanly readable names, such as tango.ece.uci.edu, to low-level network addresses, such as 128.195.174.35:

Function	Description
gethostbyname() gethostbyaddr()	Handle network address mapping between hostnames and IPv4 addresses.
getipnodebyname() getipnodebyaddr()	Handle network address mapping between hostnames and IPv4/IPv6 addresses.
getservbyname()	Identifies services by their humanly readable names.

Although the Socket API is most often used to write TCP/IP applications it's broad enough to support multiple communication domains. A communication domain is defined by a protocol family and an address family, as follows:

• **Protocol family.**   Today's networking environments include a large number of protocols that can offer a variety of communication services, such as connection-oriented reliable delivery, unreliable multicast, etc. A protocol family is a collection of protocols that offers a distinct set of related services. When creating a socket using the Socket API, the protocol is specified by a combination of the following two parameters:

1. **Protocol family**—for example, UNIX-domain (PF_UNIX), Internet-domain IPv4 (PF_INET) and IPv6 (PF_INET6), ATM (PF_ATMSVC), X.25 (PF_X25), Appletalk (PF_APPLETALK), and so on.

2. **Service type**—for example, sequenced, reliable bytestream (SOCK_STREAM), unreliable *datagram* (SOCK_DGRAM), and so on.

For example, the TCP/IP protocol is specified by passing the PF_INET (or PF_INET6) and SOCK_STREAM flags to the socket() function.

• **Address family.** An address family defines an address format that characterizes the size of an address in bytes, as well as the number, type, and order of its fields. In addition, an address family defines a set of functions that interpret the address format, for example, to determine the subnet where an IP datagram is destined. Address families correspond closely to protocol families, for example, the IPv4 address family AF_INET works only with the IPv4 protocol family PF_INET.

2.3 Limitations of the Socket API

The native Socket API has several limitations: it's error-prone, overly complex, and nonportable/nonuniform. Although the following discussion focuses on the Socket API, the critique also applies to other native OS IPC APIs.

2.3.1 Error-Prone APIs

As outlined in Section 2.2, the Socket API uses handles to identify socket endpoints. In general, operating systems use handles to identify other I/O devices, such as files, pipes, and terminals. These handles are implemented as *weakly typed* integer or pointer types, which allows subtle errors to occur at run time. To illustrate these and other problems that can occur, consider the following echo_server() function:

```
0 // This example contains bugs!  Do not copy this example!
1 #include <sys/types.h>
2 #include <sys/socket.h>
3
4 const int PORT_NUM = 10000;
5
6 int echo_server ()
7 {
8   struct sockaddr_in addr;
9   int addr_len;
10   char buf[BUFSIZ];
11   int n_handle;
12   // Create the local endpoint.
13   int s_handle = socket (PF_UNIX, SOCK_DGRAM, 0);
14   if (s_handle == -1) return -1;
15
16   // Set up the address information where the server listens.
17   addr.sin_family = AF_INET;
```

```
18    addr.sin_port = PORT_NUM;
19    addr.sin_addr.addr = INADDR_ANY;
20
21    if (bind (s_handle, (struct sockaddr *) &addr,
22              sizeof addr) == -1)
23      return -1;
24
25    // Create a new communication endpoint.
26    if (n_handle = accept (s_handle, (struct sockaddr *) &addr,
27                           &addr_len) != -1) {
28      int n;
29      while ((n = read (s_handle, buf, sizeof buf)) > 0)
30        write (n_handle, buf, n);
31
32      close (n_handle);
33    }
34    return 0;
35 }
```

This function contains at least 10 subtle and all-too-common bugs that occur when using the Socket API. See if you can locate all 10 bugs while reading the code above, then read our dissection of these flaws below. The numbers in parentheses are the line numbers where errors occur in the echo_server() function.

1. **Forgot to initialize an important variable. (8–9)** The addr_len variable must be set to sizeof(addr). Forgetting to initialize this variable will cause the accept() call on line 26 to fail at run-time.

2. **Use of nonportable handle datatype. (11–14)** Although these lines look harmless enough, they are also fraught with peril. This code isn't portable to Windows Sockets (WinSock) platforms, where socket handles are type SOCKET, not type int. Moreover, WinSock failures are indicated via a non-standard macro called INVALID_SOCKET_HANDLE rather than by returning −1. The other bugs in the code fragment above aren't obvious until we examine the rest of the function.

The next three network addressing errors are subtle, and show up only at run time.

3. **Unused struct members not cleared. (17–19)** The entire addr structure should have been initialized to 0 before setting each address member. The Socket API uses one basic addressing structure (sockaddr) with different overlays, depending on the address family, for example, sockaddr_in for IPv4. Without initializing the entire structure to 0, parts of the fields

may have indeterminate contents, which can yield random run-time failures.

4. **Address/protocol family mismatch. (17)** The addr.sin_family field was set to AF_INET, which designates the Internet addressing family. It will be used with a socket (s_handle) that was created with the UNIX protocol family, which is inconsistent. Instead, the protocol family type passed to the socket() function should have been PF_INET.

5. **Wrong byte order. (18)** The value assigned to addr.sin_port is not in network byte order; that is, the programmer forgot to use htons() to convert the *port number* from host byte order into network byte order. When run on a computer with little-endian byte order, this code will execute without error; however, clients will be unable to connect to it at the expected port number.

If these network addressing mistakes were corrected, lines 21–23 would actually work!

There's an interrelated set of errors on lines 25–27. These exemplify how hard it is to locate errors before run-time when programming directly to the C Socket API.

6. **Missing an important API call. (25)** The listen() function was omitted accidentally. This function must be called before accept() to set the socket handle into so-called "passive mode."

7. **Wrong socket type for API call. (26)** The accept() function was called for s_handle, which is exactly what should be done. The s_handle was created as a SOCK_DGRAM-type socket, however, which is an illegal socket type to use with accept(). The original socket() call on line 13 should therefore have been passed the SOCK_STREAM flag.

8. **Operator precedence error. (26–27)** There's one further error related to the accept() call. As written, n_handle will be set to 1 if accept() succeeds and 0 if it fails. If this program runs on UNIX (and the other bugs are fixed), data will be written to either stdout or stdin, respectively, instead of the connected socket. Most of the errors in this example can be avoided by using the ACE wrapper facade classes, but this bug is simply an error in operator precedence, which can't be avoided by using ACE, or any other library. It's a common pitfall [Koe88] with C and C++ programs, remedied only by knowing your operator precedence. To fix this, add a set of parentheses around the assignment expression, as follows:

```
if ((n_handle = accept (s_handle, (struct sockaddr *) &addr,
                        &addr_len)) != -1) {
```

Better yet, follow the convention we use in ACE and put the assignment to
n_handle on a separate line:

```
n_handle = accept (s_handle,
                   (struct sockaddr *) &addr, &addr_len);
if (n_handle != -1) {
```

This way, you don't have to worry about remembering the arcane C++ operator precedence rules!

   We're almost finished with our echo_server() function, but there are
still several remaining errors.

9. **Wrong handle used in API call. (29)** The read() function was called to
receive up to sizeof buf bytes from s_handle, which is the passive-mode
listening socket. We should have called read() on n_handle instead. This
problem would have manifested itself as an obscure run-time error and
could not have been detected at compile time since socket handles are
weakly typed.

10. **Possible data loss. (30)** The return value from write() was not
checked to see if all n bytes (or any bytes at all) were written, which is a
possible source of data loss. Due to socket buffering and *flow control*, a
write() to a bytestream mode socket may only send part of the requested
number of bytes, in which case the rest must be sent later.

   After being burned enough times, experienced network programmers
will be alert for most of the problems outlined above. A more fundamental
design problem, however, is the lack of adequate type safety and data abstraction in the Socket API. The source code above will compile cleanly on
some OS platforms, but not all. It will not run correctly on any platform,
however!

   Over the years, programmers and libraries have implemented numerous workarounds to alleviate these problems. A common solution is to
use typedefs to clarify to programmers what types are involved. Although
these solutions can alleviate some portability concerns, they don't cover
the other problems outlined above. In particular, the diversity of IPC addressing schemes presents more variation than a mere typedef can hide.

2.3.2   Overly Complex APIs

The Socket API provides a single interface that supports multiple:

- **Protocol families**, such as TCP/IP, IPX/SPX, X.25, ISO OSI, ATM, and UNIX-domain sockets
- **Communication/connection roles**, such as *active connection establishment* versus *passive connection establishment* versus data transfer
- **Communication optimizations**, such as the gather-write function, `writev()`, that sends multiple buffers in a single system function and
- **Options** for less common functionality, such as broadcasting, multicasting, asynchronous I/O, and urgent data delivery.

The Socket API combines all this functionality into a single API, listed in the tables in Section 2.2. The result is complex and hard to master. If you apply a careful analysis to the Socket API, however, you'll see that its interface can be decomposed into the following dimensions:

1. **Type of communication service,** such as streams versus datagrams versus connected datagrams
2. **Communication/connection role;** for example, clients often initiate connections actively, whereas servers often accept them passively
3. **Communication domain,** such as local host only versus local or remote host

Figure 2.1 clusters the related Socket functions according to these three dimensions. This natural clustering is obscured in the Socket API, however, because all this functionality is crammed into a single set of functions. Moreover, the Socket API can't enforce the correct use of its functions at compile time for different communication and connection roles, such as active versus passive connection establishment or datagram versus stream communication.

2.3.3   Nonportable and Nonuniform APIs

Despite its ubiquity, the Socket API is not portable. The following are some areas of divergence across platforms:

- **Function names**—The `read()`, `write()`, and `close()` functions in the `echo_server()` function on page 37 are not portable to all OS platforms. For example, Windows defines a different set of functions (`ReadFile()`, `WriteFile()`, and `closesocket()`) that provide these behaviors.

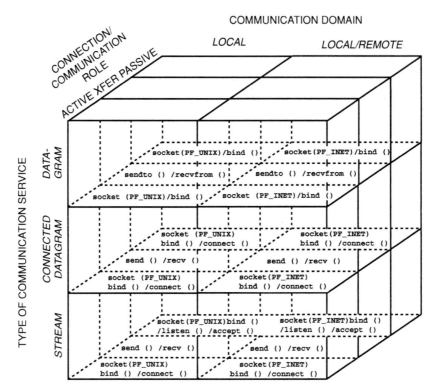

Figure 2.1: **Taxonomy of Socket Dimensions**

- **Function semantics**—Certain functions behave differently on different platforms. For example, on UNIX and Win32 the accept() function can be passed NULL pointers for the client address and client length field. On certain real-time platforms, such as VxWorks, passing NULL pointers to accept() can crash the machine.
- **Socket handle types**—Different platforms use different representations for socket handles. For example, on UNIX platforms socket handles are integers, whereas on Win32 they are actually implemented as pointers.
- **Header files**—Different OS/compiler platforms use different names for header files containing Socket API function prototypes.

Another problem with the Socket API is that its several dozen functions lack a uniform naming convention, which makes it hard to determine the scope of the API. For example, it isn't immediately obvious that `socket()`, `bind()`, `accept()`, and `connect()` functions belong to the same API. Other networking APIs address this problem by prepending a common prefix before each function. For example, a `t_` is prepended before each function in the TLI API [Rag93].

2.4 Summary

A prerequisite to performing any job well is knowing how to use your tools effectively. Many useful tools can hurt you if misused. Although no one's been hit over the head by a UNIX pipe or socket, the time and resources wasted on unnecessary development and debugging has certainly cost lots of money, caused premature hair loss, and put a damper on many social lives. Moreover, unlike tools such as wrenches and hammers, learning to use low-level tools on one platform may not help when you port your networked applications to a new platform.

Software developers building networked applications must master the concepts and tools associated with interprocess communication (IPC). This chapter presented the Socket API. It discussed the range of capabilities this ubiquitous API provides, as well as its associated set of accidental complexities. One short program illustrated the range of errors commonly made as a result of these complexities. The next chapter shows how ACE applies C++ features and the Wrapper Facade [SSRB00] pattern to resolve them.

CHAPTER 3

The ACE Socket Wrapper Facades

CHAPTER SYNOPSIS

This chapter presents the patterns and wrapper facade classes that ACE provides to resolve the accidental complexity problems with the Socket API discussed in Chapter 2. We describe the ACE classes that use the Wrapper Facade pattern to encapsulate connection-oriented Socket API functionality in portable C++ classes. We also illustrate the use of these classes using brief, familiar Web server and client examples before showing the larger networked logging service in Chapter 4.

3.1 Overview

ACE defines a set of C++ classes that address the limitations with the Socket API described in Section 2.3. These classes are designed in accordance with the Wrapper Facade design pattern [SSRB00].[1] They therefore encapsulate the functions and data provided by existing non-object-oriented APIs within more concise, robust, portable, maintainable, and cohesive object-oriented class interfaces. The ACE Socket wrapper facade classes presented in this chapter include:

---

[1] In the rest of this book, we use the term *ACE wrapper facade* to indicate an ACE class designed using the Wrapper Facade pattern.

ACE Class	Description
ACE_Addr	The root of the ACE network addressing hierarchy.
ACE_INET_Addr	Encapsulates the Internet-domain address family.
ACE_IPC_SAP	The root of the ACE IPC wrapper facade hierarchy.
ACE_SOCK	The root of the ACE Socket wrapper facade hierarchy.
ACE_SOCK_Connector	A factory that connects to a peer acceptor and then initializes a new endpoint of communication in an ACE_SOCK_Stream object.
ACE_SOCK_IO ACE_SOCK_Stream	Encapsulate the data transfer mechanisms supported by data-mode sockets.
ACE_SOCK_Acceptor	A factory that initializes a new endpoint of communication in an ACE_SOCK_Stream object in response to a connection request from a peer connector.

Figure 3.1 illustrates the key relationship between these classes. These ACE Socket wrapper facades provide the following benefits:

- **Enhance type-safety** by detecting many subtle application type errors quickly; for example, the passive and active connection establishment factories don't provide methods for sending or receiving data, so type errors are caught at compile time rather than at run time.

- **Ensure portability** via platform-independent C++ classes.

- **Simplify common use cases** by reducing the amount of application code and development effort expended on lower-level network programming details, which frees developers to focus on higher-level, application-centric concerns.

Moreover, ACE Socket wrapper facades retain efficiency by using inline functions to enhance the software qualities listed above without sacrificing performance. ACE's efficiency-related design principles are discussed further in Section A.6 on page 255.

The structure of the ACE Socket wrapper facades corresponds to the taxonomy of communication services, connection/communication roles, and communication domains shown in Figure 3.2. The classes in this figure provide the following capabilities:

- The ACE_SOCK_* classes encapsulate the Internet-domain Socket API functionality.

- The ACE_LSOCK_* classes encapsulate the UNIX-domain Socket API functionality.

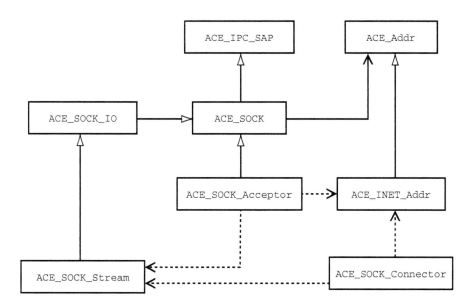

Figure 3.1: **The ACE Connection-Oriented Socket Class Relationships**

It's instructive to compare the structure of the ACE classes in Figure 3.2 with the functions shown in Figure 2.1 on page 42. The classes in Figure 3.2 are much more concise since they use the ACE Socket wrapper facades to encapsulate the behavior of multiple socket functions within C++ classes related by inheritance. In addition to the classes that support connection establishment and communication, ACE also provides a related set of addressing classes. We examine their capabilities in Section 3.2 and their underlying design principles in Section A.4.2. Figure 3.1 depicts the associations between these classes and the other ACE classes in the connection-oriented Socket API family.

The remainder of our discussion in this chapter focuses on the ACE connection-oriented Internet-domain wrapper facades because they're the most widely used ACE IPC mechanism. The classes are arranged in the hierarchy shown in Figure 3.1. To avoid duplication of code, common methods and state are factored into abstract classes, which aren't instantiated directly. Subclasses then add appropriate methods and enforce proper usage patterns. For example, connection-oriented networked applications are typified by asymmetric connection roles between clients and servers. Servers listen *passively* for clients to initiate connections *ac-*

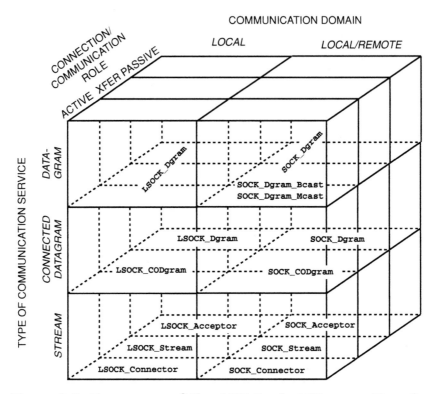

Figure 3.2: **Taxonomy of the ACE Socket Wrapper Facades**

tively [SSRB00], as shown in Figure 3.3. Even in *peer-to-peer* applications, in which applications play the role of both client and server, connections must be initiated actively by one of the peers and accepted passively by the other.

The functions in the C Socket API can be distinguished by the three different roles they play for connection-oriented protocols, such as TCP:

1. The active connection role (connector) is played by a peer application that initiates a connection to a remote peer
2. The passive connection role (acceptor) is played by a peer application that accepts a connection from a remote peer and
3. The communication role (stream) is played by both peer applications to exchange data after they are connected.

This chapter motivates and describes the capabilities of the ACE Socket classes that collectively provide the connection and communication roles

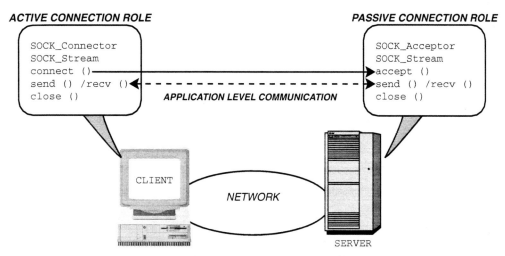

Figure 3.3: **Roles in the ACE Socket Wrapper Facade**

outlined above. Keep in mind the points noted in Sidebar 4 regarding UML diagrams and C++ code in this book.

3.2 The ACE_Addr and ACE_INET_Addr Classes

Motivation

Network addressing is a trouble spot in the Socket API. Socket API network addressing mechanisms use C structures and typecasts, which are tedious and error-prone to program. The address family is the first member of the generic addressing structure, sockaddr. Other address structures, such as sockaddr_in for Internet-domain addresses and sockaddr_un for UNIX-domain addresses, also have an address family member that occupies the same position and size as in the sockaddr struct. Applications use these specific address family structures by

1. Allocating a structure for the desired address family, for example, struct sockaddr_in
2. Filling in the address family member to indicate to the Socket API just what type it really is
3. Supplying addresses, such as IP and port numbers, and
4. Casting the type to sockaddr * to pass to Socket API functions.

Sidebar 4: Displaying ACE Classes and C++ Code

We generally provide a UML diagram and a table that describe the key methods for each ACE C++ class used in this book. Complete C++ class interfaces for ACE are available online at `http://ace.ece.uci.edu` and `http://www.riverace.com`. Complete C++ class implementations and networked logging service examples are available in the `$ACE_ROOT/ace` and `$ACE_ROOT/examples/C++NPv1` directories, respectively. We recommend that you keep a copy of the ACE source code handy for quick reference.

To save space in the book, our UML class diagrams focus on attributes and operations that are used in our code examples. Class diagrams don't show an attributes section when none of that class's attributes are directly pertinent to our discussions. If you need a quick UML introduction or refresher, we recommend *UML Distilled* (wKS00).

To further save space, we use some programming shortcuts that aren't used in ACE; for example:

- We've omitted much of the error-handling code in our C++ examples. Naturally, ACE always checks for error conditions and takes corrective action, just as your applications should.
- Some of our C++ examples implement methods within the class definition. We don't do this in ACE itself, however, since it clutters class interfaces and slows down compilation.

The ACE programming guidelines are located in `$ACE_ROOT/docs/ACE-guidelines.html`.

To minimize the complexity of all these low-level details, ACE defines a hierarchy of classes that provide a uniform interface for all ACE network addressing objects.

Class Capabilities

The `ACE_Addr` class is the root of the ACE network addressing hierarchy. The interface of this class is shown in Figure 3.4 and its key methods provide the following capabilities that are common to all the ACE network addressing classes:

```
┌─────────────────────────────────────────────────────────┐
│                        ACE_Addr                          │
├─────────────────────────────────────────────────────────┤
│  + sap any  : ACE Addr                                   │
│  # addr_type_  : int                                     │
│  # addr_size_  : int                                     │
├─────────────────────────────────────────────────────────┤
│  + ACE_Addr (type : int = -1, size : int = -1)          │
│  + operator ==(sap : const ACE_Addr&) : int             │
│  + operator!= (sap : const ACE_Addr&) : int             │
│  + hash () : int                                         │
└─────────────────────────────────────────────────────────┘
```

```
┌──────────────────────────────────────────────────────────────────┐
│                          ACE_INET_Addr                             │
├──────────────────────────────────────────────────────────────────┤
│  - inet_addr_  : sockaddr_in                                       │
├──────────────────────────────────────────────────────────────────┤
│  + ACE_INET_Addr (port : unsigned short, host : const char *)     │
│  + set (port : unsigned short, host : const char *) : int         │
│  + string_to_addr (address : const char *) : int                  │
│  + addr_to_string (s : char *, max : size_t, ipfmt : int = 1) : int│
│  + get_port_number () : u_short                                    │
│  + get_host_name (buff : char *, max : size_t) : int              │
└──────────────────────────────────────────────────────────────────┘
```

Figure 3.4: **The** ACE_Addr **and** ACE_INET_Addr **Class Diagrams**

Method	Description
operator==()	Compares addresses for equality.
operator!=()	Compares addresses for inequality.
hash()	Computes a hash value for an address.

The ACE_Addr class also defines a sap_any static data member that both client and server applications can use as a "wildcard" if they don't care what address they're assigned. For example,

- Client applications can use sap_any to create temporary OS-assigned port numbers, known as "ephemeral ports," which are recycled by the OS after connections are closed.
- Server applications can use sap_any to select their port numbers, as long as they export the assigned numbers to clients via some type of location discovery mechanism, such as a naming or trading service.

Concrete address classes for each IPC mechanism, such as Internet-domain sockets and UNIX-domain sockets, derive from ACE_Addr and add their addressing needs. For example, TCP/IP and UDP/IP addressing information is represented in the `ACE_INET_Addr` class shown in Figure 3.4. In addition to implementing the `ACE_Addr` base interface, `ACE_INET_Addr` provides the following key methods:

Method	Description
`ACE_INET_Addr()` `set()`	Initialize an `ACE_INET_Addr` with hostnames, IP addresses, and/or port numbers.
`string_to_addr()`	Converts a string to an `ACE_INET_Addr`.
`addr_to_string()`	Converts an `ACE_INET_Addr` to a string.
`get_port_number()`	Returns the port number in host byte order.
`get_host_name()`	Returns the host name.

The use of the ACE Socket wrapper facades for network addressing avoids common traps and pitfalls that can arise when using the C sockaddr family of data structures. For example, consider the `ACE_INET_Addr` constructor shown in Figure 3.4. This constructor creates an `ACE_INET_ Addr` from a port number and host name, thereby eliminating common programming errors by

- Initializing all bytes in the underlying `sockaddr_in` to 0 and
- Converting the port number and IP address to network byte order

`ACE_INET_Addr` allows developers to write networked applications without concern for low-level address initialization details. There are many other overloaded constructors and `set()` methods in `ACE_INET_Addr` that can be used to initialize Internet-domain network address objects using various combinations of host names, IP addresses, and/or TCP/UDP port names and numbers.

3.3 The ACE_IPC_SAP Class

Motivation

Section 2.3.1 on page 37 outlined the portability problems incurred by the I/O handles used in native OS IPC APIs. ACE addresses I/O handle portability by:

- Defining the `ACE_HANDLE` type definition, which designates the appropriate type of handle on each OS platform and

- Defining a portable ACE_INVALID_HANDLE macro that applications can use to test for errors

These simple ACE-defined type and value abstractions help to enhance application portability.

Object-savvy software developers will note, however, that a handle—even a portable one—is not the appropriate level of abstraction in an object-oriented networked application. Instead, a more appropriate programming abstraction would be some type of I/O handle class, which is why ACE provides the ACE_IPC_SAP class.[2]

Class Capabilities

The ACE_IPC_SAP class is the root of the ACE hierarchy of IPC wrapper facades and provides basic I/O handle manipulation capabilities to other ACE wrapper facades. Its interface is shown in Figure 3.5 (along with the ACE_SOCK class described in Section 3.4) and its key methods are shown in the table below:

Method	Description
enable() disable()	Enable or disable various I/O handle options, such as enabling/disabling non-blocking I/O.
set_handle() get_handle()	Set and get the underlying I/O handle.

Although ACE_IPC_SAP defines useful methods and data, it's not intended for direct use by applications. Instead, it's used by subclasses, such as the ACE wrapper facades for files, STREAM pipes, Named Pipes, and the System V Transport Layer Interface (TLI). To enforce this design constraint and to prevent ACE_IPC_SAP from being instantiated directly, we make ACE_IPC_SAP an *abstract class* by declaring its constructor in the protected part of the class. We use this convention instead of defining a pure virtual method to eliminate the need for a virtual pointer in each subclass instance.

---

[2]In the networking standards literature [Bla91], the acronym "SAP" stands for "service access point."

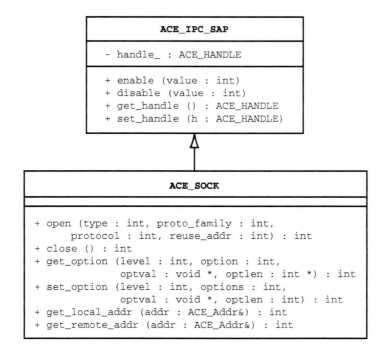

Figure 3.5: **The** ACE_IPC_SAP **and** ACE_SOCK **Class Diagrams**

3.4 The ACE_SOCK Class

Motivation

As discussed in Section 2.3, a key cause of accidental complexity in the Socket API stems from the inability of compilers to detect the misuse of socket handles during compilation. The ACE_IPC_SAP class described in Section 3.3 is the first step toward resolving this problem. The remainder of this chapter describes other ACE Socket wrapper facades that address the other problems illustrated in Section 2.3. We start by moving down the inheritance hierarchy in Figure 3.1 and discussing behavior that makes sense at each level, beginning with the ACE_SOCK class.

Class Capabilities

The ACE_SOCK class is the root of the ACE Socket wrapper facade hierarchy. In addition to exporting the methods inherited from ACE_IPC_SAP, ACE_

SOCK provides capabilities that are common to other ACE Socket wrapper facades, including the classes discussed later in this chapter. These capabilities include

- Creating and destroying socket handles

- Obtaining the network addresses of local and remote peers and

- Setting and getting socket options, such as socket queue sizes, enabling broadcast/multicast communication, and disabling Nagle's algorithm (described in Sidebar 6 on page 64)

The interface of ACE_SOCK and its relationship to the ACE_IPC_SAP base class is shown in Figure 3.5 and its key methods are shown in the following table:

Method	Description
open () close ()	Create and destroy a socket endpoint of communication.
get_local_addr () get_remote_addr ()	Return the address of the local and remote peer, respectively.
set_option () get_option ()	Set and get socket options.

To prevent accidental misuse, ACE_SOCK is defined as an abstract class; that is, its constructor is declared in the protected access control section of the class. As with ACE_IPC_SAP therefore, objects of ACE_SOCK can't be instantiated directly since they are accessible only to subclasses, such as the connection-oriented wrapper facades described in Section 3.5 through Section 3.7.

The ACE_SOCK class provides a close () method since it doesn't close the socket handle in its destructor. As described in Section A.6.1 on page 255, this design is intentional and prevents errors from occurring when an ACE_SOCK_Stream is passed by value or copied to different objects. Experienced ACE developers use higher-level classes to close the underlying socket handle automatically. For example, the Logging_Handler class described in Section 4.4.2 starting on page 86 closes its socket when the higher-level handler object is closed. The ACE_Svc_Handler class discussed in [SH] also closes the underlying socket handle automatically.

3.5 The ACE_SOCK_Connector Class

Motivation

Although there are three distinct roles for connection-oriented protocols, the Socket API only supports the following two socket modes:

1. A *data-mode socket* is used by peer applications in their communication roles to exchange data between connected peers and

2. A *passive-mode socket* is a factory used by a peer application in its passive connection role to return a handle to a connected data-mode socket.

No socket mode focuses exclusively on the active connection role, however. Instead, a data-mode socket also plays this role by convention. An application is therefore not supposed to call `send()` or `recv()` on a data-mode socket until after the `connect()` function establishes a connection successfully.

The asymmetry in the Socket API between the connection roles and the socket modes is confusing and error-prone. For example, an application may accidentally call `recv()` or `send()` on a data-mode socket handle before it's connected. Unfortunately, this problem can't be detected until run time since socket handles are weakly-typed and thus the dual role of data-mode sockets is only enforced via programming convention, rather than via the compiler's type-checking features. ACE therefore defines the `ACE_SOCK_Connector` class, which prevents accidental misuse by only exposing methods for actively establishing connections.

Class Capabilities

The `ACE_SOCK_Connector` class is a factory that establishes a new endpoint of communication actively. It provides the following capabilities:

- It initiates a connection with a peer acceptor and then initializes an `ACE_SOCK_Stream` object after the connection is established.

- Connections can be initiated in either a blocking, nonblocking, or timed manner and

- C++ traits are used to support generic programming techniques that enable the wholesale replacement of functionality via C++ parameterized types, as described in Sidebar 5 on page 57.

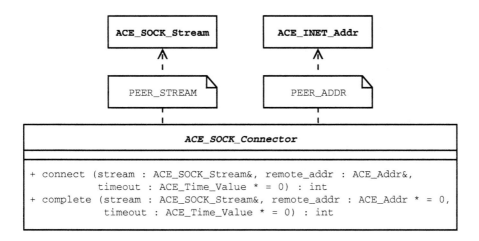

Figure 3.6: **The** ACE_SOCK_Connector **Class Diagram**

Sidebar 5: Using Traits for ACE Socket Wrapper Facades

To simplify the wholesale replacement of IPC classes and their associated addressing classes, the ACE Socket wrapper facades define *traits*. Traits are a C++ generic programming (Ale01) idiom that can be used to define and combine a set of characteristics to alter the behavior(s) of a template class (Jos99). The ACE Socket wrapper facades use traits to define the following class associations:

- PEER_ADDR—This trait defines the ACE_INET_Addr addressing class that's associated with ACE Socket wrapper facade classes and
- PEER_STREAM—This trait defines the ACE_SOCK_Stream data transfer class that's associated with the ACE_SOCK_Acceptor and ACE_SOCK_Connector factories.

ACE implements these traits as C++ type definitions, which are shown as notes in the UML figures in this chapter. Section A.5.3, page 253, illustrates how to use these traits to write concise generic functions and classes. We explore other uses of ACE traits and traits classes in (SH).

The interface of ACE_SOCK_Connector is shown in Figure 3.6. The two key methods in ACE_SOCK_Connector are outlined in the following table:

Method	Description
`connect()`	Actively connects an `ACE_SOCK_Stream` at a particular network address using either blocking, nonblocking, or timed mode.
`complete()`	Tries to complete a nonblocking connection and initialize an `ACE_SOCK_Stream`.

`ACE_SOCK_Connector` supports blocking, nonblocking, and timed connections, where blocking is the default. Nonblocking and timed connections are useful when establishing connections over high-latency links, using single-threaded applications, or initializing many peers that can be connected in an arbitrary order. Three types of `ACE_Time_Value` values can be passed to the `connect()` method to control its behavior:

Value	Behavior
NULL `ACE_Time_Value` pointer	Indicates `connect()` should wait indefinitely, that is, block until the connection is established or the OS deems the server host unreachable.
Non-NULL `ACE_Time_Value` pointer whose `sec()` and `usec()` methods return 0	Indicates `connect()` should perform a nonblocking connection, that is, if the connection isn't established immediately, return −1 and set errno to `EWOULDBLOCK`.
A non-NULL `ACE_Time_Value` pointer whose `sec()` or `usec()` method returns > 0	Indicates `connect()` should only wait a relative amount of time to establish the connection, returning −1 with errno set to `ETIME` if it can't establish the connection by then.

The `ACE_SOCK_Connector`'s connection time-out support is particularly useful in practice since the ways in which Socket APIs implement connection time-outs differs widely across OS platforms.

Since the underlying socket API doesn't use a factory socket to connect data-mode sockets, the `ACE_SOCK_Connector` class needn't inherit from the `ACE_SOCK` class described on page 54 in Section 3.4. It therefore doesn't have its own socket handle. Instead, an `ACE_SOCK_Connector` borrows the handle from the `ACE_SOCK_Stream` passed to its `connect()` method and uses it to establish the connection actively. As a result, instances of `ACE_SOCK_Connector` don't store any state, so they can be used reentrantly in multithreaded programs without the need for additional locks.

Example

Sidebar 2 on page 19 describes how to build the ACE library so that you can experiment with the examples we show in the book. Our first example illustrates how the ACE_SOCK_Connector can be used to connect a client application to a Web server. We start by including the necessary ACE Socket wrapper header files:

```
#include "ace/INET_Addr.h"
#include "ace/SOCK_Connector.h"
#include "ace/SOCK_Stream.h"
```

We then define the main() function, which establishes a connection with a Web server listening at port 80. This is the standard port number used by Web servers that support the Hypertext Transport Protocol (HTTP) [Ste96]. HTTP is a simple protocol layered on top of TCP and used by clients to download content from a Web server.

```
int main (int argc, char *argv[])
{
  const char *pathname =
    argc > 1 ? argv[1] : "/index.html";
  const char *server_hostname =
    argc > 2 ? argv[2] : "ace.ece.uci.edu";

  ACE_SOCK_Connector connector;
  ACE_SOCK_Stream peer;
  ACE_INET_Addr peer_addr;

  if (peer_addr.set (80, server_hostname) == -1)
    return 1;
  else if (connector.connect (peer, peer_addr) == -1)
    return 1;
  // ...
```

We complete the rest of this example on page 63 in Section 3.5 after first describing the capabilities of the ACE_SOCK_Stream data transfer class.

Note that the connector.connect() call above is synchronous; that is, it will block until either the connection is established or connect request fails. As shown in the table on page 58, the ACE Socket wrapper facades make it easy to perform nonblocking or timed connections portably. For example, the following code illustrates how to modify our client application to perform a nonblocking connect() to a Web server:

```
// Designate a nonblocking connect.
if (connector.connect (peer,
                       peer_addr,
                       &ACE_Time_Value::zero) == -1) {
  if (errno == EWOULDBLOCK) {
    // Do some other work ...

    // Now, try to complete the connection establishment,
    // but don't block if it isn't complete yet.
    if (connector.complete (peer,
                            0,
                            &ACE_Time_Value::zero) == -1)
      // ...
```

Likewise, a timed `connect()` can be performed as follows:

```
ACE_Time_Value timeout (10); // Set time-out to 10 seconds

if (connector.connect (peer, peer_addr, &timeout) == -1) {
  if (errno == ETIME)
    // Time-out, do something else...
}
```

3.6   The ACE_SOCK_IO and ACE_SOCK_Stream Classes

Motivation

An area of accidental complexity identified in Section 2.3 is the inability to detect socket misuse at compile-time. As described in Section 3.1, connection management involves three roles: *active connection role*, *passive connection role*, and *communication role*. The Socket API, however, defines only two socket modes: *data mode* and *passive mode*. Developers can therefore misuse sockets in ways that can't be detected during compilation. The ACE_SOCK_Connector class took the first step toward resolving this area of complexity; the ACE_SOCK_Stream class takes the next step. ACE_SOCK_Stream defines a data-mode "transfer-only" object. An ACE_SOCK_Stream object can't be used in any role other than data transfer without intentionally violating its interface.

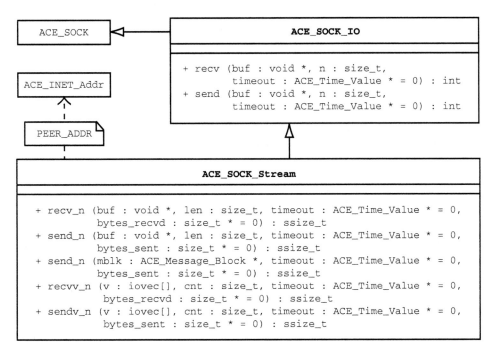

Figure 3.7: **The** ACE_SOCK_Stream **and** ACE_SOCK_IO **Class Diagrams**

Class Capabilities

The ACE_SOCK_Stream class encapsulates the data transfer mechanisms supported by data-mode sockets. This class provides the following capabilities:

- Support for sending and receiving up to n bytes or exactly n bytes
- Support for "scatter-read" operations, which populate multiple caller-supplied buffers instead of a single contiguous buffer
- Support for "gather-write" operations, which transmit the contents of multiple noncontiguous data buffers in a single operation
- Support for blocking, nonblocking, and timed I/O operations and
- Support for generic programming techniques [Ale01] that enable the wholesale replacement of functionality via C++ parameterized types, as described in Sidebar 5 on page 57

ACE_SOCK_Stream instances are initialized by the ACE_SOCK_Acceptor or ACE_SOCK_Connector factories. The interface of the ACE_SOCK_Stream and `ACE_SOCK_IO` classes are shown in Figure 3.7 on page 61. `ACE_SOCK_Stream` derives from `ACE_SOCK_IO`, which itself derives from `ACE_SOCK` and defines basic data transfer methods that are reused by the ACE UDP wrapper facades.

The key methods exported through `ACE_SOCK_Stream` are outlined in the following table:

Method	Description
`send()` `recv()`	Transmit and receive buffers of data. They may write or read less than the number of bytes requested due to buffering in the OS and flow control in the transport protocol.
`send_n()` `recv_n()`	Transmit and receive data buffers of exactly n bytes to simplify application handling of "short-writes" and "short-reads."
`recvv_n()`	Receives multiple buffers of data efficiently and completely using an OS "scatter-read" system function.
`sendv_n()`	Sends multiple buffers of data efficiently and completely using an OS "gather-write" system function.

The `ACE_SOCK_Stream` class supports blocking, timed, and nonblocking I/O. With blocking I/O, the calling thread waits until the I/O completes. Timed I/O is useful when communicating with peers that can hang or block indefinitely. Two types of `ACE_Time_Value` values can be passed to the `ACE_SOCK_Stream` I/O methods to control their time-out behavior:

Value	Behavior
`NULL ACE_Time_Value` pointer	Indicates that an I/O method should block until data are transferred or until an error occurs.
A non-`NULL` `ACE_Time_Value` pointer	Indicates that the I/O method should wait a relative amount of time to transfer the data. If the time-out expires before the data is sent or received a -1 is returned with `errno` set to `ETIME`.

Nonblocking I/O is useful for applications that can't afford to block when data isn't sent or received immediately. Blocking versus nonblocking I/O can be controlled via the `enable()` and `disable()` methods inherited from `ACE_IPC_SAP`:

```
peer.enable (ACE_NONBLOCK); // Enable nonblocking I/O.
peer.disable (ACE_NONBLOCK); // Disable nonblocking I/O.
```

If an I/O method is invoked on an instance of `ACE_SOCK_Stream` that's in nonblocking mode and the call would block, a -1 is returned and `errno` is set to `EWOULDBLOCK`.

Example

Now that we've examined the capabilities of ACE_SOCK_Stream, we can show the data transfer portion of our Web client example begun on page 59 in Section 3.5. This code sends an HTTP GET request for a particular URL path name and then prints out the contents of the file that's downloaded from the Web server.

```
// ...Connection code from example in Section 3.5 omitted...
char buf[BUFSIZ];
iovec iov[3];
iov[0].iov_base = (char *) "GET ";
iov[0].iov_len = 4; // Length of "GET ".
iov[1].iov_base = (char *) pathname;
iov[1].iov_len = strlen (pathname);
iov[2].iov_base = (char *) " HTTP/1.0\r\n\r\n";
iov[2].iov_len = 13; // Length of " HTTP/1.0\r\n\r\n";

if (peer.sendv_n (iov, 3) == -1)
  return 1;

for (ssize_t n; (n = peer.recv (buf, sizeof buf)) > 0; )
  ACE::write_n (ACE_STDOUT, buf, n);

  return peer.close () == -1 ? 1 : 0;
}
```

We use an array of iovec structures to transmit the HTTP GET request to the Web server efficiently using the ACE_SOCK_Stream::sendv_n() gather-write method. This avoids performance issues with Nagle's algorithm [Ste93] described in Sidebar 6. On UNIX/POSIX platforms this method is implemented via writev() and on WinSock2 platforms it's implemented via WSASend().

The I/O methods in the portion of the main() function above will block if they encounter TCP flw control or if the Web server misbehaves. To prevent the client from hanging indefinitely, we can add time-outs to these method calls. In the following code, for instance, if the server doesn't receive the data in 10 seconds, a −1 will be returned with errno set to ETIME:

```
// Wait no more than 10 seconds to send or receive data.
ACE_Time_Value timeout (10);

peer.sendv_n (iov, 3, &timeout);

while (peer.recv (buf, sizeof buf, &timeout) > 0)
  // ... process the contents of the downloaded file.
```

Sidebar 6: Working With—and Around—Nagle's Algorithm

By default, most TCP/IP implementations use Nagle's algorithm (Ste93), which buffers small, sequentially sent packets in the sender's TCP/IP stack. Although this algorithm minimizes network congestion, it can increase latency and decrease throughput if you're unaware of how and when it takes effect. These problems can arise when several small buffers are sent in successive one-way operations; for example, the following code will trigger Nagle's algorithm:

```
peer.send_n ("GET ", 4);
peer.send_n (pathname, strlen (pathname));
peer.send_n (" HTTP/1.0\r\n\r\n", 13);
```

Application developers can disable Nagle's algorithm by calling `peer.set_option()` with the TCP_NODELAY flag, which forces TCP to send packets out as soon as possible. The `main()` function code on page 63 shows an even more efficient solution using `sendv_n()` to transfer all data buffers in a single system function. This method is passed an array of `iovec` structures, which are defined as follows:

```
struct iovec {
  // Pointer to a buffer.
  char *iov_base;

  // Length of buffer pointed to by <iov_base>.
  int iov_len;
};
```

Some OS platforms define `iovec` natively, whereas in other platforms it's defined by ACE. Member names are the same in all cases, but they're not always in the same order, so set them explicitly rather than via `struct` initialization.

3.7 The ACE_SOCK_Acceptor Class

Motivation

The ACE_SOCK_Connector and ACE_SOCK_Stream classes resolve complexity issues that arise from the mismatch of communication roles and Socket API functions. Although the Socket API defines a single set of functions to

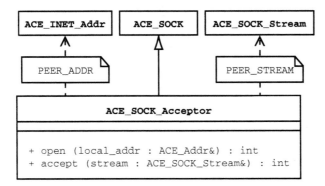

Figure 3.8: **The** ACE_SOCK_Acceptor **Class Diagram**

fill the passive connection establishment role, there's an additional set of complexities. The C functions in the Socket API are weakly typed, which makes it easy to apply them incorrectly.

For example, the accept() function can be called on a data-mode socket handle that's intended to transfer data via the recv() and send() I/O operations. Likewise, the I/O operations can be called on a passive-mode socket handle factory that's intended only to accept connections. Unfortunately, these mistakes can't be detected until run time. ACE resolves these complexities with the strongly typed ACE_SOCK_Acceptor class. As opposed to direct Socket API calls, the compiler can easily detect misuse of an ACE_SOCK_Acceptor at compile time.

Class Capabilities

The ACE_SOCK_Acceptor class is a factory [GHJV95] that establishes a new endpoint of communication passively. It provides the following capabilities:

- It accepts a connection from a peer connector and then initializes an ACE_SOCK_Stream object after the connection is established.
- Connections can be accepted in either a blocking, nonblocking, or timed manner.
- C++ traits are used to support generic programming techniques that enable the wholesale replacement of functionality via C++ parameterized types, as described in Sidebar 5 on page 57.

The interface of the ACE_SOCK_Acceptor class is shown in Figure 3.8 on page 65 and its two key methods are outlined in the following table:

Method	Description
open()	Initializes the passive-mode factory socket to listen passively at a designated ACE_INET_Addr address.
accept()	Initializes the ACE_SOCK_Stream parameter with a newly accepted client connection.

The ACE_SOCK_Acceptor open() and accept() methods use the socket handle inherited from ACE_IPC_SAP. This design employs the C++ type system to protect application developers from the following sources of accidental misuse:

- The low-level socket(), bind(), and listen() functions are always called in the right order by the ACE_SOCK_Acceptor's open() method.
- These functions are called only on a socket handle that's been initialized as a passive-mode socket handle factory.

The principles that underlie these and other ACE wrapper facade design choices are described in Appendix A.

Example

We illustrate the ACE_SOCK_Acceptor by showing the passive connection establishment and content downloading portions of an iterative Web server, which processes client requests as follows:

1. Accept a new connection from client on port 80.
2. Read path name from GET request and download requested file.
3. Close the connection.
4. Go back to step 1.

To read the file efficiently we use an ACE_Mem_Map, which is described in Sidebar 7 on page 68. To use the ACE_Mem_Map capabilities, we include ace/Mem_Map.h along with the other ACE Socket wrapper facade header files needed to write our Web server.

```
#include "ace/Auto_Ptr.h"
#include "ace/INET_Addr.h"
#include "ace/SOCK_Acceptor.h"
```

```
#include "ace/SOCK_Stream.h"
#include "ace/Mem_Map.h"

// Return a dynamically allocated path name buffer.
extern char *get_url_pathname (ACE_SOCK_Stream *);
```

Our Web server supports HTTP version 1.0, so each client request will have a separate TCP connection. In the following Web server code, we first initialize our ACE_SOCK_Acceptor factory to listen for connections on port 80. We then run an event loop that iteratively accepts a new client connection, memory-maps the file, downloads it to the client, and closes the connection when it's finished transmitting the file.

```
int main ()
{
  ACE_INET_Addr server_addr;
  ACE_SOCK_Acceptor acceptor;
  ACE_SOCK_Stream peer;

  if (server_addr.set (80) == -1) return 1;
  if (acceptor.open (server_addr) == -1) return 1;

  for (;;) {
    if (acceptor.accept (peer) == -1) return 1;
    peer.disable (ACE_NONBLOCK); // Ensure blocking <send_n>.

    ACE_Auto_Array_Ptr<char> pathname (get_url_pathname (&peer));
    ACE_Mem_Map mapped_file (pathname.get ());

    if (peer.send_n (mapped_file.addr (),
                     mapped_file.size ()) == -1) return 1;
    peer.close ();
  }

  return acceptor.close () == -1 ? 1 : 0;
}
```

The primary drawback with our iterative Web server will arise when many clients send it requests simultaneously. In this case, the OS Socket implementation will queue a small number (e.g., 5–10) of connection requests while the Web server processes the current one. In a production Web server, the OS can be overwhelmed quickly. When this happens, clients can encounter errors when the Web server's OS refuses their connection attempts. Chapters 8 and 9 describe patterns and ACE wrapper facades that address this drawback.

Sidebar 7: The ACE_Mem_Map Class

The `ACE_Mem_Map` wrapper facade encapsulates the memory-mapped file mechanisms available on Win32 and POSIX platforms. These calls use OS virtual memory mechanisms to map files into the address space of a process. Mapped file contents can be accessed directly via a pointer, which is more convenient and efficient than accessing blocks of data via read and write system I/O functions. In addition, the contents of memory-mapped files can be shared by multiple processes on the same machine, as described in Section 1.3 on page 29.

The native Win32 and POSIX memory-mapped file APIs are non-portable and complex. For instance, developers must perform many bookkeeping details manually, such as explicitly opening a file, determining its length, and performing multiple mappings. In contrast, the `ACE_Mem_Map` wrapper facade offers an interface that simplifies common memory-mapped file usage via default values and multiple constructors with several type signature variants, for example, "map from an open file handle" or "map from a filename."

3.8 Summary

This chapter showed how ACE uses C++ features and the Wrapper Facade pattern to make it easier to program connection-oriented TCP/IP mechanisms correctly and portably in networked applications. We focused on ACE Socket wrapper facades that simplify the use of

- Network addresses, I/O handles, and basic socket operations and
- TCP connection establishment and data transfer operations

The next chapter shows how these Socket wrapper facades are used to develop the first iteration of our networked logging service.

The ACE Socket wrapper facades resolve the following problems with the Socket API discussed in Section 2.3:

- **Error-prone APIs**—The ACE Socket wrapper facades ensure that all arguments to Socket APIs are type-safe. Likewise, byte-ordering issues that must be dealt with during address lookup functions are handled by ACE transparently.

- **Overly complex APIs**—By clustering the Socket API into separate classes for actively connecting, passively accepting, and transferring data, the ACE Socket wrapper facades reduce the amount of complexity that's exposed to developers of networked applications. Thus, developers needn't understand all of the ACE Socket wrapper facades to write a networked application, only the parts they use.
- **Nonportable and nonuniform APIs**—The client application and Web server source code compiles and runs correctly and efficiently on all platforms that ACE supports.

The object-oriented design of the ACE Socket wrapper facades also makes it easy to change an application's IPC mechanism without having to modify API arguments and manually change addressing structures and functions. For example, the classes within each communication service type (stream, connected datagram, or datagram) in Figure 3.2 expose a common set of methods that allows them to be interchanged easily using *generic programming* techniques [Ale01]. As described in Sidebar 5 on page 57, generic programming and the C++ trait *idiom* enable the wholesale replacement of functionality via parameterized types. These techniques are also applied to other ACE IPC wrapper facade classes, which are described at the ACE Web site at `http://ace.ece.uci.edu`.

## CHAPTER 4

Implementing the Networked Logging Service

This chapter presents the first implementation of our networked logging service. We illustrate how to send, receive, and process log records in a portable, correct, and efficient manner by combining the ACE Socket wrapper facades from Chapter 3 with other ACE classes that handle message buffering and (de)marshaling. We refine this example throughout the rest of the book to illustrate common issues and problems that need to be resolved when developing object-oriented networked applications.

4.1 Overview

Most networked applications perform the following activities:

- Establish connections actively and passively
- Exchange data with peer applications
- Manage buffers of data and
- Marshal and demarshal typed data so that it can be processed correctly in heterogeneous systems

This chapter illustrates how the ACE Socket wrapper facades from Chapter 3 can be augmented with ACE message buffering and (de)marshaling classes to simplify the first implementation of our networked logging service. The participants in this service are shown in Figure 0.6 on page 18.

4.2 The ACE_Message_Block Class

Motivation

Many networked applications require a means to manipulate messages efficiently [SS93]. Standard message management operations include

- Storing messages in buffers as they are received from the network or from other processes on the same host
- Adding and/or removing headers and trailers from messages as they pass through a user-level protocol stack
- Fragmenting and reassembling messages to fit into network maximum transmission units (MTUs)
- Storing messages in buffers for transmission or retransmission
- Reordering messages that were received out-of-sequence

To improve efficiency, these operations must minimize the overhead of dynamic memory management and avoid unnecessary data copying, which is why ACE provides the `ACE_Message_Block` class.

Class Capabilities

The `ACE_Message_Block` class enables efficient manipulation of fixed- and variable-sized messages. `ACE_Message_Block` implements the Composite pattern [GHJV95] and provides the following capabilities:

- Each `ACE_Message_Block` contains a pointer to a reference-counted `ACE_Data_Block`, which in turn points to the actual data associated with a message. This design allows flexible and efficient sharing of data and minimizes excessive memory copying overhead.
- It allows multiple messages to be chained together into a singly linked list to support composite messages, which can be used for polymorphic lists and for layered protocol stacks that require headers/trailers to be inserted/removed efficiently.
- It allows multiple messages to be joined together in a doubly linked list that forms the basis of the `ACE_Message_Queue` class outlined on page 228 and described in [SH].
- It treats synchronization and memory management properties as *aspects* [Kic97, CE00] that applications can vary without changing the underlying `ACE_Message_Block` implementation.

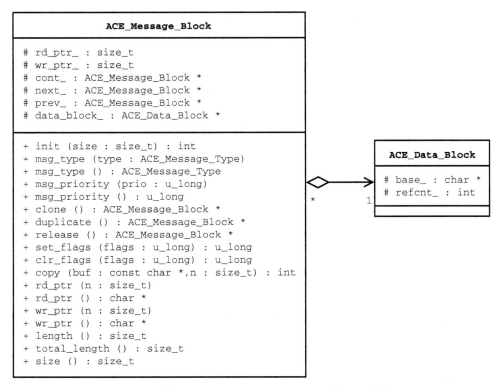

Figure 4.1: **The** ACE_Message_Block **Class Diagram**

The interface of the ACE_Message_Block class is shown in Figure 4.1. Its design is modeled loosely on the System V STREAMS [Rag93] message buffering mechanism, and it supports two kinds of messages:

- **Simple messages** contain a single ACE_Message_Block, as shown in Figure 4.2 (1).

- **Composite messages** contain multiple ACE_Message_Blocks linked together in accordance with the Composite pattern [GHJV95], which provides a structure for building recursive aggregations, as shown in Figure 4.2 (2). Composite messages often consist of a control message that contains bookkeeping information, such as destination addresses, followed by one or more data messages that contain the actual contents of the message.

The key methods of ACE_Message_Block are outlined in the following table:

Method	Description
ACE_Message_Block() init()	Initialize the message.
msg_type()	Set and get the message type.
msg_priority()	Set and get the message priority.
clone()	Returns an exact "deep copy" of the entire message.
duplicate()	Returns a "shallow" copy of the message that increments its reference count by 1.
release()	Decrements the reference count by 1 and releases the message resources if the count drops to 0.
set_flags()	Bitwise-OR the specified bits into the existing set of flags that determine the message semantics, for example, whether to delete the buffer when the message is released, and so on.
clr_flags()	Clears the designated flag bits.
copy()	Copies *n* bytes from a buffer into the message.
rd_ptr()	Set and get the read pointer.
wr_ptr()	Set and get the write pointer.
cont()	Set and get the message continuation field, which chains together composite messages.
next() prev()	Set and get the pointers to the doubly linked list of messages in an ACE_Message_Queue.
length()	Set and get the current length of the message, which is defined as wr_ptr() − rd_ptr().
total_length()	Gets the length of the message, including all chained message blocks.
size()	Set and get the total capacity of the message, which includes the amount of storage allocated before and beyond the [rd_ptr(), wr_ptr()) range.

Each ACE_Message_Block contains a pointer to a reference-counted ACE_Data_Block, which in turn points to the actual data payload, as shown in Figure 4.2 (1). Note how the rd_ptr() and wr_ptr() point to the beginning and end of the active portion of the data payload, respectively. Figure 4.2 (2) shows how the ACE_Message_Block::duplicate() method can be used to make a "shallow copy" of a message. This allows them to share the same data flexibly and efficiently by minimizing memory allocation and copying overhead. Since the message block itself is copied, the rd_ptr()s and wr_ptr()s can point to different parts of the same shared data payload.

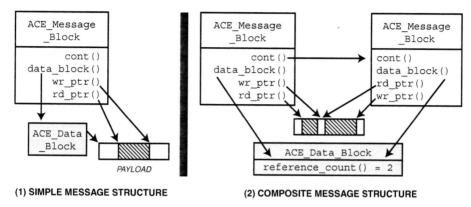

(1) SIMPLE MESSAGE STRUCTURE   **(2) COMPOSITE MESSAGE STRUCTURE**

Figure 4.2: **Two Kinds of** ACE_Message_Block

Example

The following program reads all data from standard input into a singly
linked list of dynamically allocated ACE_Message_Blocks that are chained
together by their continuation pointers. It then prints the contents of all
the chained message blocks to the standard output and releases their dynamically allocated memory.

```
#include "ace/ACE.h"
#include "ace/Message_Block.h"

int main (int, char *[])
{
  ACE_Message_Block *head = new ACE_Message_Block (BUFSIZ);
  ACE_Message_Block *mblk = head;

  for (size_t recvd = 0; ; recvd = 0) {
    ssize_t nbytes = ACE::read_n (ACE_STDIN,
                                  mblk->wr_ptr (),
                                  mblk->size (),
                                  &recvd);
    // Advance the write pointer to the end of the buffer.
    mblk->wr_ptr (recvd);
    if (nbytes <= 0)
      break; // Break out at EOF or error.

    // Allocate message block and chain it at the end of list.
    mblk->cont (new ACE_Message_Block (BUFSIZ));
    mblk = mblk->cont ();
  }
```

```
// Print the contents of the list to the standard output.
for (mblk = head; mblk != 0; mblk = mblk->cont ())
  ACE::write_n (ACE_STDOUT, mblk->rd_ptr (), mblk->length ());

head->release (); // This releases all the memory in the chain.
return 0;
}
```

The `for` loop that prints the contents of the list to the standard output can be replaced by a single call to `ACE::write_n(ACE_STDOUT,head)`. This method prints out all the message blocks chained through their `cont()` pointers using a highly efficient gather-write operation. A similar optimization is used in the `Logging_Handler::write_log_record()` method on page 90.

We use the `ACE::read_n()` and `ACE::write_n()` methods rather than the C++ iostreams mechanism since not all OS platforms that ACE runs on support C++ iostreams adequately. It's possible to substitute `cin` and `cout` on platforms that do support them properly. They may incur additional data copying due to internal buffering, however, and can't take advantage of the gather-write optimization described in the preceding paragraph.

4.3   The ACE_InputCDR and ACE_OutputCDR Classes

Motivation

Networked applications that send and receive messages often require support for

- *Linearization* to handle the conversion of richly typed data, such as arrays, linked lists, or graphs, to/from raw memory buffers
- *Marshaling/demarshaling* to correctly interoperate in environments with heterogeneous compiler alignment constraints and hardware instructions with different byte-ordering rules

Since it's hard to manually perform linearization, marshaling, and demarshaling correctly and efficiently, these operations are best encapsulated in reusable classes, which is why ACE provides `ACE_OutputCDR` and `ACE_InputCDR`.

Class Capabilities

The ACE_OutputCDR and ACE_InputCDR classes provide a highly optimized, portable, and convenient means to marshal and demarshal data using the standard CORBA *Common Data Representation (CDR)* format [Obj01]. ACE_OutputCDR creates a CDR buffer from a data structure (marshaling) and ACE_InputCDR extracts data from a CDR buffer (demarshaling).

The ACE_OutputCDR and ACE_InputCDR classes support the following features:

- They provide operations to (de)marshal the following types:

  - **Primitive types**, for example, booleans; 16-, 32-, and 64-bit integers; 8-bit octets; single and double precision floating point numbers; characters; and strings
  - **Arrays of primitive types**

- The insertion (<<) and extraction (>>) operators can be used to marshal and demarshal primitive types, using the same syntax as the C++ iostream components.

- They use ACE_Message_Block chains internally to avoid expensive memory copies.

- They take advantage of CORBA CDR alignment and byte-ordering rules to avoid expensive memory copying and byte-swapping operations, respectively.

- They provide optimized byte swapping code that uses inline assembly language instructions for common hardware platforms, such as Intel x86, and the standard htons(), htonl(), ntohs(), and ntohl() macros/functions on other platforms.

- They support zero copy marshaling and demarshaling of octet buffers.

- Users can define custom character set translators for platforms that do not use ASCII or UNICODE as their native character sets.

The interfaces for the ACE CDR streaming classes are shown in Figure 4.3. The key methods in ACE_OutputCDR class are shown in the following table:

Method	Description
`ACE_OutputCDR()`	Creates an empty CDR stream for insertion.
`write_*()`	Inserts a primitive into the stream, for example, `write_ushort()`.
`write_*_array()`	Inserts an array of primitives into the stream, for example, `write_long_array()`.
`operator<<()`	An insertion operator is defined for each primitive type.
`good_bit()`	Returns 0 if the stream has detected an error.
`total_length()`	Returns the number of bytes in the stream.
`begin()`	Returns a pointer to the first message block in the chain.
`end()`	Returns a pointer to the last message block in the chain.

Likewise, the key methods for the `ACE_InputCDR` class are shown in the following table:

Method	Description
`ACE_InputCDR()`	Creates an empty CDR stream for extraction.
`read_*()`	Extracts a primitive from the stream, for example, `read_char()`.
`read_*_array()`	Extracts an array of primitives from the stream, for example, `read_octet_array()`.
`operator>>()`	An extraction operator is defined for each primitive type.
`good_bit()`	Returns 0 if the stream has detected an error.
`steal_contents()`	Returns a copy of the underlying `ACE_Message_Block` containing the current CDR stream.

The `ACE_OutputCDR` and `ACE_InputCDR` classes transform typed data into untyped buffers and vice versa. As a result, programmers must be careful when using these classes to prevent type system violations. One way to avoid these problems altogether is to program using distribution middleware, such as CORBA [Obj01] and The ACE ORB (TAO) [SLM98] described in Section B.1.4 on page 264.

Example

The ACE CDR streaming classes predefine operators `<<` and `>>` for primitive types and arrays. ACE applications are responsible for defining these operators for their own data types.[1] To illustrate these operators, we show

---

[1]These operators can also be generated automatically by tools, such as the CORBA Interface Definition Language (IDL) compiler [AOSK00] provided by TAO.

```
+-----------------------------------+
|           ACE_InputCDR            |
+-----------------------------------+
| - start_ : ACE_Message_Block      |
| - good_bit_ : int                 |
+-----------------------------------+
| + read_char (x : Char &)          |
|       : Boolean                   |
| + read_octet_array (x : Octet*,   |
|               size : ULong)       |
|     : Boolean                     |
| + operator>> (s: ACE_InputCDR&,   |
|           x : Char)               |
|     : Boolean                     |
| + good_bit () : int               |
| + steal_contents ()               |
|       : ACE_Message_Block *       |
+-----------------------------------+
```

```
+-----------------------------------+
|          ACE_OutputCDR            |
+-----------------------------------+
| - start_ : ACE_Message_Block      |
| - current_ : ACE_Message_Block *  |
| - good_bit_ : int                 |
+-----------------------------------+
| + write_ushort (x : UShort)       |
|       : Boolean                   |
| + write_long_array (x : Long *,   |
|               size : ULong)       |
|     : Boolean                     |
| + operator<< (s : ACE_OutputCDR&, |
|           x : UShort)             |
|     : Boolean                     |
| + good_bit () : int               |
| + total_length () : size_t        |
| + begin () : ACE_Message_Block *  |
| + end () : ACE_Message_Block *    |
+-----------------------------------+
```

Figure 4.3: **The** ACE_InputCDR **and** ACE_OutputCDR **Class Diagrams**

the ACE CDR insertion and extraction operators for the ACE_Log_Record class that's used by both the client application and logging server. This C++ class contains several fields and a variable-sized message buffer. Our insertion operation therefore marshals each field into an ACE_OutputCDR object, as shown below:

```
int operator<< (ACE_OutputCDR &cdr,
                const ACE_Log_Record &log_record)
{
  size_t msglen = log_record.msg_data_len ();

  // Insert each <log_record> field into the output CDR stream.
  cdr << ACE_CDR::Long (log_record.type ());
  cdr << ACE_CDR::Long (log_record.pid ());
  cdr << ACE_CDR::Long (log_record.time_stamp ().sec ());
  cdr << ACE_CDR::Long (log_record.time_stamp ().usec ());
  cdr << ACE_CDR::ULong (msglen);

  cdr.write_char_array (log_record.msg_data (), msglen);

  return cdr.good_bit ();
}
```

Our extraction operator demarshals each field from an ACE_InputCDR object and fills in an ACE_Log_Record object accordingly:

```
int operator>> (ACE_InputCDR &cdr,
                ACE_Log_Record &log_record)
{
  ACE_CDR::Long type;
  ACE_CDR::Long pid;
  ACE_CDR::Long sec, usec;
  ACE_CDR::ULong buffer_len;

  // Extract each field from input CDR stream into <log_record>.
  if ((cdr >> type) && (cdr >> pid) && (cdr >> sec)
      && (cdr >> usec) && (cdr >> buffer_len)) {
    ACE_TCHAR log_msg[ACE_Log_Record::MAXLOGMSGLEN+1];
    log_record.type (type);
    log_record.pid (pid);
    log_record.time_stamp (ACE_Time_Value (sec, usec));
    cdr.read_char_array (log_msg, buffer_len);
    log_msg[buffer_len] = '\0';
    log_record.msg_data (log_msg);
  }

  return cdr.good_bit ();
}
```

We'll use these two insertion and extraction operators to simplify our networked logging application shortly.

4.4   The Initial Logging Server

Our first networked logging service implementation defines the initial design and the core reusable class implementations. The logging server listens on a TCP port number defined in the operating system's network services file as `ace_logger`, which is a practice used by many networked servers. For example, the following line might exist in the UNIX `/etc/ services` file:

```
ace_logger     9700/tcp     # Connection-oriented Logging Service
```

Client applications can optionally specify the TCP port and the IP address where the client application and logging server should rendezvous to exchange log records. If this information is not specified, however, the port number is located in the services database, and the host name is assumed to be the ACE_DEFAULT_SERVER_HOST, which is defined as "localhost" on most OS platforms. Once it's connected, the client sends log records to the logging server, which writes each record to a file. This section presents a

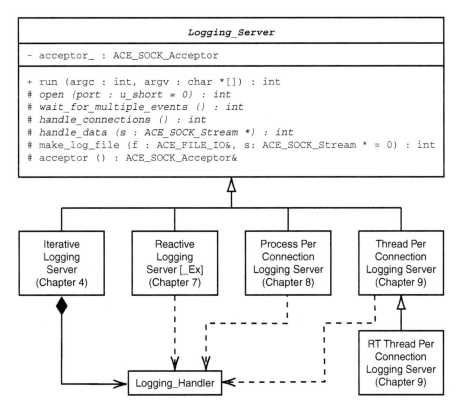

Figure 4.4: **Logging Server Example Classes**

set of reusable classes that handle passive connection establishment and data transfer for all the logging servers shown in this book.

4.4.1   The Logging_Server Base Class

Now that previous sections described ACE_Message_Block, ACE_Output_ CDR, and ACE_InputCDR, we'll use these classes in a new base class that will simplify our logging server implementations throughout the book. Figure 4.4 illustrates our Logging_Server abstract base class, the Logging_ Handler class we'll develop in Section 4.4.2, and the concrete logging server classes that we'll develop in future chapters. We put the definition of the Logging_Server base class into the following header file called Logging_Server.h:

```cpp
#include "ace/FILE_IO.h"
#include "ace/SOCK_Acceptor.h"

// Forward declaration.
class ACE_SOCK_Stream;

class Logging_Server
{
public:
  // Template Method that runs logging server's event loop.
  virtual int run (int argc, char *argv[]);

protected:
  // The following four methods are ``hooks'' that can be
  // overridden by subclasses.
  virtual int open (u_short logger_port = 0);
  virtual int wait_for_multiple_events () { return 0; }
  virtual int handle_connections () = 0;
  virtual int handle_data (ACE_SOCK_Stream * = 0) = 0;

  // This helper method can be used by the hook methods.
  int make_log_file (ACE_FILE_IO &, ACE_SOCK_Stream * = 0);

  // Close the socket endpoint and shutdown ACE.
  virtual ~Logging_Server () {
    acceptor_.close ();
  }

  // Accessor.
  ACE_SOCK_Acceptor &acceptor () {
    return acceptor_;
  }

private:
  // Socket acceptor endpoint.
  ACE_SOCK_Acceptor acceptor_;
};
```

All the subsequent networked logging service examples will include this
header file, subclass Logging_Server, and override and reuse its methods, each of which we describe below. The implementation file Logging_
Server.cpp includes the following ACE header files:

```cpp
#include "ace/FILE_Addr.h"
#include "ace/FILE_Connector.h"
#include "ace/FILE_IO.h"
#include "ace/INET_Addr.h"
#include "ace/SOCK_Stream.h"
#include "Logging_Server.h"
```

The Logging_Server::run() Template Method

This public method performs the canonical initialization and event loop steps used by most of the logging servers in this book.

```
int Logging_Server::run (int argc, char *argv[])
{
  if (open (argc > 1 ? atoi (argv[1]) : 0) == -1)
    return -1;

  for (;;) {
    if (wait_for_multiple_events () == -1) return -1;
    if (handle_connections () == -1) return -1;
    if (handle_data () == -1) return -1;
  }
  return 0;
}
```

The code above is an example of the Template Method pattern [GHJV95], which defines the skeleton of an algorithm in an operation, deferring some steps to hook methods that can be overridden by subclasses. The calls to open(), wait_for_multiple_events(), handle_data(), and handle_connections() in the run() template method are all hook methods that can be overridden by subclasses.

The Logging_Server Hook Methods

Each hook method in the Logging_Server class has a role and a default behavior that's described briefly below.

Logging_Server::open(). This method initializes the server address and the Logging_Server's acceptor endpoint to listen passively on a designated port number. Although it can be overridden by subclasses, the default implementation shown below suffices for all the examples in this book:

```
int Logging_Server::open (u_short logger_port)
{
  // Raises the number of available socket handles to
  // the maximum supported by the OS platform.
  ACE::set_handle_limit ();

  ACE_INET_Addr server_addr;
  int result;
```

```
  if (logger_port != 0)
    result = server_addr.set (logger_port, INADDR_ANY);
  else
    result = server_addr.set ("ace_logger", INADDR_ANY);
  if (result == -1)
    return -1;

  // Start listening and enable reuse of listen address
  // for quick restarts.
  return acceptor_.open (server_addr, 1);
}
```

Although an `ACE_INET_Addr` constructor accepts the port number and host name as arguments, we avoid it here for the following reasons:

1. We allow the user to either pass a port number or use the default service name, which requires different calls

2. Networking addressing functions such as `gethostbyname()` may be called, which can surprise programmers who don't expect a constructor to delay its execution until the server host address is resolved and

3. We need to issue the proper diagnostic if there was an error.

Section A.6.3 on page 256 explains why ACE doesn't use native C++ exceptions to propagate errors.

Note the second argument on the `acceptor_.open` call. It causes the SO_REUSEADDR socket option to be set on the acceptor socket, allowing the program to restart soon after it has been stopped. This avoids any clashes with sockets in TIME_WAIT state left from the previous run that would otherwise prevent a new logging server from listening for logging clients for several minutes.

Logging_Server::wait_for_multiple_events(). The role of this method is to wait for multiple events to occur. It's default implementation is a no-op; that is, it simply returns 0. This default behavior is overridden by implementations of the logging server that use the `select()`-based synchronous event demultiplexing mechanisms described in Chapter 7.

Logging_Server::handle_connections(). The role of this hook method is to accept one or more connections from clients. We define it as a pure virtual method to ensure that subclasses implement it.

Logging_Server::handle_data(). The role of this hook method is to receive a log record from a client and write it to a log file. We also define it as a pure virtual method to ensure that subclasses implement it.

Sidebar 8: The ACE File Wrapper Facades

ACE encapsulates platform mechanisms for unbuffered file operations in accordance with the Wrapper Facade pattern. Like most of the ACE IPC wrapper facades families, the ACE File classes decouple the

- **Initialization factories,** such as `ACE_FILE_Connector`, which open and/or create files, from
- **Data transfer classes,** such as the `ACE_FILE_IO`, which applications use to read and write data to a file opened by `ACE_FILE_Connector`.

The symmetry of the ACE IPC and file wrapper facades demonstrates the generality of ACE's design and provides the basis for strategizing IPC mechanisms into the higher-level ACE frameworks described in (SH).

The Logging_Server::make_log_file() Method

This helper method can be used by the hook methods to initialize a log file using the ACE File wrapper facades outlined in Sidebar 8.

```
int Logging_Server::make_log_file (ACE_FILE_IO &logging_file,
                                   ACE_SOCK_Stream *logging_peer)
{
  char filename[MAXHOSTNAMELEN + sizeof (".log")];

  if (logging_peer != 0) { // Use client host name as file name.
    ACE_INET_Addr logging_peer_addr;
    logging_peer->get_remote_addr (logging_peer_addr);
    logging_peer_addr.get_host_name (filename, MAXHOSTNAMELEN);
    strcat (filename, ".log");
  }
  else
    strcpy (filename, "logging_server.log");

  ACE_FILE_Connector connector;
  return connector.connect (logging_file,
                            ACE_FILE_Addr (filename),
                            0, // No time-out.
                            ACE_Addr::sap_any, // Ignored.
                            0, // Don't try to reuse the addr.
                            O_RDWR|O_CREAT|O_APPEND,
                            ACE_DEFAULT_FILE_PERMS);
}
```

We name the log file `"logging_server.log"` by default. This name can
be overridden by using the host name of the connected client, as we show
on page 156 in Section 7.4.

Sidebar 9: The Logging Service Message Framing Protocol

Since TCP is a bytestream protocol, we need an application-level message framing protocol to delimit log records in the data stream. We use
an 8-byte, CDR-encoded header that contains the byte-order indication and payload length, followed by the log record contents, as shown
below:

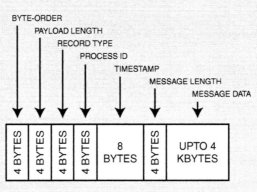

4.4.2   The Logging_Handler Class

This class is used in logging servers to encapsulate the I/O and processing
of log records in accordance with the message framing protocol described
in Sidebar 9. The sender side of this protocol implementation is shown
in the `Logging_Client::send()` method on page 96, and the receiver
side is shown in the `Logging_Handler::recv_log_record()` method on
page 88.

   The `Logging_Handler` class definition is placed in a header file called
`Logging_Handler.h`.

```
#include "ace/FILE_IO.h"
#include "ace/SOCK_Stream.h"

class ACE_Message_Block; // Forward declaration.
```

```
class Logging_Handler
{
protected:
  // Reference to a log file.
  ACE_FILE_IO &log_file_;

  // Connected to the client.
  ACE_SOCK_Stream logging_peer_;

public:
  // Initialization and termination methods.
  Logging_Handler (ACE_FILE_IO &log_file)
    : log_file_ (log_file) {}
  Logging_Handler (ACE_FILE_IO &log_file,
                   ACE_HANDLE handle)
    : log_file_ (log_file) { logging_peer_.set_handle (handle); }
  Logging_Handler (ACE_FILE_IO &log_file,
                   const ACE_SOCK_Stream &logging_peer)
    : log_file_ (log_file), logging_peer_ (logging_peer) {}

  int close () { return logging_peer_.close (); }

  // Receive one log record from a connected client.  Returns
  // length of record on success and <mblk> contains the
  // hostname, <mblk->cont()> contains the log record header
  // (the byte order and the length) and the data. Returns -1 on
  // failure or connection close.
  int recv_log_record (ACE_Message_Block *&mblk);

  // Write one record to the log file. The <mblk> contains the
  // hostname and the <mblk->cont> contains the log record.
  // Returns length of record written on success; -1 on failure.
  int write_log_record (ACE_Message_Block *mblk);

  // Log one record by calling <recv_log_record> and
  // <write_log_record>. Returns 0 on success and -1 on failure.
  int log_record ();

  ACE_SOCK_Stream &peer () { return logging_peer_; } // Accessor.
};
```

Below, we show the implementation of the recv_log_record(), write_log_record(), and log_record() methods.

Logging_Handler::recv_log_record(). This method implements the receiving side of the networked logging service's message framing protocol (see Sidebar 9, page 86). It uses the ACE_SOCK_Stream, ACE_Message_Block, and ACE_InputCDR classes along with the extraction operator>> defined on page 79 to read one complete log record from a connected client. This code is portable and interoperable since we demarshal the contents received from the network using the ACE_InputCDR class.

```
1  int Logging_Handler::recv_log_record (ACE_Message_Block *&mblk)
2  {
3    ACE_INET_Addr peer_addr;
4    logging_peer_.get_remote_addr (peer_addr);
5    mblk = new ACE_Message_Block (MAXHOSTNAMELEN + 1);
6    peer_addr.get_host_name (mblk->wr_ptr (), MAXHOSTNAMELEN);
7    mblk->wr_ptr (strlen (mblk->wr_ptr ()) + 1); // Go past name.
8
9    ACE_Message_Block *payload =
10     new ACE_Message_Block (ACE_DEFAULT_CDR_BUFSIZE);
11   // Align Message Block for a CDR stream.
12   ACE_CDR::mb_align (payload);
13
14   if (logging_peer_.recv_n (payload->wr_ptr (), 8) == 8) {
15     payload->wr_ptr (8);      // Reflect addition of 8 bytes.
16
17     ACE_InputCDR cdr (payload);
18
19     ACE_CDR::Boolean byte_order;
20     // Use helper method to disambiguate booleans from chars.
21     cdr >> ACE_InputCDR::to_boolean (byte_order);
22     cdr.reset_byte_order (byte_order);
23
24     ACE_CDR::ULong length;
25     cdr >> length;
26
27     ACE_CDR::grow
28       (payload, 8 + ACE_CDR::MAX_ALIGNMENT + length);
29     if (logging_peer_.recv_n (payload->wr_ptr(), length) > 0) {
30       payload->wr_ptr (length);   // Reflect additional bytes.
31       mblk->cont (payload);
32       return length; // Return length of the log record.
33     }
34   }
35   payload->release ();
36   mblk->release ();
37   payload = mblk = 0;
38   return -1;
39 }
```

Lines 3–7 We allocate a new ACE_Message_Block in which to store the logging_peer_'s host name. We're careful to NUL-terminate the host name and to ensure that only the host name is included in the current length of the message block, which is defined as `wr_ptr() - rd_ptr()`.

Lines 9–12 We create a separate `ACE_Message_Block` to hold the log record. The size of the header is known (8 bytes), so we receive that first. Since we'll use the CDR facility to demarshal the header after it's received, we take some CDR-related precautions with the new message block. CDR's ability to demarshal data portably requires the marshaled data start on an 8-byte alignment boundary. `ACE_Message_Block` doesn't provide any alignment guarantees, so we call `ACE_CDR::mb_align()` to force proper alignment before using `payload->wr_ptr()` to receive the header. The alignment may result in some unused bytes at the start of the block's internal buffer, so we must initially size `payload` larger than the 8 bytes it will receive (`ACE_DEFAULT_CDR_BUFSIZE` has a default value of 512).

Lines 14–15 Following a successful call to `recv_n()` to obtain the fixed-sized header, `payload`'s write pointer is advanced to reflect the addition of 8 bytes to the message block.

Lines 17–25 We create a CDR object to demarshal the 8-byte header located in the `payload` message block. The CDR object copies the header, avoiding any alteration of the `payload` message block as the header is demarshaled. Since the byte order indicator is a `ACE_CDR::Boolean`, it can be extracted regardless of the client's byte order. The byte order of the CDR stream is then set according to the order indicated by the input, and the length of the variable-sized log record payload is extracted.

Lines 27–32 Now that we know the length of the log record payload, the `payload` message block is resized to hold the complete record. The second `recv_n()` call appends the remainder of the log record to the `payload` message block, immediately following the header. If all goes well, we update the write pointer in `payload` to reflect the added data, chain `payload` to `mblk` via its continuation field, and return the length of the log record.

Lines 35–38 Error cases end up here, so we need to release the memory in `mblk` and `payload` to prevent leaks.

The `recv_log_record()` method makes effective use of a CDR stream and a message block to portably and efficiently receive a log record. It leverages the message block's continuation chain to store the host name of the client application, followed by the message block holding the log record.

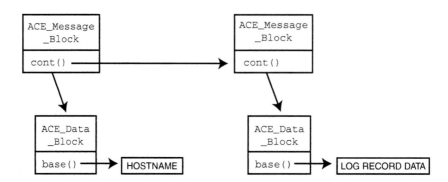

Figure 4.5: **Message Block Chain of Log Record Information**

These two items are kept separate, yet are passed around the application as a single unit, as shown in Figure 4.5.

Logging Handler::write log record(). This method uses the `ACE_FILE_IO`, `ACE_Message_Block`, and `ACE_InputCDR` classes together with the extraction `operator>>` defined on page 79 to format and write the host name and log record data received from a client into a log file.

```
 1 int Logging_Handler::write_log_record (ACE_Message_Block *mblk)
 2 {
 3   if (log_file_->send_n (mblk) == -1) return -1;
 4
 5   if (ACE::debug ()) {
 6     ACE_InputCDR cdr (mblk->cont ());
 7     ACE_CDR::Boolean byte_order;
 8     ACE_CDR::ULong length;
 9     cdr >> ACE_InputCDR::to_boolean (byte_order);
10     cdr.reset_byte_order (byte_order);
11     cdr >> length;
12     ACE_Log_Record log_record;
13     cdr >> log_record;  // Extract the <ACE_log_record>.
14     log_record.print (mblk->rd_ptr (), 1, cerr);
15   }
16
17   return mblk->total_length ();
18 }
```

Line 3 The peer host name is in `mblk` and the log record is in `mblk`'s continuation chain. We use the `send_n()` method from `ACE_FILE_IO` to write all the message blocks chained through their `cont()` pointers. Internally, this method uses an OS gather-write operation to reduce the *domain-*

crossing penalty. Since the log file is written out in CDR format, we'd need to write a separate program to read the file and display its values in a humanly readable format.

Lines 5–18 If we're in debugging mode, we build a CDR stream from the log record data and print its contents to `cerr`. Since the log record's header is still in the log record message block, the byte order must be extracted to ensure that the log record itself is demarshaled correctly. Although the header's `length` is not used, we extract it to ensure that the CDR stream is positioned correctly at the start of the log record when the extraction operator is called to demarshal the log record. The method returns the number of bytes written to the log file.

Logging_Handler::log_record(). This method uses both the `recv_log_record()` and the `write_log_record()` methods to read a log record from a socket and write it to a log file, respectively.

```
int Logging_Handler::log_record ()
{
  ACE_Message_Block *mblk = 0;
  if (recv_log_record (mblk) == -1)
    return -1;
  else {
    int result = write_log_record (mblk);
    mblk->release (); // Free up the entire contents.
    return result == -1 ? -1 : 0;
  }
}
```

The `release()` call deletes the client host name in `mblk` and the log record in `mblk->cont()`.

4.4.3 The Iterative Logging Server Class

The following code shows how to implement an iterative logging server using the ACE Socket wrapper facades. This example subclasses the various hook methods in the `Logging_Server` base class to process client logging requests iteratively as follows:

1. The `handle_connections()` hook method accepts a new connection from a client.
2. The `handle_data()` hook method reads and processes log records from that client until the connection is closed or a failure occurs.

3. Go back to step 1.

We first include the header files we'll need for this example.

```
#include "ace/FILE_IO.h"
#include "ace/INET_Addr.h"
#include "ace/Log_Msg.h"

#include "Logging_Server.h"
#include "Logging_Handler.h"
```

We next create an `Iterative_Logging_Server` class that inherits from `Logging_Server` and put this class into a header file called `Iterative_Logging_Server.h`. We define data members that receive log records from a client and write the data to a log file.

```
class Iterative_Logging_Server : public Logging_Server
{
protected:
  ACE_FILE_IO log_file_;
  Logging_Handler logging_handler_;

public:
  Iterative_Logging_Server (): logging_handler_ (log_file_) {}

  Logging_Handler &logging_handler () {
    return logging_handler_;
  }

protected:
  // Other methods shown below...
};
```

The `open()` hook method creates and/or opens a log file using the `make_log_file()` helper method defined on page 85. If the call to `make_log_file()` fails, we use the ACE_ERROR_RETURN macro described in Sidebar 10 to print the reason and return a failure value. If it succeeds, we call our parent's `open()` hook to initialize the `ACE_INET_Addr` networking address where the logging server listens for client connections.

```
  virtual int open (u_short logger_port) {
    if (make_log_file (log_file_) == -1)
      ACE_ERROR_RETURN ((LM_ERROR, "%p\n", "make_log_file()"),
                        -1);
    return Logging_Server::open (logger_port);
  }
```

The destructor closes down the log file, as shown below:

```
virtual ~Iterative_Logging_Server () {
  log_file_.close ();
}
```

Sidebar 10: ACE Debugging and Error Macros

ACE provides a set of macros that consolidate the printing of debugging and error messages via a `printf()`-like format. The most common macros are ACE_DEBUG, ACE_ERROR, and ACE_ERROR_RETURN, which encapsulate the `ACE_Log_Msg::log()` method. This method takes a variable number of arguments, so the first argument to all these macros is actually a compound argument wrapped in an extra set of parentheses to make it appear as one argument to the C++ preprocessor.

The first argument to the `ACE_Log_Msg::log()` method is the severity code, for example, LM_ERROR for general errors and LM_DEBUG for diagnostic information. The next parameter is a format string that accepts most `printf()` conversion specifiers. ACE defines some additional format specifiers that are useful for tracing and logging operations, including

Format	Action
%1	Displays the line number where the error occurred
%N	Displays the filename where the error occurred
%n	Displays the name of the program
%P	Displays the current process ID
%p	Takes a `const char *` argument and displays it and the error string corresponding to `errno` (like `perror()`)
%T	Displays the current time
%t	Displays the calling thread's ID

The ACE_ERROR_RETURN macro is a shortcut for logging an error message and returning a value from the current function. Hence, it takes two arguments: the first is the same as the other macros and the second is the value to return from the function after logging the message.

We can reuse the inherited `wait_for_multiple_events()` method since we're implementing an iterative server. Thus, the `handle_connections()` method simply blocks until it can accept the next client connection.

```
virtual int handle_connections () {
  ACE_INET_Addr logging_peer_addr;

  if (acceptor ().accept (logging_handler_.peer (),
                          &logging_peer_addr) == -1)
    ACE_ERROR_RETURN ((LM_ERROR, "%p\n", "accept()"), -1);
  ACE_DEBUG ((LM_DEBUG, "Accepted connection from %s\n",
             logging_peer_addr.get_host_name ()));
  return 0;
}
```

After the server accepts a new connection from a client, its `handle_data()` hook method continues to receive log records from that client until the connection closes or a failure occurs.

```
virtual int handle_data (ACE_SOCK_Stream *) {
  while (logging_handler_.log_record () != -1)
    continue;

  logging_handler_.close (); // Close the socket handle.
  return 0;
}
```

The `main()` function instantiates an `Iterative_Logging_Server` object and calls its `run()` method to process all client requests iteratively. This code is in file `Iterative_Logging_Server.cpp`.

```
#include "ace/Log_Msg.h"
#include "Iterative_Logging_Server.h"

int main (int argc, char *argv[])
{
  Iterative_Logging_Server server;

  if (server.run (argc, argv) == -1)
    ACE_ERROR_RETURN ((LM_ERROR, "%p\n", "server.run()"), 1);
  return 0;
}
```

This example illustrates how much easier it is to program networked applications using ACE instead of the native C Socket API calls. All the Socket API's accidental complexities identified in Section 2.3 have been removed via the use of ACE wrapper facade classes. With this complexity removed, application developers are freed to focus on strategic application logic. Note that most of the source code we've shown is concerned with application-specific (de)marshaling and I/O code in the `Logging_Handler` methods shown in Section 4.4.1, and none of the "traditional" socket manipulation, buffer management, or byte ordering code found in applications programmed directly to the Socket API.

Despite its many improvements, however, our first logging server's implementation is limited by its iterative server design. Subsequent examples in this book illustrate how concurrency patterns and ACE wrapper facades help to overcome these problems. Since the logging server decouples the `Logging_Server` and `Logging_Handler` roles, we can modify its implementation details without changing its overall design.

4.5 The Client Application

The following client application illustrates how to use the ACE wrapper facades to establish connections, marshal log records, and send the data to our logging server. This example reads lines from standard input, sends each line to the logging server in a separate log record, and stops when it reads EOF from standard input. We first include the ACE header files needed for the classes this code uses. It's a good idea to specifically include all ACE headers corresponding to the classes used. For example, `ace/OS.h` includes a definition of ACE_DEFAULT_SERVER_HOST, which we use as the default host name.

```
#include "ace/OS.h"
#include "ace/CDR_Stream.h"
#include "ace/INET_Addr.h"
#include "ace/SOCK_Connector.h"
#include "ace/SOCK_Stream.h"
#include "ace/Log_Record.h"
#include "ace/streams.h"
#include <string>
```

We include `ace/streams.h`, which contains the conditional code to make the use of C++ iostreams more portable. Based on configuration settings in ACE, it includes the proper form of header file (e.g., `<iostream>` vs. `<iostream.h>`). If the iostreams are supplied in the `std` namespace, the `ace/streams.h` file brings the classes used into the global namespace.

We start by defining a `Logging_Client` class whose `send()` method transmits one `ACE_Log_Record` over a connected `ACE_SOCK_Stream`. This class also implements a helper method that returns a reference to its ACE_

`SOCK_Stream` instance and a destructor that closes the underlying socket handle.

```
class Logging_Client
{
public:
  // Send <log_record> to the server.
  int send (const ACE_Log_Record &log_record);

  // Accessor method.
  ACE_SOCK_Stream &peer () { return logging_peer_; }

  // Close the connection to the server.
  ~Logging_Client () { logging_peer_.close (); }

private:
  ACE_SOCK_Stream logging_peer_; // Connected to server.
};
```

The `Logging_Client::send()` method implements the sender side of the message framing mechanism described in Sidebar 9 on page 86. This method is portable and interoperable since it uses the insertion operator (`operator<<`) defined on page 79 to marshal the contents of the log record into an `ACE_OutputCDR` stream.

```
 1 int Logging_Client::send (const ACE_Log_Record &log_record) {
 2   const size_t max_payload_size =
 3         4 // type()
 4       + 8 // timestamp
 5       + 4 // process id
 6       + 4 // data length
 7       + MAXLOGMSGLEN // data
 8       + ACE_CDR::MAX_ALIGNMENT; // padding;
 9
10   ACE_OutputCDR payload (max_payload_size);
11   payload << log_record;
12   ACE_CDR::ULong length = payload.total_length ();
13
14   ACE_OutputCDR header (ACE_CDR::MAX_ALIGNMENT + 8);
15   header << ACE_OutputCDR::from_boolean (ACE_CDR_BYTE_ORDER);
16   header << ACE_CDR::ULong (length);
17
18   iovec iov[2];
19   iov[0].iov_base = header.begin ()->rd_ptr ();
20   iov[0].iov_len  = 8;
21   iov[1].iov_base = payload.begin ()->rd_ptr ();
22   iov[1].iov_len  = length;
```

```
23
24   return logging_peer_.sendv_n (iov, 2);
25 }
```

Lines 2–12 We allocate enough space for a complete ACE_Log_Record, insert the contents of log_record into the payload CDR stream, and get the number of bytes used by the stream.

Lines 14–16 We next create a CDR-encoded header so the receiver can determine the byte order and size of the incoming CDR stream.

Lines 18–24 We use an iovec to efficiently send the header and payload CDR streams using a single sendv_n() gather-write method call.

Finally, we show the client application's main() function.

```
 1 int main (int argc, char *argv[])
 2 {
 3   u_short logger_port =
 4     argc > 1 ? atoi (argv[1]) : 0;
 5   const char *logger_host =
 6     argc > 2 ? argv[2] : ACE_DEFAULT_SERVER_HOST;
 7   int result;
 8
 9   ACE_INET_Addr server_addr;
10
11   if (logger_port != 0)
12     result = server_addr.set (logger_port, logger_host);
13   else
14     result = server_addr.set ("ace_logger", logger_host);
15   if (result == -1)
16     ACE_ERROR_RETURN((LM_ERROR,
17                       "lookup %s, %p\n",
18                       logger_port == 0 ? "ace_logger" : argv[1],
19                       logger_host), 1);
20
21   ACE_SOCK_Connector connector;
22   Logging_Client logging_client;
23
24   if (connector.connect (logging_client.peer (),
25                          server_addr) < 0)
26     ACE_ERROR_RETURN ((LM_ERROR,
27                        "%p\n",
28                        "connect()"),
29                        1);
30
31   // Limit the number of characters read on each record.
32   cin.width (ACE_Log_Record::MAXLOGMSGLEN);
```

```
33   for (;;) {
34     std::string user_input;
35     getline (cin, user_input, '\n');
36
37     if (!cin || cin.eof ()) break;
38
39     ACE_Time_Value now (ACE_OS::gettimeofday ());
40     ACE_Log_Record log_record (LM_INFO, now,
41                                ACE_OS::getpid ());
42     log_record.msg_data (user_input.c_str ());
43
44     if (logging_client.send (log_record) == -1)
45       ACE_ERROR_RETURN ((LM_ERROR,
46                          "%p\n", "logging_client.send()"), 1);
47   }
48
49   return 0; // Logging_Client destructor closes TCP connection.
50 }
```

Lines 3–19 If the TCP port and host name are passed as command-line arguments, we use them to initialize the network endpoint where the logging server listens passively to accept connections. Otherwise, we use the default settings.

Lines 21–29 We next try to connect to the logging server using the ACE_ INET_Addr initialized above. The connection is attempted via an ACE_ SOCK_Connector. If successful, the logging_client object's socket is connected.

Lines 31–47 Finally, we show the main client event loop, which keeps reading buffers from the standard input and forwarding them to the logging server until an EOF occurs. The ACE_Log_Record class holds the information for logging one record and contains methods to set and get log record data. We use the Logging_Client::send() method defined on page 96 to simplify the ACE_Log_Record marshaling and transmission.

This client logging application is a simplification of the networked logging service in ACE. The actual ACE logging facility is based on the ACE_ Log_Msg class. The macros described in Sidebar 10 use the ACE_Log_Msg class (particularly its ACE_Log_Msg::log() method). The logging client code itself is relatively simple after the accidental complexities have been removed. As we continue to develop the logging service in the book, therefore, the examples will focus on servers since they illustrate the most interesting demultiplexing, concurrency, and synchronization challenges.

4.6 Summary

In this chapter, we applied the ACE Socket wrapper facades and the ACE message buffering and (de)marshaling classes to the initial client/server implementation of our networked logging service. We'll continue to use these ACE classes throughout the book to keep our networked logging service implementations portable, concise, and efficient. A complete logging service is available as part of ACE's networked service components, which are outlined in Section 0.4.4 on page 16.

Part II

Concurrent Object-Oriented Network Programming

CHAPTER 5

Concurrency Design Dimensions

CHAPTER SYNOPSIS

Concurrency is essential to develop scalable and robust networked applications, particularly servers. This chapter presents a domain analysis of concurrency design dimensions that address the policies and mechanisms governing the proper use of processes, threads, and synchronizers. We cover the following design dimensions in this chapter:

- Iterative versus concurrent versus reactive servers
- Processes versus threads
- Process/thread spawning strategies
- User versus kernel versus hybrid threading models
- Time-shared versus real-time scheduling classes
- Task- versus message-based architectures

5.1 Iterative, Concurrent, and Reactive Servers

Servers can be categorized as either iterative, concurrent, or reactive. The primary trade-offs in this dimension involve simplicity of programming versus the ability to scale to increased service offerings and host loads.

Iterative servers handle each client request in its entirety before servicing subsequent requests. While processing a request, an iterative server therefore either queues or ignores additional requests. Iterative servers are best suited for either

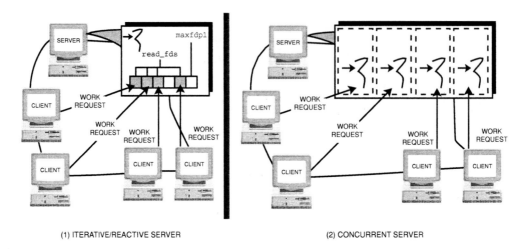

(1) ITERATIVE/REACTIVE SERVER   (2) CONCURRENT SERVER

Figure 5.1: **Iterative/Reactive versus Concurrent Servers**

- **Short-duration services,** such as the standard Internet ECHO and DAYTIME services, that have minimal execution time variation or
- **Infrequently run services,** such as a remote file system backup service that runs nightly when platforms are lightly loaded

Iterative servers are relatively straightforward to develop. Figure 5.1 (1) illustrates how they often execute their service requests internally within a single process address space, as shown by the following pseudo-code:

```
void iterative_server ()
{
  initialize listener endpoint(s)

  for (each new client request) {
    retrieve next request from an input source
    perform requested service
    if (response required) send response to client
  }
}
```

Due to this iterative structure, the processing of each request is serialized at a relatively coarse-grained level, for example, at the interface between the application and an OS synchronous event demultiplexer, such as `select()` or `WaitForMultipleObjects()`. However, this coarse-grained level of concurrency can underutilize certain processing resources (such as multiple CPUs) and OS features (such as support for parallel DMA transfer to/from I/O devices) that are available on a host platform.

Iterative servers can also prevent clients from making progress while they are blocked waiting for a server to process their requests. Excessive server-side delays complicate application and middleware-level retransmission time-out calculations, which can trigger excessive network traffic. Depending on the types of protocols used to exchange requests between client and server, duplicate requests may also be received by a server.

Concurrent servers handle multiple requests from clients simultaneously, as shown in Figure 5.1 (2). Depending on the OS and hardware platform, a concurrent server either executes its services using multiple threads or multiple processes. If the server is a single-service server, multiple copies of the same service can run simultaneously. If the server is a multiservice server, multiple copies of different services may also run simultaneously.

Concurrent servers are well-suited for I/O-bound services and/or long-duration services that require variable amounts of time to execute. Unlike iterative servers, concurrent servers allow finer grained synchronization techniques that serialize requests at an application-defined level. This design requires synchronization mechanisms, such as semaphores or mutex *locks* [EKB+92], to ensure robust cooperation and data sharing between processes and threads that run simultaneously. We examine these mechanisms in Chapter 6 and show examples of their use in Chapter 10.

As we'll see in Section 5.2, concurrent servers can be structured various ways, for example, with multiple processes or threads. A common concurrent server design is *thread-per-request*, where a master thread spawns a separate worker thread to perform each client request concurrently:

```
void master_thread ()
{
  initialize listener endpoint(s)

  for (each new client request) {
    receive the request
    spawn new worker thread and pass request to this thread
  }
}
```

The master thread continues to listen for new requests, while the worker thread processes the client request, as follows:

```
void worker_thread ()
{
  perform requested service
```

```
    if (response required) send response to client
    terminate thread
}
```

It's straightforward to modify this thread-per-request model to support other concurrent server models, such as *thread-per-connection*:

```
void master_thread ()
{
  initialize listener endpoint(s)

  for (each new client connection) {
    accept connection
    spawn new worker thread and pass connection to this thread
  }
}
```

In this design, the master thread continues to listen for new connections, while the worker thread processes client requests from the connection, as follows:

```
void worker_thread ()
{
  for (each request on the connection) {
    receive the request
    perform requested service
    if (response required) send response to client
  }
}
```

Thread-per-connection provides good support for prioritization of client requests. For instance, connections from high-priority clients can be associated with high-priority threads. Requests from higher-priority clients will therefore be served ahead of requests from lower-priority clients since the OS can preempt lower-priority threads.

Section 5.3 illustrates several other concurrent server models, such as *thread pool* and process pool.

Reactive servers process multiple requests virtually simultaneously, although all processing is actually done in a single thread. Before multithreading was widely available on OS platforms, concurrent processing was often implemented via a synchronous event demultiplexing strategy where multiple service requests were handled in round-robin order by a single-threaded process. For instance, the standard X Windows server operates this way.

A reactive server can be implemented by explicitly time-slicing attention to each request via synchronous event demultiplexing mechanisms, such as `select()` and `WaitForMultipleObjects()` described in Chapter 6. The following pseudo-code illustrates the typical style of programming used in a reactive server based on `select()`:

```
void reactive_server ()
{
  initialize listener endpoint(s)

  // Event loop.
  for (;;) {
    select() on multiple endpoints for client requests
    for (each active client request) {
      receive the request
      perform requested service
      if (response is necessary) send response to client
    }
  }
}
```

Although this server can service multiple clients over a period of time, it's fundamentally iterative from the server's perspective. Compared with taking advantage of full-fledged OS support for multithreading, therefore, applications developed using this technique possess the following limitations:

• **Increased programming complexity.** Certain types of networked applications, such as I/O-bound servers, are hard to program with a reactive server model. For example, developers are responsible for yielding the event loop thread explicitly and saving and restoring context information manually. For clients to perceive that their requests are being handled concurrently rather than iteratively, therefore, each request must execute for a relatively short duration. Likewise, long-duration operations, such as downloading large files, must be programmed explicitly as finite state machines that keep track of an object's processing steps while reacting to events for other objects. This design can become unwieldy as the number of states increases.

• **Decreased dependability and performance.** An entire server process can hang if a single operation fails, for example, if a service goes into an infinite loop or hangs indefinitely in a *deadlock*. Moreover, even if the entire process doesn't fail, its performance will degrade if the OS blocks the whole process whenever one service calls a system function or incurs a page fault. Conversely, if only nonblocking methods are used, it can be hard to improve performance via advanced techniques, such as DMA, that benefit from locality of reference in *data and instruction caches*. As discussed in Chapter 6, OS multithreading mechanisms can overcome these performance limitations by automating preemptive and parallel execution of independent services running in separate threads. One way to work around these problems without going to a full-blown concurrent server solution is to use asynchronous I/O, which is described in Sidebar 11.

Sidebar 11: Asynchronous I/O and Proactive Servers

Yet another mechanism for handling multiple I/O streams in a single-threaded server is *asynchronous I/O*. This mechanism allows a server to initiate I/O requests via one or more I/O handles without blocking for completion. Instead, the OS notifies the caller when requests are complete, and the server can then continue processing on the completed I/O handles. Asynchronous I/O is available on the following OS platforms:

- It's supported on Win32 via overlapped I/O and I/O completion ports (Ric97, Sol98).
- Some POSIX-compliant platforms implement the `aio_*()` family of asynchronous I/O functions (POS95, Gal95).

Since asynchronous I/O isn't implemented as portably as multithreading or synchronous event demultiplexing, however, we don't consider it further in this book.

Asynchronous I/O is discussed in (SH) when we present the ACE Proactor framework, which implements the *Proactor pattern* (SSRB00). This pattern allows event-driven applications to demultiplex and dispatch service requests efficiently when they are triggered by the completion of asynchronous operations, thereby achieving the performance benefits of concurrency without incurring certain of its liabilities. The ACE Proactor framework runs on Win32 and on POSIX-compliant platforms that support the `aio_*()` family of asynchronous I/O functions.

Logging service ⇒ For simplicity, the initial implementation of our networked logging service in Chapter 4 used an iterative server design. Subse-

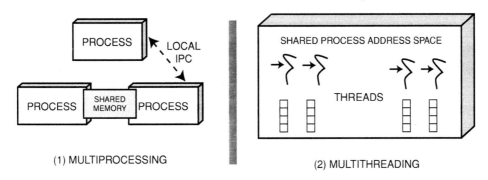

Figure 5.2: **Multiprocessing versus Multithreading**

quent chapters extend the capabilities and scalability of our logging server as follows: Chapter 7 extends the server to show a reactive style, Chapter 8 illustrates a concurrent style using multiple processes, and Chapter 9 shows several concurrent designs using multiple threads.

5.2 Processes versus Threads

Section 5.1 described the benefits of concurrent servers, which can be implemented using multiple *processes* or multiple *threads*. The primary tradeoffs in this dimension involve robustness, efficiency, and scalability.

Multiprocessing. A process is the OS entity that provides the context for executing program instructions. Each process manages certain resources, such as virtual memory, I/O handles, and signal handlers, and is protected from other OS processes via *memory management unit (MMU)* hardware. Processes created by `fork()` on UNIX and by `CreateProcess()` on Win32 execute concurrently in different address spaces than their callers. These mechanisms are examined closely in Chapter 8.

Earlier-generation operating systems, such as BSD UNIX [MBKQ96], provided processes with just one thread of control. This single-threaded process model can enhance robustness since processes can't interfere with one another without explicit programmer intervention. For example, processes can collaborate with each other only via shared memory or local IPC mechanisms, as shown in Figure 5.2 (1).

It's hard to use single-threaded processes, however, to develop certain types of applications, particularly high-performance or real-time servers.

Servers that need to communicate with each other or respond to management requests must use some form of IPC, which adds to their complexity. It's also hard to exert efficient, fine-grain control over scheduling and process priority using multiprocessing.

Multithreading.   To alleviate the problems with processes outlined above, most OS platforms now support multiple threads within a process. A thread is a single sequence of instruction steps executed in the context of a process's protection domain, as shown in Figure 5.2 (2). In addition to an instruction pointer, a thread manages certain resources, such as a run-time stack of function activation records, a set of registers, signal masks, priorities, and thread-specific data. If multiple CPUs are available, services in multithreaded servers can execute in parallel [EKB+92]. On many versions of UNIX, threads are spawned by `pthread_create()`; on Win32 they are spawned by `CreateThread()`.

Implementing concurrent networked applications that perform multiple operations in separate threads rather than in separate processes can reduce the following sources of concurrency overhead:

• **Thread creation and context switching.**   Since threads maintain less state than processes, thread creation and context switching overhead can be lower than the corresponding process lifecycle activities. For example, process-wide resources, such as virtual address mappings and caches, needn't change when switching between threads in a process.

• **Synchronization.**   It may not be necessary to switch between kernel mode and user mode when scheduling and executing an application thread. Likewise, intraprocess synchronization is often less expensive than interprocess synchronization because the objects being synchronized are local to a process and may therefore require no kernel intervention. In contrast, interprocess thread synchronization generally involves the OS kernel.

• **Data copying.**   Threads can share information using process-local memory, which has the following benefits:

1. It's often more efficient than using shared memory or local IPC mechanisms to communicate between processes because data needn't be copied through the kernel.
2. It's easier to use C++ objects in process-local memory since there's no problem with class virtual table layouts (see Sidebar 3 on page 30).

For example, cooperating database services that reference common data structures resident in process-local memory are simpler and more efficient to implement with multiple threads than with multiple processes.

As a result of these optimizations, multithreading can often improve application performance significantly. For example, I/O-bound applications can benefit from multithreading since compute-intensive services can be overlapped with disk and network operations. Just because an OS platform supports threads, however, doesn't imply that all applications should be multithreaded. In particular, the following limitations arise when using multithreading to implement concurrent applications:

• **Performance degradation.** A common misconception is that threading inherently improves application performance. Many times, however, threading doesn't improve performance for several reasons, including:

1. Compute-bound applications on a uniprocessor won't benefit from multithreading since computations and communication can't run in parallel.

2. Fine-grained locking strategies can yield high synchronization overhead, which prevents applications from fully exploiting the benefits of parallel processing [SS95].

• **Reduced robustness.** To reduce context switching and synchronization overhead, threads receive little or no MMU protection from each other. Executing all tasks via threads within a single process address space can reduce application robustness for several reasons, including:

1. Separate threads within the same process address space aren't well protected from each other. One faulty service in a process can therefore corrupt global data shared by services running on other threads in the process. This, in turn, may produce incorrect results, crash an entire process, or cause an application to hang indefinitely.

2. Certain OS functions invoked in one thread can have undesirable side effects on an entire process; for example, the UNIX `exit()` and Win32 `ExitProcess()` functions have the side effect of terminating all the threads within a process.

• **Lack of fine-grained access control.** On most operating systems, a process is the granularity of access control. Another limitation with multithreading, therefore, is that all threads within a process share the same user ID and access privileges to files and other protected resources. To prevent accidental or intentional access to unauthorized resources, network services, such as TELNET, that base their security mechanisms on process ownership often run in separate processes.

Logging service ⇒ The concurrent implementations of the logging server in our networked logging service can be implemented in a variety of ways. Chapters 8 and 9 use multiple processes and multiple threads, respectively, to implement concurrent logging servers.

5.3   Process/Thread Spawning Strategies

There are various strategies for spawning processes and threads. Different strategies can be used to optimize concurrent server performance under different circumstances, thereby enabling developers to tune server concurrency levels to match client demands and available OS processing resources. As shown below, the different strategies trade off decreased startup overhead for increased resource consumption.

Eager spawning.   This strategy prespawns one or more OS processes or threads at server creation time. These "warm-started" execution resources form a pool that improves response time by incurring service startup overhead before requests must be serviced. This pool can be expanded or contracted statically and/or dynamically depending on various factors, such as number of available CPUs, current machine load, or the length of a client request queue. Figure 5.3 (1) depicts an eager spawning strategy for threads. This design uses the Half-Sync/Half-Async pattern [SSRB00], which feeds requests from an I/O layer up to a worker in the pool of threads.

An alternative eager spawning strategy is to manage a thread pool using the *Leader/Followers pattern* [SSRB00], as shown in Figure 5.3 (2). This pattern defines an efficient concurrency model where multiple threads take turns sharing a set of event sources to detect, demultiplex, dispatch, and process service requests that occur on the event sources. The Leader/Followers pattern can be used in lieu of the Half-Sync/Half-Async pattern to improve performance when there are no synchronization or ordering constraints on the processing of requests by pooled threads.

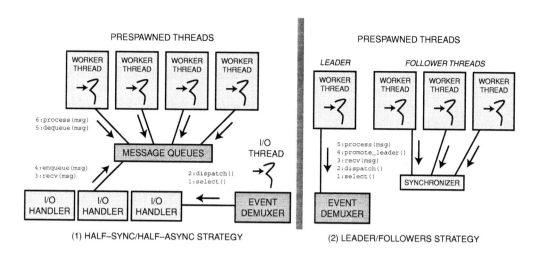

Figure 5.3: **Thread Pool Eager Spawning Strategies**

On-demand spawning creates a new process or thread in response to the arrival of client connection and/or data requests, as the thread-per-request and thread-per-connection models shown in Section 5.1. Figure 5.4 illustrates this strategy for threads. The primary benefit of on-demand spawning strategies is their reduced consumption of resources. The drawbacks, however, are that these strategies can degrade performance in heavily loaded servers and determinism in real-time systems due to the costs incurred when spawning processes/threads and starting services.

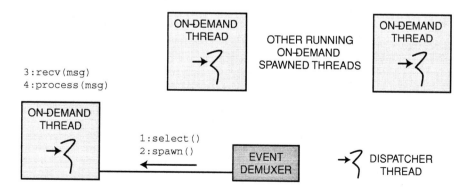

Figure 5.4: **Thread-per-Request On-Demand Spawning Strategy**

Logging service ⇒ Section 9.2 on page 191 presents a logging server implemented with a thread-per-connection, on-demand spawning strategy. Examples that illustrate eager spawning strategies are presented in [SH]. In that book, we show how ACE frameworks can be applied to implement both half-sync/half-async and leader/followers thread pool models.

5.4   User, Kernel, and Hybrid Threading Models

Scheduling is the primary mechanism an OS provides to ensure that applications use host CPU resources appropriately. Threads are the units of scheduling and execution in multithreaded processes. Modern OS platforms provide various models for scheduling threads created by applications. A key difference between the models is the *contention scope* in which threads compete for system resources, particularly CPU time. There are two different contention scopes:

- *Process contention scope*, where threads in the same process compete with each other (but not directly with threads in other processes) for scheduled CPU time.
- *System contention scope*, where threads compete directly with other system-scope threads, regardless of what process they are associated with.

Three thread scheduling models are implemented in commonly available operating systems today:

- N:1 user-threading model
- 1:1 kernel-threading model
- N:M hybrid-threading model

We describe these models below, discuss their trade-offs, and show how they support various contention scopes.

The N:1 user-threading model.   Early threading implementations were layered atop the native OS process control mechanisms and handled by libraries in user space. The OS kernel therefore had no knowledge of threads at all. The kernel scheduled the processes and the libraries managed n threads within one process, as shown in Figure 5.5 (1). Hence, this model is referred to as "N:1" user-threading model, and the threads are called "user-space threads" or simply "user threads." All threads operate in pro-

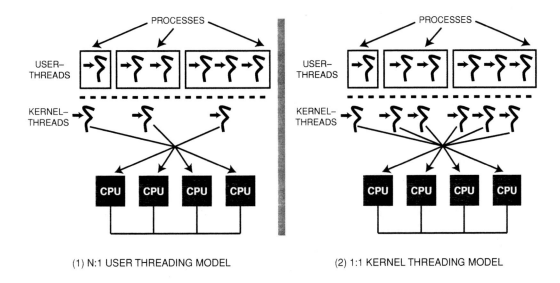

(1) N:1 USER THREADING MODEL   (2) 1:1 KERNEL THREADING MODEL

Figure 5.5: **The N:1 and 1:1 Threading Models**

cess contention scope in the N:1 thread model. HP-UX 10.20 and SunOS 4.x are examples of platforms that provide an N:1 user-threading model.

In the N:1 threading model, the kernel isn't involved in any thread life-cycle events or context switches within the same process. Thread creation, deletion, and context switches can therefore be highly efficient. The two main problems with the N:1 model, ironically, also stem from the kernel's ignorance of threads:

1. Regardless of the number of host CPUs, each process is scheduled onto only one. All threads in a process contend for that CPU, sharing any time-slice allocation the kernel may use in its process scheduling.

2. If one thread issues a blocking operation, for example, to read() from or write() to a file, all threads in that process block until the operation completes. Many N:1 implementations, most notably DCE Threads, provide wrappers around OS system functions to alleviate this restriction. These wrappers aren't entirely transparent, however, and they have restrictions on your program's behavior. You must therefore be aware of them to avoid adversely affecting your application.

The 1:1 kernel-threading model. Most modern OS kernels provide direct support for threads. In the "1:1" kernel-threading model, each thread created by an application is handled directly by a kernel thread. The OS kernel schedules each kernel thread onto the system's CPU(s), as shown in Figure 5.5 (2). In the "1:1" model, therefore, all threads operate in system contention scope. HP-UX 11, Linux, and Windows NT/2000 are examples of platforms that provide a 1:1 kernel-threading model.

The 1:1 model fixes the following two problems with the N:1 model outlined above:

- Multithreaded applications can take advantage of multiple CPUs if they are available.

- If the kernel blocks one thread in a system function, other threads can continue to make progress.

Since the OS kernel is involved in thread creation and scheduling, however, thread life-cycle operations can be more costly than with the N:1 model, though generally still cheaper than process life-cycle operations.

The N:M hybrid-threading model. Some operating systems, such as Solaris [EKB$^+$92], offer a combination of the N:1 and 1:1 models, referred to as the "N:M" hybrid-threading model. This model supports a mix of user threads and kernel threads. The hybrid model is shown in Figure 5.6. When an application spawns a thread, it can indicate in which contention scope the thread should operate (the default on Solaris is process contention scope). The OS threading library creates a user-space thread, but only creates a kernel thread if needed or if the application explicitly requests the system contention scope. As in the 1:1 model, the OS kernel schedules kernel threads onto CPUs. As in the N:1 model, however, the OS threading library schedules user-space threads onto so-called "lightweight processes" (LWPs), which themselves map 1-to-1 onto kernel threads.

The astute reader will note that a problem resurfaces in the N:M model, where multiple user-space threads can block when one of them issues a blocking system function. When the OS kernel blocks an LWP, all user threads scheduled onto it by the threads library also block, though threads scheduled onto other LWPs in the process can continue to make progress. The Solaris kernel addresses this problem via the following two-pronged approach based on the concept of scheduler activations [ABLL92]:

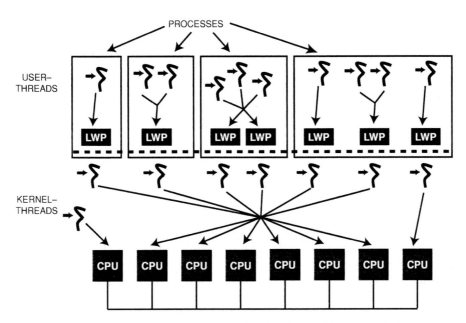

Figure 5.6: **The N:M Hybrid Threading Model**

1. The OS threading library maintains a pool of LWPs that it uses to run all the process-scoped user threads. It can reschedule these user threads onto LWPs in the pool as the need arises. The size of this pool can be adjusted via the Pthreads `pthread_setconcurrency()` function.

2. When the OS kernel notices that all kernel threads in a process are blocked, it sends the SIGWAITING signal to the affected process. The threading library catches the signal and can start a new LWP. It can then reschedule a process-scope thread onto the new LWP, allowing the application to continue making progress.

Not all OS platforms allow you to influence how threads are mapped to, and how they allocate, system resources. You should know what your platform(s) do allow and how they behave to make the most of what you have to work with. Detailed discussions of OS concurrency mechanisms appear in [Lew95, But97, Ric97, Sol98, Sch94]. As with any powerful, full-featured tool, it's possible to hurt yourself when misusing threads. So, when given a choice between contention scope, which should you choose? The answer lies in which of the following reasons corresponds most closely to why you're spawning a thread, as well as how independent it must be of other threads in your program:

- **Spawn threads to avoid interference from other tasks.** Some tasks must execute with minimal interference from other threads in your process, or even other threads in the system. Some examples are

    - A thread that must react quickly to some stimulus, such as tracking mouse movement or closing a valve in a power plant
    - A CPU-intensive task that should be isolated from other tasks
    - An I/O-intensive task on a multiprocessor system.

    In these cases, each thread should be scheduled on its own and have minimal contention from the other threads in your application. To achieve this aim, use a system-scoped thread to avoid scheduling the new thread against other threads on the same kernel thread and enable the OS to utilize multiple CPUs. If your system supports the N:M model, request system contention scope explicitly. If your system offers the 1:1 model, you're in luck because you get a system-scoped thread anyway. On N:1 systems, however, you may be out of luck.

- **Spawn threads to simplify application design.** It's often wise to conserve your available OS resources for demanding situations. Your primary motivation for creating threads may be to simplify your application design by decomposing it into separate logical tasks, such as processing stages that operate on data and pass it to the next stage. In this case, you needn't incur the cost of a kernel-thread if you can employ process-scoped threads, which are always used in N:1 systems or by request in the N:M model. Process-scoped threads have the following consequences:

    - They avoid extra kernel involvement in thread creation, scheduling, and synchronization, while still separating concerns in your application.
    - As long as the wait states of process-scoped threads are induced by synchronization, such as waiting on a mutex, rather than blocking system functions, your entire process or kernel thread won't block inadvertently.

Although multithreading may seem intimidating at first, threads can help to simplify your application designs once you've mastered synchronization patterns [SSRB00] and OS concurrency mechanisms. For example, you can perform *synchronous I/O* from one or more threads, which can yield more straightforward designs compared with synchronous or asynchronous event handling patterns, such as Reactor or Proactor, respectively. We discuss OS concurrency mechanisms in Chapter 6 and the ACE threading and synchronization wrapper facades that encapsulate these mechanisms in Chapters 9 and 10.

Logging service ⇒ Our logging server implementations in the rest of this book illustrate various ACE concurrency wrapper facades. These examples use threads with system contention scope, that is, 1:1 kernel threads, when the thread's purpose is to perform I/O, such as receiving log records from clients. This design ensures that a blocking call to receive data from a socket doesn't inadvertently block any other thread or the whole process!

5.5   Time-Shared and Real-Time Scheduling Classes

In addition to the contention scopes and threading models described in Section 5.4, OS platforms often define policies and priority levels that further influence scheduling behavior [But97]. These capabilities enable modern operating systems to run a mix of applications with a range of general-purpose and real-time scheduling needs. OS kernels can assign threads to different scheduling classes and schedule these threads using several criteria, such as their priority and their resource usage. The different scheduling class strategies described below trade off fairness for increased predictability and control.

Time-shared scheduling class. General-purpose OS *schedulers* target traditional time-sharing, interactive environments. Schedulers for these operating systems are typically

- **Priority-based**—the highest-priority runnable thread is the next one scheduled for execution.

- **Fair**—the priority of threads in a time-shared scheduler can be varied as a function of their CPU usage. For example, as a long-running compute-bound thread uses more CPU time, a time-shared scheduler can decrease its priority progressively until a lower limit is reached.

- **Preemptive**—if a lower-priority thread is executing when a higher-priority thread becomes runnable, the scheduler should preempt the lower-priority thread and allow the higher-priority thread to run.

- **Time-sliced,** which is used to cycle among threads with the same priority. With this technique, each thread runs for up to a finite period of time (e.g., 10 milliseconds). After the time slice of the currently running thread has elapsed, the scheduler selects another available thread, performs a context switch, and places the preempted thread onto a queue.

Real-time scheduling class. Although time-shared schedulers are suitable for conventional networked applications, they rarely satisfy the needs of applications with real-time requirements. For example, there's usually no fixed order of execution for threads in a time-shared scheduler class since the scheduler can vary thread priorities over time. Moreover, time-shared schedulers don't try to bound the amount of time needed to preempt a lower-priority thread when a higher-priority thread becomes ready to run.

Therefore, real-time operating systems (such as VxWorks or LynxOS) and some general-purpose operating systems (such as Solaris and Windows NT) provide a real-time scheduling class [Kha92] that bounds the worst-case time required to dispatch user threads or kernel threads. An OS with a real-time scheduling class often supports one or both of the following scheduling policies [Gal95]:

- **Round-robin**, where a time quantum specifies the maximum time a thread can run before it's preempted by another real-time thread with the same priority.

- **First-in, first-out (FIFO)**, where the highest-priority thread can run for as long as it chooses, until it voluntarily yields control or is preempted by a real-time thread with an even higher priority.

When an OS supports both time-shared and real-time scheduling classes, the real-time threads always run at a higher priority than any time-shared threads.

A CPU-bound real-time program can take over the system and starve all other system activities. Most general-purpose operating systems therefore regulate this undesirable situation by restricting the use of the real-time scheduling class to applications running with superuser privileges.

Logging service ⇒ Since a logging service isn't usually time critical, most of our examples in this book simply use the default OS time-shared scheduling class. For completeness, however, the networked logging server example on page 200 in Section 9.3 shows how to use ACE to write a portable logging server that runs in the real-time scheduling class.

5.6 Task- versus Message-Based Architectures

A concurrency architecture is a binding between:

1. **CPUs,** which provide the execution context for application code

2. **Data and control messages,** which are sent and received from one or more applications and network devices

3. **Service processing tasks,** which perform services upon messages as they arrive and depart.

A networked application's concurrency architecture is one of several factors[1] that most impact its performance by affecting context switching, synchronization, scheduling, and data movement costs. There are two canonical types of concurrency architectures: task-based and message-based [SS93]. The primary trade-offs in this dimension involve simplicity of programming versus performance.

Task-based concurrency architectures structure multiple CPUs according to units of service functionality in an application. In this architecture, tasks are active and messages processed by the tasks are passive, as shown in Figure 5.7 (1). Concurrency is achieved by executing service tasks in separate CPUs and passing data messages and control messages between the tasks/CPUs. Task-based concurrency architectures can be implemented using producer/consumer patterns, such as Pipes and Filters [BMR+96] and Active Object [SSRB00], which we illustrate in [SH].

Message-based concurrency architectures structure the CPUs according to the messages received from applications and network devices. In this architecture, messages are active and tasks are passive, as shown

---

[1]Other key factors that affect performance include protocol, bus, memory, and network hardware device characteristics.

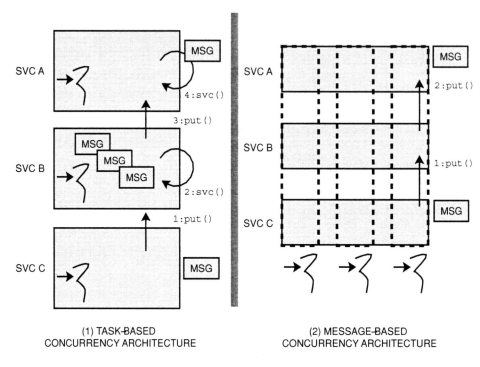

(1) TASK-BASED
CONCURRENCY ARCHITECTURE

(2) MESSAGE-BASED
CONCURRENCY ARCHITECTURE

Figure 5.7: **Task-Based vs. Message-Based Concurrency Architectures**

in Figure 5.7 (2). Concurrency is achieved by shepherding multiple messages on separate CPUs through a stack of service tasks simultaneously. Thread-per-request, thread-per-connection, and thread pool models can be used to implement message-based concurrency architectures. Chapter 9 illustrates the use of thread-per-connection, and thread pools are shown in [SH].

Logging service ⇒ We structure the networked logging service threading designs in this book using message-based concurrency architectures, in particular thread-per-connection, which are often more efficient than task-based architectures [HP91, SS95]. Task-based architectures are often easier to program, however, since synchronization within a task or layer is often unnecessary since concurrency is serialized at the task access points, such as between layers in a protocol stack. In contrast, message-based architectures can be harder to implement due to the need for more sophisticated concurrency control.

5.7 Summary

Networked servers may associate one or more OS processes or threads with one or more application services. These factors require design decisions in a number of dimensions that affect thread and process usage, CPU resource usage, scheduling behavior, and application performance. This chapter provided a domain analysis of the rich set of concurrency dimensions that can be used to design networked applications. The remaining chapters in this book describe the ACE wrapper facades that resulted from this domain analysis. There we focus on the pros and cons of encapsulating and using synchronous event demultiplexing, multiprocessing, threading, and synchronization mechanisms available on today's operating systems.

CHAPTER 6

An Overview of Operating System Concurrency Mechanisms

CHAPTER SYNOPSIS

Networked applications, particularly servers, must often process requests concurrently to meet their quality of service requirements. Chapter 5 describes general design tradeoffs related to concurrency alternatives. This chapter presents an overview of the synchronous event demultiplexing, multiprocessing, multithreading, and synchronization mechanisms available to implement those designs. We also discuss common portability and programming problems that arise when networked applications are developed using native C-level concurrency APIs.

6.1 Synchronous Event Demultiplexing

A synchronous event demultiplexer is a function supplied by an OS that waits for specified events to occur on a set of event sources. When one or more of the event sources become active, the function returns to its caller. The caller can then process the events originating from many sources. Synchronous event demultiplexers are often used as the basis of reactive server *event loops* that examine and react to events from clients in a continuous and orderly way.

Most operating systems support one or more synchronous event demultiplexing functions, such as

- The `poll()` function [Rag93], which stems from System V UNIX
- The `WaitForMultipleObjects()` function [Sol98], which is provided by Win32 and
- The `select()` function [Ste98], which demultiplexes event sources on I/O handles[1]

We focus on `select()` because it's the most common. Event-driven networked applications can use `select()` to determine which handles can have I/O operations invoked on them synchronously without blocking the application thread that calls them. The C API for the `select()` function is outlined below:

```
int select (int width,           // Maximum handle plus 1
            fd_set *read_fds,    // Set of "read" handles
            fd_set *write_fds,   // Set of "write" handles
            fd_set *except_fds,  // Set of "exception" handles
            struct timeval *timeout);// Time to wait for events
```

An `fd_set` is a structure representing a set of handles to check for I/O events (a handle set). The three `fd_set` parameters whose addresses are passed in `read_fds`, `write_fds`, and `except_fds` are examined by `select()` to see if any of their handles are active for reading, writing, or exceptional conditions (such as *out-of-band data*), respectively. The `select()` function informs its caller about active and inactive handles by modifying its `fd_set` arguments as outlined below:

- If a handle value is *not* active in the `fd_set`, that handle is ignored and its value won't be active in the `fd_set` returned from `select()`.
- If a handle value is active in the `fd_set`, the corresponding handle is examined for pending events. If the handle has an event pending, its corresponding value will be active in the `fd_set` returned from `select()`. If the handle does not have a pending event, its value will be inactive in the returned `fd_set`.

Each OS platform supplies a basic set of operations that allows applications to query and manipulate `fd_set`s. Although these operations are macros on some platforms and functions on others, they have a consistent set of names and behaviors:

---

[1]The Win32 version of `select()` works only on socket handles.

Function	Description
FD_ZERO()	Mark all handle values as inactive in an fd_set.
FD_CLR()	Mark a handle as inactive in an fd_set.
FD_SET()	Mark a handle as active in an fd_set.
FD_ISSET()	Test to see if a specified handle is active in an fd_set.

The final parameter to select() is a pointer to struct timeval, which contains the following two fields:

```
struct timeval
{
  long tv_sec;   /* seconds */
  long tv_usec; /* microseconds */
};
```

The following three types of timeval values can be passed to select() to control its time-out behavior:

Value	Behavior
NULL timeval pointer	Indicates that select() should wait indefinitely, until at least one I/O event occurs or a signal interrupts the call.
Non-NULL timeval pointer whose tv_sec and tv_usec fields are 0	Indicates that select() should perform a "poll," that is, check all the handles and return immediately with any results.
timeval whose tv_sec or tv_usec fields is > 0	Indicates that select() should wait up to that amount of time for I/O events to occur.

6.2 Multiprocessing Mechanisms

All modern, general-purpose operating systems provide mechanisms to create and manage the execution of multiple processes. A process is a unit of resource management and protection. Some embedded operating systems, such as many versions of VxWorks and pSoS, support only a single address space, which is akin to a single process. This limitation is often reasonable; for example, your cell phone's computer may not need to run multiple processes. Most of these embedded-type systems do facilitate multithreading, however, which we'll examine in Section 6.3.

The process control functionality offered by different operating systems varies greatly. On multiprocessing operating systems, however, the following areas of capability are common:

Process lifetime operations. Processes come into existence when either the OS or application programs call process creation and execution functions, such as `fork()` and the `exec*()` family of functions (POSIX) or `CreateProcess()` (Win32). These functions create a new address space to run a particular program. The initiating process can also set the new program's command-line arguments and environment variables to pass information, such as commands, parameters, and file or directory locations, to a new process. A process runs until it terminates either

- **Voluntarily,** for example, by reaching the end of its `main()` function or by calling a process exit API, such as `ExitProcess()` (Win32) or `exit()` (POSIX), which allows a process to set its exit status to a specified value, or

- **Involuntarily,** for example, by being killed via a signal (POSIX) or by an external cancelation operation, such as `TerminateProcess()` (Win32).

Process synchronization operations. Most operating systems retain the identity and exit status of a process when it exits, which allows its parent process to synchronize with it and obtain its exit status. Common examples of process synchronization functions include:

- The POSIX `wait()` and `waitpid()` functions and
- The Win32 functions `WaitForSingleObject()` and `WaitForMultipleObjects()`

Many operating systems also maintain the inherent parent/child relationship between creator and created processes. This relationship is used by some operating systems to help notify a possibly-interested parent process that one of its child processes has exited. On POSIX systems, for instance, the OS sends a `SIGCHLD` signal to a parent process when one of its child processes exits.

Process property operations. Most operating systems provide functions to get and set various process properties. Properties that can be set at the process level include default file access permissions, user identification, resource limits, scheduling priority, and the current working directory. Some operating systems also allow a process to lock down regions of its virtual memory to avoid page faulting or to enable memory-based exchanges with I/O devices.

6.3 Multithreading Mechanisms

A thread is a unit of execution within a process. Most modern operating systems provide mechanisms that handle thread lifetime, synchronization, and various other thread-related properties, such as priorities and thread-specific storage. We outline each of these mechanisms below.

Thread lifetime operations. The main thread in a program is created implicitly when a process begins its execution. Most other threads come into existence via explicit calls to thread creation functions, such as `pthread_create()` (Pthreads) or `CreateThread()` (Win32). These functions create and start a new thread running a particular entry-point function specified by the caller. As with processes, threads run until they terminate either

- **Voluntarily,** for example, by reaching the end of their entry-point functions or calling a thread exit function, such as `pthread_exit()` (Pthreads) or `ExitThread()` (Win32), which allows a thread to set its exit status to a specified value or
- **Involuntarily,** for example, by being killed via a signal or by an asynchronous thread cancelation operation, such as `pthread_cancel()` (Pthreads) or `TerminateThread()` (Win32).

Thread synchronization operations. Many OS threading mechanisms allow threads to be created as either:

- **Detached**—When a detached thread exits, the OS reclaims storage used for the thread's state and exit status automatically, or
- **Joinable**—When a joinable thread exits, the OS retains its identity and exit status so that another thread can subsequently synchronize with it to obtain its exit status.

Examples of common thread synchronization mechanisms include

- The `pthread_join()` function in Pthreads
- The Win32 functions `WaitForSingleObject()` and `WaitForMultipleObjects()`

Some OS platforms provide synchronization functions that allow threads to suspend and resume each other. Some allow threads to send signals to other threads in the same process. However, these operations are generally nonportable and hard to use correctly [But97]; therefore, we don't consider them further in this book, although ACE does encapsulate them on platforms where they exist.

Thread property operations.   Most operating systems provide functions to get and set various thread properties. For example, a thread's priority can be examined and changed using the pthread_getschedparam() and pthread_setschedparam() functions in Pthreads as well as the GetThreadPriority() and SetThreadPriority() functions in Win32. Likewise, many operating systems allow applications to select more fundamental properties, such as the thread's scheduling class. For instance, Solaris supports both the real-time and time-shared scheduling classes [Kha92] described in Section 5.5.

Thread-specific storage.   Thread-specific storage (TSS) is similar in scope to global data; that is, it isn't local to any specific function or object. Unlike global data, however, each thread actually has a separate copy of TSS data. TSS can be used by applications to maintain data that many functions or objects need to access, but that's private to a given thread. A common example is errno, which conveys the error status of system functions. In a multithreaded program, each thread contains a separate copy of errno.

Each TSS item is associated with a key that's global to all threads within a process. These keys are created by a factory function, such as pthread_key_create() (Pthreads) or TlsAlloc() (Win32). Any thread can use the key to access its copy of the storage via a pointer. The key/pointer relationship is managed by TSS functions, such as pthread_setspecific() and pthread_getspecific() in Pthreads or TlsGetValue() and TlsSetValue() in Win32.

6.4   Synchronization Mechanisms

As described in Sections 6.2 and 6.3, OS platforms provide rudimentary synchronization mechanisms that allow processes and threads to wait for other processes and threads to finish. These mechanisms are sufficient for relatively coarse-grained applications that execute multiple independent execution paths concurrently. Many concurrent applications require more fine-grained synchronization mechanisms, however, to allow processes and threads to coordinate their execution order and the order that they access shared resources, such as files, database records, network devices, object members, and shared memory. Access to these resources must be synchronized to prevent *race conditions*.

A race condition can occur when the execution order of two or more concurrent threads yields unpredictable and erroneous results. One way to prevent race conditions is to use *synchronization mechanisms* that serialize access to critical sections of code that access shared resources. Common OS synchronization mechanisms include mutexes, readers/writer locks, semaphores, and condition variables.

To illustrate the need for these mechanisms, consider the following addition to the `Iterative_Logging_Server::handle_data()` method defined in Section 4.4.3 on page 94.

```
typedef u_long COUNTER;

// File scope global variable.
static COUNTER request_count;

// ...

  virtual int handle_data (ACE_SOCK_Stream *) {
    while (logging_handler_.log_record () != -1)
      // Keep track of number of requests.
      ++request_count;

    ACE_DEBUG ((LM_DEBUG,
                "request_count = %d\n", request_count));
    logging_handler_.close ();
    return 0;
  }
```

The `handle_data()` method waits for log records to arrive from a client. When a record arrives, it's removed and processed. The `request_count` variable keeps track of the number of incoming client log records.

The code above works fine as long as `handle_data()` executes in just one thread in a process. Incorrect results can occur on many platforms, however, when multiple threads execute `handle_data()` simultaneously in the same process. The problem is that the code's not *thread-safe* due to race conditions on the global variable `request_count`. In particular, different threads can increment and print "stale" versions of the `request_count` variable on platforms where

- Auto-increment operations compile into multiple assembly language `load`, `add`, and `store` assignments and/or

- Total memory ordering is not enforced by the hardware.

Operating systems offer a range of synchronization mechanisms to ensure correct results in this and similar situations. The following are the most common synchronization mechanisms.

6.4.1 Mutual Exclusion (Mutex) Locks

Mutual exclusion (*mutex*) locks can be used to protect the integrity of a shared resource that's accessed concurrently by multiple threads. A mutex serializes the execution of multiple threads by defining a *critical section* of code that can be executed by only one thread at a time. Mutex semantics are "bracketed"; that is, the thread owning a mutex is responsible for releasing it. This semantic simplicity helps ensure efficient mutex implementations, for example, via hardware spin locks.[2]

There are two general types of mutexes:

- *Nonrecursive mutex* that will deadlock or otherwise fail if the thread currently owning the mutex tries to reacquire it without first releasing it and
- *Recursive mutex* that will allow the thread owning the mutex to acquire it multiple times without self-deadlock, as long as the thread ultimately releases the mutex the same number of times.

6.4.2 Readers/Writer Locks

A *readers/writer lock* allows access to a shared resource by either

- Multiple threads reading a resource concurrently without modifying it or
- Only one thread at a time modifying the resource and excluding all other threads from both read and write access.

This type of lock can improve the performance of concurrent applications in which resources protected by a readers/writer lock are read from much more frequently than they are written to. Readers/writer locks can be implemented to give preference either to readers or to writers [BA90].

Readers/writer locks share some properties with mutexes; for example, the thread that acquires a lock must also release it. When a writer wishes

---

[2]Although spin locks have low individual overhead they can consume excessive CPU resources if a thread must *busy wait* a long period of time for a particular condition to occur.

to acquire the lock, the thread waits for all other lock holders to release the lock, then the writer thread gains an exclusive hold on the lock. Unlike mutexes, however, multiple threads may acquire a readers/writer lock for reading simultaneously.

6.4.3 Semaphore Locks

A *semaphore* is conceptually a non-negative integer that can be incremented and decremented atomically. A thread blocks when it tries to decrement a semaphore whose value equals 0. A blocked thread will be released only after another thread "posts" the semaphore, causing its count to become greater than 0.

Semaphores retain state to keep track of the count and the number of blocked threads. They are often implemented using *sleep locks*, which trigger a context switch that allows other threads to execute. Unlike mutexes, they need not be released by the same thread that acquired them initially. This capability allows semaphores to be used in a broader range of execution contexts, such as signal handlers or interrupt handlers.

6.4.4 Condition Variables

A *condition variable* provides a different flavor of synchronization than a mutex, readers/writer, or semaphore lock. The latter three mechanisms make other threads wait while the thread holding the lock executes code in a critical section. In contrast, a thread can use a condition variable to coordinate and schedule its own processing.

For example, a condition variable can make itself wait until a condition expression involving data shared by other threads attains a particular state. When a cooperating thread indicates that the shared data state has changed, a thread that's blocked on a condition variable is awakened. The newly awakened thread then reevaluates its condition expression and can resume its processing if the shared data has attained the desired state. Since arbitrarily complex condition expressions can be waited for using a condition variable, they permit more complex scheduling decisions than the other synchronization mechanisms outlined above.

Condition variables provide the core synchronization mechanisms for advanced concurrency patterns, such as *Active Object* and *Monitor Object* [SSRB00], and intraprocess communication mechanisms, such as synchronized message queues. Pthreads and UNIX International (UI) threads (implemented on Solaris) support condition variables natively, but other platforms, such as Win32 and many real-time operating systems, do not.

Sidebar 12 evaluates the relative performance characteristics of the OS synchronization mechanisms outlined above. You should generally try to use the most efficient synchronization mechanism that provides the semantics you require. When efficiency is important, look up the reference information for platforms targeted by your application. You can tune your application to take advantage of platform differences by varying the ACE synchronization classes. Moreover, your code can remain portable by using the *Strategized Locking pattern* [SSRB00] and conforming to the method signature of the ACE_LOCK* pseudo-class described on page 209 in Section 10.1.

Sidebar 12: Evaluating Synchronization Mechanism Performance

Operating systems provide a range of synchronization mechanisms to handle the needs of different applications. Although the performance of the synchronization mechanisms discussed in this chapter varies according to OS implementations and hardware, the following are general issues to consider:

- Condition variables and semaphores often have higher overhead than mutexes since their implementations are more complicated. Native OS mechanisms nearly always perform better than user-created substitutes, however, since they can take advantage of internal OS characteristics and hardware-specific tuning.
- Mutexes generally have lower overhead than readers/writer locks because they don't need to manage multiple waiter sets. Multiple reader threads can proceed in parallel, however, so readers/writer locks can scale better on multiprocessors when they are used to access data that are read much more than they are updated.
- Nonrecursive mutexes are more efficient than recursive mutexes. Moreover, recursive mutexes can cause subtle bugs if programmers forget to release them (But97), whereas nonrecursive mutexes reveal these problems by deadlocking immediately.

6.5 Limitations with OS Concurrency Mechanisms

Developing networked applications using the native OS concurrency mechanisms outlined above can cause portability and reliability problems. To illustrate some of these problems, consider a function that uses a UI threads mutex to solve the auto-increment serialization problem we observed with `request_count` on page 131 in Section 6.4:

```
typedef u_long COUNTER;

static COUNTER request_count; // File scope global variable.

static mutex_t m; // Protects request_count (initialized to zero).
// ...
   virtual int handle_data (ACE_SOCK_Stream *) {
      while (logging_handler_.log_record () != -1) {
         // Keep track of number of requests.
         mutex_lock (&m);    // Acquire lock
         ++request_count;    // Count # of requests
         mutex_unlock (&m);  // Release lock
      }

      mutex_lock (&m);
      int count = request_count;
      mutex_unlock (&m);
      ACE_DEBUG ((LM_DEBUG, "request_count = %d\n", count));
      logging_handler_.close ();
      return 0;
   }
```

In the code above, `m` is a variable of type `mutex_t`, which is automatically initialized to 0. In UI threads, any synchronization variable that's set to zero is initialized implicitly with its default semantics [EKB$^+$92]. For example, the `mutex_t` variable `m` is a static variable that's initialized by default in the unlocked state. The first time the `mutex_lock()` function is called, it will therefore acquire ownership of the lock. Any other thread that attempts to acquire the lock must wait until the thread owning lock `m` releases it.

Although the code above solves the original synchronization problem, it suffers from the following drawbacks:

- **Obtrusive.** The solution requires changing the source code to add the mutex and its associated C functions. When developing a large software system, making these types of modifications manually will cause maintenance problems if changes aren't made consistently.

- **Error-prone.** Although the `handle_data()` method is relatively simple, it's easy for programmers to forget to call `mutex_unlock()` in more complex methods. Omitting this call will cause *starvation* for other threads that are blocked trying to acquire the mutex. Moreover, since a `mutex_t` is nonrecursive, deadlock will occur if the thread that owns mutex m tries to reacquire it before releasing it. In addition, we neglected to check the return value of `mutex_lock()` to make sure it succeeded, which can yield subtle problems in production applications.

- **Unseen side-effects.** It's also possible that a programmer will forget to initialize the mutex variable. As mentioned above, a static `mutex_t` variable is implicitly initialized on UI threads. No such guarantees are made, however, for `mutex_t` fields in objects allocated dynamically. Moreover, other OS thread implementations, such as Pthreads and Win32 threads, don't support these implicit initialization semantics; that is, all synchronization objects must be initialized explicitly.

- **Non-portable.** This code will work only with the UI threads synchronization mechanisms. Porting the `handle_data()` method to use Pthreads and Win32 threads will therefore require changing the locking code to use different synchronization APIs altogether.

In general, native OS concurrency APIs exhibit many of the same types of problems associated with the Socket API in Section 2.3. In addition, concurrency APIs are even less standardized across OS platforms. Even where the APIs are similar, there are often subtle syntactic and semantic variations from one implementation to another. For example, functions in different drafts of the Pthreads standard implemented by different operating system providers have different parameter lists and return different error indicators.

Sidebar 13 outlines some of the differences between error propagation strategies for different concurrency APIs. This lack of portability increases the accidental complexity of concurrent networked applications. Therefore, it's important to design higher-level programming abstractions, such as those in ACE, to help developers avoid problems with nonportable and nonuniform APIs.

Sidebar 13: Concurrency API Error Propagation Strategies

Different concurrency APIs report errors to callers differently. For example, some APIs, such as UI threads and Pthreads, return 0 on success and a non-0 error value on failure. Other APIs, such as Win32 threads, return 0 on failure and indicate the error value via thread-specific storage. This diversity of behaviors is confusing and nonportable. In contrast, the ACE concurrency wrapper facades define and enforce a uniform approach that always returns −1 if a failure occurs and sets a thread-specific `errno` value to indicate the cause of the failure.

6.6 Summary

Operating systems provide concurrency mechanisms that manage multiple processes on an end system and manage multiple threads within a process. Any decent general-purpose OS allows multiple processes to run concurrently. Modern general-purpose and real-time operating systems also allow multiple threads to run concurrently. When used in conjunction with the appropriate patterns and application configurations, concurrency helps to improve performance and simplify program structure.

The concurrency wrapper facade classes provided by ACE are described in the following four chapters:

- Chapter 7 describes ACE classes for synchronous event demultiplexing.
- Chapter 8 describes ACE classes for OS process mechanisms.
- Chapter 9 describes ACE classes for OS threading mechanisms.
- Chapter 10 describes ACE classes for OS synchronization mechanisms.

Throughout these four chapters we'll examine how ACE uses C++ features and the Wrapper Facade pattern to overcome problems with native OS concurrency APIs and improve the functionality, portability, and robustness of concurrent networked applications. Where appropriate, we'll show ACE concurrency wrapper facade implementations to illustrate how they are mapped onto underlying OS concurrency mechanisms. We also point out where the features of OS platforms differ and how ACE shields developers from these differences.

CHAPTER 7

The ACE Synchronous Event Demultiplexing Wrapper Facades

CHAPTER SYNOPSIS

This chapter describes the ACE wrapper facades that encapsulate OS synchronous event demultiplexing mechanisms with portable C++ classes. We also present several new and improved versions of our networked logging server that apply these ACE wrapper facades.

7.1 Overview

Section 5.1 discussed server concurrency dimensions, with the reactive server on page 106 being one of the design choices. The reactive server model can be thought of as "lightweight multitasking," where a single-threaded server communicates with multiple clients in a round-robin manner without introducing the overhead and complexity of threading and synchronization mechanisms. This server concurrency strategy uses an event loop that examines and reacts to events from its clients continuously. An event loop demultiplexes input from various event sources so they can be processed in an orderly way.

Event sources in networked applications are primarily socket handles. The most portable synchronous event demultiplexer for socket handles is the select() function and its handle sets, discussed on page 125 in Section 6.1. This chapter describes the following classes that can be applied to simplify and optimize the use of these facilities in reactive servers:

139

ACE Class/Method	Description
ACE_Handle_Set	Encapsulates an `fd_set` and the common operations that manipulate it.
ACE_Handle_Set_Iterator	Provides a portable and efficient mechanism for iterating through the set of active handles in an `ACE_Handle_Set` object.
ACE::select()	Simplify the most common uses of `select()` and enhance its portability.

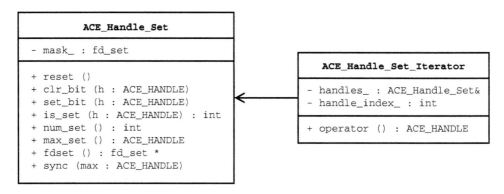

Figure 7.1: ACE_Handle_Set **&** ACE_Handle_Set_Iterator **Class Diagrams**

The interfaces of the `ACE_Handle_Set` and `ACE_Handle_Set_Iterator` classes are shown in Figure 7.1. These wrapper facades provide the following benefits:

- **Ensure portability across OS platforms.** The `ACE_Handle_Set` and `ACE_Handle_Set_Iterator` classes can be used on all OS platforms that support `select()` and `fd_set`. These classes simplify the correct use of I/O handles to demultiplex network events synchronously.

- **Iterate through the set of active handles efficiently without compromising portability.** Iterating through the set of active handles efficiently is an important factor in enhancing the performance of reactive server event loops. The need to optimize event loop performance often tempts programmers to examine the internals of `fd_set` to find ways to scan them more efficiently. The `ACE_Handle_Set_Iterator` is highly optimized to alleviate the need for networked applications to rely on internal `fd_set` representations.

The ACE::select() wrapper methods encapsulate the select() system function and use the ACE_Handle_Set class to simplify handle passing. A reactive version of the logging server is used to illustrate how these ACE wrappers can simplify networked application programming.

7.2 The ACE_Handle_Set Class

Motivation

Section 2.3 on page 37 described the complexities associated with direct use of I/O handles. The fd_set represents another source of accidental complexity in the following areas:

- The macros or functions that platforms supply to manipulate and scan an fd_set must be used carefully to avoid processing handles that aren't active and to avoid corrupting an fd_set inadvertently.

- The code to scan for active handles is often a *hot spot* because it executes continually in a tight loop. It's therefore an obvious candidate for optimization to improve performance.

- The fd_set is defined in system-supplied header files, so its representation is exposed to programmers. Naturally, it's tempting to make use of this platform-internal knowledge in "creative" ways. However, doing so causes portability problems because representations vary widely across platforms.

- There are subtle nonportable aspects of fd_set when used in conjunction with the select() function.

To illustrate the latter point, let's revisit the function signature for the select() function:

```
int select (int width,              // Maximum handle plus 1
            fd_set *read_fds,       // Set of "read" handles
            fd_set *write_fds,      // Set of "write" handles
            fd_set *except_fds,     // Set of "exception" handles
            struct timeval *timeout);// Time to wait for events
```

The three fd_set arguments specify the handles to use when selecting for each event type. The timeout argument is used to specify a time limit to wait for events to occur. The particular details concerning these parameters vary in only minor ways across platforms. Due to the changing nature of I/O handles (and, thus, `fd_set`) across platforms, however, the meaning of the first argument (`width`) varies widely across operating systems:

- On UNIX, I/O handles start at the value 0 and increase to an OS-defined maximum limit. The meaning of the `width` parameter on UNIX is therefore "how far into the `fd_set` to scan for handles"; that is, it's defined as the highest numbered handle in any of the three `fd_set` parameters, plus 1.

- On Win32, socket handles are implemented as pointers rather than as low-numbered integers. The `width` argument to `select()` is therefore ignored completely. Instead, each `fd_set` contains its own handle count.

- On other platforms, where handles may be integers that don't start at 0, the definition may differ yet again.

The size-related values in an `fd_set` are also computed differently depending on the characteristics of the platform's representation and its `select()` semantics. Any applications written directly to native OS APIs must therefore adapt to all these subtle differences, and each project may end up redesigning and reimplementing code that manages the proper value to supply for `width`. Addressing these portability differences in each application is tedious and error prone, which is why ACE provides the `ACE_Handle_Set` class.

Class Capabilities

The `ACE_Handle_Set` class uses the Wrapper Facade pattern [SSRB00] to guide the encapsulation of `fd_sets`. This class provides the following capabilities:

- It enhances the portability, ease of use, and type safety of event-driven applications by simplifying the use of `fd_set` and `select()` across OS platforms

- It tracks and adjusts the `fd_set` size-related values automatically as handles are added and removed

Since differences in `fd_set` representations are hidden in the implementation of `ACE_Handle_Set`, application code can be written once and then simply recompiled when it's ported to a new platform.

The interface for `ACE_Handle_Set` is shown in Figure 7.1 and its key methods are shown in the following table:

Method	Description
`ACE_Handle_Set()` `reset()`	Initializes the handle set to its default values.
`clr_bit()`	Clears one handle in the set.
`set_bit()`	Sets one handle in the set.
`is_set()`	Tests to see if a specified handle is active in the set.
`num_set()`	Returns the number of active handles in the set.
`max_set()`	Returns the value of the largest handle in the set.
`fdset()`	Returns a pointer to the underlying `fd_set()` or a NULL pointer if there are no active handles in the set.
`sync()`	Resynchronizes the handle set to find the new highest active handle and the number of active handles, which is useful after the handle set has changed as the result of an external operation, such as a call to `select()`.

Example

Sections 4.4.3 and 5.1 outlined some of the problems associated with iterative servers. Using synchronous event demultiplexing to implement the reactive server model is one strategy to avoid these problems. We now show an example that enhances the iterative logging server implementation from Chapter 4 by using `select()` together with the `ACE_Handle_Set` class. This server demultiplexes the following two types of events:

1. Arrival of new connections from clients
2. Arrival of log records on client connections

We put our implementation in a header file named `Reactive_Logging_Server.h`, which starts by including ACE's `Handle_Set.h` file and the `Iterative_Logging_Server.h` file. We derive a new class, `Reactive_Logging_Server`, from the `Iterative_Logging_Server` class defined on page 92. We reuse its data members and define two more that are used to manage multiple clients.

```
#include "ace/Handle_Set.h"
#include "Iterative_Logging_Server.h"

class Reactive_Logging_Server : public Iterative_Logging_Server
```

```
{
protected:
  // Keeps track of the acceptor socket handle and all the
  // connected stream socket handles.
  ACE_Handle_Set master_handle_set_;

  // Keep track of handles marked as active by <select>.
  ACE_Handle_Set active_handles_;

  // Other methods shown below...
};
```

To implement reactive server semantics, we override the hook methods in Iterative_Logging_Server, starting with open():[1]

```
virtual int open (u_short logger_port) {
  Iterative_Logging_Server::open (logger_port);
  master_handle_set_.set_bit (acceptor ().get_handle ());
  acceptor ().enable (ACE_NONBLOCK);
  return 0;
}
```

After calling down to its parent class's open() method to initialize the acceptor, we call the set_bit() method on the master_handle_set_ to keep track of the acceptor's socket handle. We also set the acceptor into non-blocking mode for the reasons described in Sidebar 14.

Next, we implement the wait_for_multiple_events() method for the reactive server. We copy master_handle_set_ into active_handles_, which will be modified by select(). We need to calculate the width argument for select() using a cast to compile on Win32 (the actual value passed to select() is ignored on that platform). The second parameter to select() is a pointer to the underlying fd_set in active_handles_ accessed via the ACE_Handle_Set::fdset() method.

```
virtual int wait_for_multiple_events () {
  active_handles_ = master_handle_set_;
  int width = (int) active_handles_.max_set () + 1;
  if (select (width,
              active_handles_.fdset (),
              0,           // no write_fds
              0,           // no except_fds
              0) == -1) // no timeout
      return -1;
```

---

[1]To save space, we omit more of the error handling than in our earlier iterative logging server implementation.

Sidebar 14: Motivation for Nonblocking Acceptors

When an acceptor socket is passed to `select()`, it's marked as "active" when a connection is received. Many servers use this event to indicate that it's okay to call `accept()` without blocking. Unfortunately, there's a race condition that stems from the asynchronous behavior of TCP/IP. In particular, after `select()` indicates an acceptor socket is active (but before `accept()` is called) a client can close its connection, whereupon `accept()` can block and potentially hang the entire application process. To avoid this problem, acceptor sockets should always be set into non-blocking mode when used with `select()`. In ACE, this is handled portably and conveniently by passing the ACE_NONBLOCK flag to the `enable()` method exported by ACE_IPC_SAP and, thus, by ACE_SOCK_Acceptor.

```
    active_handles_.sync
      ((ACE_HANDLE) active_handles_.max_set () + 1);
    return 0;
}
```

If an error occurs, `select()` returns −1, which we return as the value of the method. If it succeeds, the number of active handles is returned and the `active_handles_` fd_set is modified to indicate each handle that's now active. The call to `ACE_Handle_Set::sync()` resets the handle count and size-related values in `active_handles_` to reflect the changes made by `select()`.

We now show the implementation of the `handle_connections()` hook method. If the acceptor's handle is active, we accept all the connections that have arrived and add them to the `master_handle_set_`. Since we set the acceptor into non-blocking mode, it returns −1 and sets `errno` to EWOULDBLOCK when all pending connections have been accepted, as described in Sidebar 14. We therefore needn't worry about the process hanging indefinitely.

```
virtual int handle_connections () {
  if (active_handles_.is_set (acceptor ().get_handle ())) {
    while (acceptor ().accept (logging_handler ().peer ()) == 0)
      master_handle_set_.set_bit
        (logging_handler ().peer ().get_handle ());
```

```
      // Remove acceptor handle from further consideration.
      active_handles_.clr_bit (acceptor ().get_handle ());
    }
  return 0;
}
```

Note our use of the `get_handle()` method here, as well as the use of `set_handle()` in the `handle_data()` method below. This direct use of a low-level socket handle is permitted by the *Allow Controlled Violations of Type Safety* design principle explained in Section A.2.2 on page 237.

The `handle_data()` hook method loops over the set of handles that may be active; for each active handle it calls the `log_record()` method defined on page 91. This method processes one log record from each active connection.

```
      // This method has problems. Do not copy this example!
      virtual int handle_data (ACE_SOCK_Stream *) {
        for (ACE_HANDLE handle = acceptor ().get_handle () + 1;
             handle < active_handles_.max_set () + 1;
             handle++) {
          if (active_handles_.is_set (handle)) {
            logging_handler ().peer ().set_handle (handle);

            if (logging_handler ().log_record () == -1) {
              // Handle connection shutdown or comm failure.
              master_handle_set_.clr_bit (handle);
              logging_handler ().close ();
            }
          }
        }

        return 0;
      }
```

In `handle_data()` we use `ACE_Handle_Set` methods to

- Check if a handle is active

- Clear the handle in the `master_handle_set_` when a client closes its connection

Although this method is fairly concise, there are several drawbacks with using `ACE_Handle_Set` in the manner shown above. The next section describes how the `ACE_Handle_Set_Iterator` addresses these problems, so make sure to read it before applying the solution above in your own code!

Our `main()` function is almost identical to the iterative server in Section 4.4.3. The only difference is we define an instance of `Reactive_Logging_Server` rather than `Iterative_Logging_Server`.

```
#include "ace/Log_Msg.h"
#include "Reactive_Logging_Server.h"

int main (int argc, char *argv[])
{
  Reactive_Logging_Server server;

  if (server.run (argc, argv) == -1)
    ACE_ERROR_RETURN ((LM_ERROR, "%p\n", "server.run()"), 1);
  return 0;
}
```

7.3 The ACE_Handle_Set_Iterator Class

Motivation

The preceding example showed how reactive servers demultiplex events to event handlers via the following steps:

1. The `select()` function returns the number of handles whose values are active in its modified handle set(s).

2. The server's event loop then scans through the handle sets, identifies the active handles, and runs the event handling code for each handle.

Although these steps seem simple, complications arise in practice since `select()` returns the total number of active handle values, but doesn't indicate in which handle set(s) they reside. Applications must therefore scan through the contents of each handle set to find the active handles. One way to scan a handle set is to call `ACE_Handle_Set::is_set()` on each handle that may be active, as we did in the `handle_data()` method on page 146. There are two problems with this approach, however:

- The `for` loop technique used to iterate through the handles works only on OS platforms that represent socket handles as a contiguous range of unsigned integers. While POSIX/UNIX platforms support this technique, it doesn't work on Win32, so the code is non-portable. Moreover, the loop assumes that the acceptor socket has the lowest socket handle. In complex applications this property may not be true if handles were opened before the acceptor socket and later closed, in which case their handle values will be recycled.

- Even on platforms that do support contiguous handle values, each is_set() operation is called sequentially on all possible handle values. In networked applications it's often the case, however, that only some of the many possible socket handles are active at any point. Searching the sparsely populated handle sets sequentially is inefficient, particularly if the potential number of handles is large; for example, many UNIX platforms default to 1,024 handles per fd_set. Although the ACE_Handle_Set max_set() and num_set() methods can be used to limit the scope of a search, there are still unnecessary inefficiencies associated with scanning handle sets sequentially.

Addressing these portability concerns and optimizing these bottlenecks in each application is tedious and error prone, which is why ACE provides the ACE_Handle_Set_Iterator class.

Class Capabilities

The ACE_Handle_Set_Iterator is based on the Iterator pattern [GHJV95] that provides ways to access elements of an aggregate object sequentially without exposing the underlying structure of the object. This class scans efficiently through the handles in an ACE_Handle_Set, returning only the active handles one at a time through its operator() method. The interface of ACE_Handle_Set_Iterator and its relationship with the ACE_Handle_Set class is shown in Figure 7.1 on page 140. Its key methods are shown in the following table:

Method	Description
ACE_Handle_Set_Iterator()	Initializes the handle set iterator to iterate over an ACE_Handle_Set.
operator()	Returns the next unseen handle in the handle set or ACE_INVALID_HANDLE if all handles have been seen.

Since the ACE_Handle_Set_Iterator is not designed as a "robust iterator" [Kof93] it's important to not clear handles from an ACE_Handle_Set that's being iterated over.

Although `ACE_Handle_Set_Iterator` has a simple interface, it's implementation is more powerful than the ACE Socket wrapper facades described in Chapter 3. In particular, `ACE_Handle_Set_Iterator` encapsulates all the platform-specific `fd_set` representation details that help to iterate through all active handles in an `ACE_Handle_Set` portably and efficiently, as follows:

- Winsock's `fd_set` has a field containing the number of handle values in the set. The handles themselves are stored in adjacent locations in an array of handle values. `ACE_Handle_Set_Iterator` uses this knowledge to access each handle without having to search for the next handle, and without having to search all possible handle values for active handles.

- Most UNIX `fd_set` representations take advantage of the *0–n* range of possible handle values by assigning each possible handle value to a single bit. An `fd_set` thus contains an array of integers that's large enough to cover the entire range of bit values. The `ACE_Handle_Set_Iterator` class is designed to scan past large sequences of inactive handle values rapidly by skipping integer array elements that have zero values. Nonzero array elements can be scanned quickly by shifting and masking bits, using private class members to remember the array element and shift position between `operator()` invocations.

- Different sizes and bit orders of underlying `fd_set` are adapted to by using more appropriate shifting and array element access strategies. For example, the `ACE_Handle_Set_Iterator` can be configured to use a highly optimized bit manipulation algorithm based on the following two assumptions:

  - The `fd_set` is represented by an array of words (this is the case on most UNIX platforms).
  - If n is a word, the expression $n \& \sim(n-1)$ computes a word in which the only set bit is the least-signficant set bit (lssb) of n.

The key optimization in this algorithm is that the number of bits tested in each word in an `fd_set` is exactly the number of bits active, rather than the total number of bits in the word. When there are few active handles, this algorithm can improve server performance significantly.

In this algorithm, the ACE_Handle_Set_Iterator starts by finding the first word with an active bit in fd_set. Since the expression *word* &~(*word*−1) tests the lsb active in a word, we must find n such that $lsb = 2^n$. For each word in fd_set we have a cost of O(number of bits active in word). Thus, if a word consists of 64 bits and there's only one bit active, the run-time cost is 1, rather than 64.

- ACE_Handle_Set can be configured to use another fast algorithm that generates a count of active handles after select() sets them. It maintains a 256 element array of characters, with each element containing the number of active bits required to produce the index value. For example, element 5 contains the value of 2 (2 bits, 0 and 2, are set for the binary number 5). By skimming through the fd_set elements and summing the corresponding array values, the number of active bits in the fd_set can be calculated quickly without scanning them all sequentially.

- Since ACE_Handle_Set_Iterator is a friend of ACE_Handle_Set, it can use the calculated number of active handles and the maximum handle value to limit its search space. This design allows an ACE_ Handle_Set_Iterator to scan the smallest necessary subset of handle values that may be active.

By hiding all these optimization details in ACE_Handle_Set_Iterator, ACE can greatly improve the performance of key synchronous event demultiplexing operations without compromising application portability. This class illustrates how the appropriate levels of abstraction can improve application performance significantly.

Example

This example illustrates how we can use the ACE_Handle_Set_Iterator to solve the drawbacks with the reactive logging server alluded to near the end of Section 7.2 on page 146. We focus our attention on the handle_ data() method shown on page 146, replacing much of its code with an ACE_Handle_Set_Iterator that iterates over the active_handles_ as follows:

```
virtual int handle_data (ACE_SOCK_Stream *) {
  ACE_Handle_Set_Iterator peer_iterator (active_handles_);
```

```
for (ACE_HANDLE handle;
     (handle = peer_iterator ()) != ACE_INVALID_HANDLE;
     ) {
  logging_handler ().peer ().set_handle (handle);

  if (logging_handler ().log_record () == -1) {
    // Handle connection shutdown or comm failure.
    master_handle_set_.clr_bit (handle);
    logging_handler ().close ();
  }
 }
}
```

Not only is this code more concise and portable, but it's also more efficient due to the ACE_Handle_Set_Iterator optimizations.

7.4 The ACE::select() Methods

Motivation

The select() function is available on most OS platforms. Yet even this common function has subtleties that make it harder to use than necessary. For example, consider how select() is used on page 144. Even though the most common use case for select() in a reactive server is to wait indefinitely for input on a set of socket handles, programmers must provide NULL pointers for the write and exception fd_sets and for the timeout pointer. Moreover, programmers must remember to call the sync() method on active_handles_ to reflect changes made by select(). Addressing these issues in each application can be tedious and error prone, which is why ACE provides the ACE::select() wrapper methods.

Method Capabilities

ACE defines overloaded static wrapper methods for the native select() function that simplify its use for the most common cases. These methods are defined in the utility class ACE as follows:

```
class ACE {
public:
  static int select (int width,
                     ACE_Handle_Set &rfds,
                     const ACE_Time_Value *tv = 0);
```

```
static int select (int width,
                   ACE_Handle_Set *rfds,
                   ACE_Handle_Set *wfds = 0,
                   ACE_Handle_Set *efds = 0,
                   const ACE_Time_Value *tv = 0);
  // ... Other methods omitted ...
};
```

The first overloaded `select()` method in class `ACE` omits certain parameters and specifies a default value of no time-out value, that is, wait indefinitely. The second method supplies default values of 0 for the infrequently used write and exception `ACE_Handle_Set`s. They both automatically call `ACE_Handle_Set::sync()` when the underlying `select()` method returns to reset the handle count and size-related values in the handle set to reflect any changes made by `select()`.

We devised these wrapper functions by paying attention to design details and common usages to simplify programming effort and reduce the chance for errors in application code. The design was motivated by the following factors:

- **Simplify for the common case.** As mentioned above, the most common use case for `select()` in a reactive server is to wait indefinitely for input on a set of socket handles. The `ACE::select()` methods simplify this common use case. We discuss this design principle further in Section A.3.

- **Encapsulate platform variation.** All versions of `select()` accept a timeout argument; however, only Linux's version modifies the time-out value on return to reflect how much time was left in the time-out period when one of the handles was selected. The `ACE::select()` wrapper functions declare the timeout `const` to unambiguously state its behavior, and include internal code to work around the nonstandard time-out-modifying extensions on Linux. We discuss this design principle further in Section A.5.

- **Provide type portability.** The `ACE_Time_Value` class is used instead of the native timer type for the platform since timer types aren't consistent across all platforms.

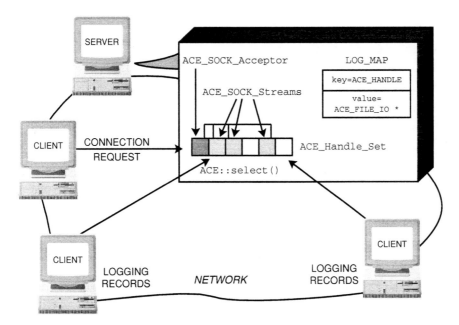

Figure 7.2: **Architecture of a Reactive Logging Server**

Example

The more useful and portable we make our logging server, the more client applications will want to use it and the greater its load will become. We therefore want to think ahead and design our subsequent logging servers to avoid becoming a bottleneck. In the next few chapters, we'll explore OS concurrency mechanisms and their associated ACE wrapper facades. As our use of concurrency expands, however, the single log record file we've been using thus far will become a bottleneck since all log records converge to that file.

In preparation for adding different forms of concurrency therefore, we extend our latest reactive server example to write log records from different clients to different log files, one for each connected client. Figure 7.2 illustrates the potentially more scalable reactive logging server architecture that builds upon and enhances the two earlier examples in this chapter. As shown in the figure, this reactive server implementation maintains a map container that allows a logging server to keep separate log files for each of its clients. The figure also shows how we use the ACE::select() wrapper method and the ACE_Handle_Set class to service multiple clients via a reactive server model.

Our implementation starts by including several new header files that provide various new capabilities we'll use in our logging server.

```
#include "ace/ACE.h"
#include "ace/Handle_Set.h"
#include "ace/Hash_Map_Manager.h"
#include "ace/Synch.h"
#include "Logging_Server.h"
#include "Logging_Handler.h"
```

We next define a type definition of the `ACE_Hash_Map_Manager` template, which is explained in Sidebar 15.

```
typedef ACE_Hash_Map_Manager<ACE_HANDLE,
                             ACE_FILE_IO *,
                             ACE_Null_Mutex> LOG_MAP;
```

We'll use an instance of this template to map an active `ACE_HANDLE` socket connection efficiently onto the `ACE_FILE_IO` object that corresponds to its log file. By using `ACE_HANDLE` as the map key, we address an important portability issue: socket handles on UNIX are small unsigned integers, whereas on Win32 they are pointers.

We create a new header file named `Reactive_Logging_Server_Ex.h` that contains a subclass called `Reactive_Logging_Server_Ex`, which inherits from `Logging_Server`. The main difference between this implementation and the one in Section 7.2 is that we construct a `log_map` to associate active handles to their corresponding `ACE_FILE_IO` pointers efficiently. To prevent any doubt that an active handle is a stream socket the `ACE_SOCK_Acceptor` isn't added to the `log_map`.

```
class Reactive_Logging_Server_Ex : public Logging_Server
{
protected:
  // Associate an active handle to an <ACE_FILE_IO> pointer.
  LOG_MAP log_map_;

  // Keep track of acceptor socket and all the connected
  // stream socket handles.
  ACE_Handle_Set master_handle_set_;

  // Keep track of read handles marked as active by <select>.
  ACE_Handle_Set active_read_handles_;

  // Other methods shown below...
};
```

Sidebar 15: The ACE Container Classes

ACE provides a suite of containers classes, including

- Singly and doubly linked lists
- Sets and multisets
- Stacks and queues
- Dynamic arrays
- String manipulation classes

Where possible, these classes are modeled after the C++ standard library classes so that it's easy to switch between them as C++ compilers mature.

The `ACE_Hash_Map_Manager` defines a set abstraction that associates keys to values efficiently. We use this class instead of the "standard" `std::map` (Aus98) for several reasons:

1. The `std::map` isn't so standard—not all compilers that ACE works with implement it, and those that do don't all implement its interface the same way.
2. The `ACE_Hash_Map_Manager` performs efficient lookups based on hashing, something `std::map` doesn't yet support.

More coverage of the ACE container classes appears in (HJS).

The `open()` hook method simply performs the steps necessary to initialize the reactive server.

```
virtual int open (u_short logger_port) {
  Logging_Server::open (logger_port);
  master_handle_set_.set_bit (acceptor ().get_handle ());
  acceptor ().enable (ACE_NONBLOCK);
  return 0;
}
```

The `wait_for_multiple_events()` hook method in this reactive server is similar to the one in Section 7.2. In this method, though, we call `ACE::select()`, which is a static wrapper method in ACE that provides default arguments for the less frequently used parameters to the `select()` function.

```
virtual int wait_for_multiple_events () {
  active_read_handles_ = master_handle_set_;
  int width = (int) active_read_handles_.max_set () + 1;

  return ACE::select (width, active_read_handles_);
}
```

The `handle_connections()` hook method implementation is similar to the one in `Reactive_Logging_Server`. We accept new connections and update the `log_map_` and `master_handle_set_`.

```
virtual int handle_connections () {
  ACE_SOCK_Stream logging_peer;

  while (acceptor ().accept (logging_peer) != -1) {
    ACE_FILE_IO *log_file = new ACE_FILE_IO;

    // Use the client's hostname as the logfile name.
    make_log_file (*log_file, &logging_peer);

    // Add the new <logging_peer>'s handle to the map and
    // to the set of handles we <select> for input.
    log_map_.bind (logging_peer.get_handle (), log_file);
    master_handle_set_.set_bit (logging_peer.get_handle ());
  }
  active_read_handles_.clr_bit (acceptor ().get_handle ());
  return 0;
}
```

Note that we use the `make_log_file()` method (see page 85) inherited from the `Logging_Server` base class described in Section 4.4.1.

The `handle_data()` hook method iterates over only the active connections, receives a log record from each, and writes the record to the log file associated with the client connection.

```
virtual int handle_data (ACE_SOCK_Stream *) {
  ACE_Handle_Set_Iterator peer_iterator (active_read_handles_);

  for (ACE_HANDLE handle;
       (handle = peer_iterator ()) != ACE_INVALID_HANDLE;
       ) {
    ACE_FILE_IO *log_file;

    log_map_.find (handle, log_file);
    Logging_Handler logging_handler (*log_file, handle);
```

```
    if (logging_handler.log_record () == -1) {
      logging_handler.close ();
      master_handle_set_.clr_bit (handle);
      log_map_.unbind (handle);
      log_file->close ();
      delete log_file;
    }
  }
}
  return 0;
}
```

When a client closes its connection, we close the corresponding Logging_
Handler, clear the handle from the master_handle_set_, remove the
handle-to-file association from the log_map_, and delete the dynamically
allocated ACE_FILE_IO object. Although we don't show much error handling code in this example, a production implementation should take appropriate corrective action if failures occur.

Finally, we show the main() program, which is essentially identical to
the ones we showed earlier, except that this time we define an instance of
Reactive_Logging_Server_Ex.

```
int main (int argc, char *argv[])
{
  Reactive_Logging_Server_Ex server;

  if (server.run (argc, argv) == -1)
    ACE_ERROR_RETURN ((LM_ERROR, "%p\n", "server.run()"), 1);
  return 0;
}
```

7.5 Summary

This chapter examined the accidental complexities, sources of performance
degradation, and portability problems that arise when designing a networked application using a reactive server model. The ACE_Handle_Set
and ACE_Handle_Set_Iterator wrapper facades were described as one
way to resolve these problems. These classes help ensure portable and
robust server programming without compromising the performance of networked applications.

Reactive servers are a common programming model that allows one
server to handle interactions with multiple peers or clients concurrently.
Although the new versions of the networked logging server in this chapter

showed how easy it is to do so portably, there's still room for further improvement. The example in Section 7.4 decides whether to accept a new connection or receive log records based on whether or not a socket handle is active in an `ACE_Handle_Set`. Although this design works, it tightly couples the event demultiplexing and connection management code. Application developers are therefore required to rewrite this code, which is actually general purpose and should therefore be refactored into a reusable framework.

The fundamental issue here is that `select()` and `fd_set` form the basis for powerful event demultiplexing and event handling capabilities that are hard to encapsulate within a simple wrapper facade. ACE therefore provides a framework based on the *Reactor pattern* [SSRB00] to refactor and reuse the generic event demultiplexing and dispatching behavior more flexibly. We cover the ACE Reactor framework thoroughly in [SH].

## CHAPTER 8

The ACE Process Wrapper Facades

CHAPTER SYNOPSIS

This chapter describes the ACE wrapper facades that encapsulate OS multiprocessing mechanisms with portable C++ classes. It illustrates the wide variation in multiprocessing facilities among popular operating systems and the techniques ACE uses to abstract portable concepts into useful classes. Finally, it shows how to apply these classes in a multiprocess version of our networked logging service.

8.1 Overview

OS support for multiprocessing is important for networked applications because it helps to

- **Enable concurrency** by allowing the OS to schedule and run separate processes on different CPUs

- **Increase robustness** by using MMU hardware to protect separate process address spaces from accidental or malicious corruption by other active processes in the system

- **Enhance security** by allowing each process to verify or control per-user or per-session security and authentication information

This chapter describes the following ACE classes that networked applications can use to spawn and manage one or more processes:

ACE Class	Description
ACE_Process	Creates and synchronizes processes portably.
ACE_Process_Options	Specifies both platform-independent and platform-specific options.
ACE_Process_Manager	Creates and synchronizes the completion of groups of processes portably.

Figure 8.1 shows the relationships among these classes. These wrapper facades provide the following benefits:

- **Enhance portability across heterogeneous OS platforms.** Process management capabilities vary widely among OS platforms. ACE's multiprocessing wrapper facades offer portable access to a common subset of these capabilities. For example, the ACE_Process and ACE_Process_Options classes can spawn, manage, and synchronize processes consistently, regardless of the underlying OS multiprocessing mechanisms.

- **Easy-to-use access to OS-specific mechanisms.** Certain platforms offer powerful process creation mechanisms, such as POSIX fork(). The ACE wrapper facades described in this chapter allow developers to access these mechanisms without changing their application code for different projects.

- **Manage a group of processes as a cohesive collection.** Networked applications that make use of multiprocessing often require multiple processes to begin and end as a group. The ACE_Process_Manager class adds this capability to the individual process management offered by ACE_Process.

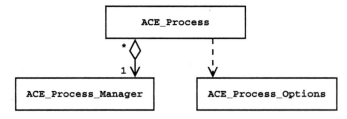

Figure 8.1: **The ACE Process Management Class Relationships**

This chapter motivates and describes the capabilities of the ACE multiprocessing classes. We present examples of each class to illustrate how they can simplify and ruggedize various aspects of our networked logging service.

8.2 The ACE_Process Class

Motivation

Process creation and management is a core part of most general-purpose operating systems (though Section 6.2 describes why some embedded operating systems don't provide process capabilities). Operating systems that do support multiple processes provide functionality to

- Create a process to run a particular program image
- End a process voluntarily or involuntarily
- Synchronize with the exit of another process

Given the maturity of these OS process management capabilities, you might expect a unified standard to govern this area. For a variety of factors, unfortunately, that's not the case. For instance, the following table outlines the key differences between POSIX/UNIX and Win32 process management:

POSIX/UNIX	Win32
fork() duplicates the calling process, including open I/O handles; a subsequent (optional) call to an exec*() function replaces the current program image with a new one.	CreateProcess() both spawns a new process and runs a designated program image in a single system function call.
The kill() function sends a signal to a process to stop it. Processes can intercept some signals and interpret them as requests to shut down and exit gracefully.	TerminateProcess() forces a process to exit without giving the process an opportunity to clean itself up.
The waitpid() function can be used to wait for child processes to exit. A parent process can also catch the SIGCHLD signal, which the OS delivers to the parent process when a child process exits.	Either the WaitForMultipleObjects() or WaitForSingleObject() function can be used to wait on a process's handle, which is signaled when it exits.

Although a complete discussion of OS multiprocessing mechanisms is beyond the scope of this book (see [Sch94, Ste92, Ric97] for more information), this comparison shows key differences between two popular operating environments. As you can see, OS process management mechanisms differ syntactically and semantically. Addressing these platform variations in each application is difficult, tedious, error prone, and unnecessary because ACE provides the ACE_Process class.

Class Capabilities

The ACE_Process class encapsulates the variation among different OS multiprocessing APIs in accordance with the Wrapper Facade pattern. This class defines uniform and portable methods whose capabilities enable applications to

- Spawn and terminate processes
- Synchronize on process exit
- Access process properties, such as process ID

The interface of the ACE_Process class is shown in Figure 8.2; its key platform-independent methods are outlined in the following table:

Method	Description
prepare()	Called by spawn() before the child process is spawned. Enables inspection and/or modification of the options to be used for the new process, and is a convenient place to set platform-specific options.
spawn()	Creates a new process address space and runs a specified program image.
unmanage()	Called by ACE_Process_Manager when a process it manages exits.
getpid()	Returns the process id of the new child process.
exit_code()	Returns the exit code of the child process.
wait()	Waits for the process we created to exit.
terminate()	Terminates the process abruptly, without giving the process a chance to clean up (so use with caution).

The ACE_Process class provides portable access to the common capability of spawning a new process and executing a new program image in the new process. Process management is one of the few functional areas,

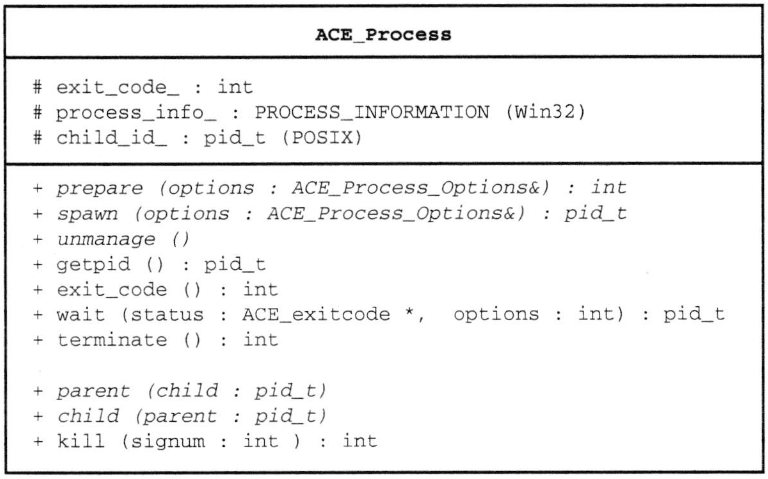

```
                         ACE_Process
─────────────────────────────────────────────────────────
 # exit_code_ : int
 # process_info_ : PROCESS_INFORMATION (Win32)
 # child_id_ : pid_t (POSIX)
─────────────────────────────────────────────────────────
 + prepare (options : ACE_Process_Options&) : int
 + spawn (options : ACE_Process_Options&) : pid_t
 + unmanage ()
 + getpid () : pid_t
 + exit_code () : int
 + wait (status : ACE_exitcode *,  options : int) : pid_t
 + terminate () : int

 + parent (child : pid_t)
 + child (parent : pid_t)
 + kill (signum : int ) : int
```

Figure 8.2: **The** ACE_Process **Class Diagram**

however, where wrapper facades can't encapsulate all the OS differences into one unified class that offers portability across the full range of OS platforms supported by ACE. For example, Sidebar 16 describes some key portability challenges associated with servers that use certain unique semantics of the POSIX fork() mechanism.

Since UNIX is a key platform for networked applications, the ACE_Process class offers a number of methods that only work in a POSIX/UNIX environment. These methods are useful (indeed, necessary) in many design situations. To avoid confusion, they are listed in the table below, separate from the portable methods that ACE_Process offers.

Method	Description
parent()	Can be overridden to supply application-specific behavior; called in the parent's process context after the fork() call if the child process was successfully forked.
child()	Can be overridden to supply application-specific behavior; called in the child's process context after the fork() and before exec().
kill()	Sends the process a signal. This is only portable to UNIX/POSIX operating systems that can send signals to designated processes.

Sidebar 16: POSIX Portability Challenges

Many UNIX applications use the POSIX `fork()` system function to create concurrent process-based servers. It can be hard to port these servers if they rely on the ability of `fork()` to both

1. Have a parent process `fork()` a child process with a duplicate of its parent's address space and copies of all the parent's I/O handles (including sockets) and
2. Have both parent and child process return from `fork()` at the same location but with different return values, which then run different parts of the server processing within the same program image.

There's no facility for duplicating an address space on platforms without the `fork()` function. However, most popular OS platforms, including Win32, support the more important capability of obtaining the needed I/O handles in the child process. The `ACE_Process_Options` class provides a portable way to use this capability, as shown in logging server example in Section 8.4.

Example

This example illustrates how to use `ACE_Process` to portably spawn a new process that runs a specified program image. The program we implement computes factorials "recursively" by

1. Having a parent process spawn a child process that runs the program image itself to compute the factorial of a number passed in the FAC-TORIAL environment variable, defaulting to factorial of 10 (10!) if no environment variable is set.
2. Each parent process then waits for its child process to finish, uses its child's exit code to compute the factorial for n, and returns this as the exit code for the process.

Although this is clearly *not* an efficient way to compute factorials, it illustrates the `ACE_Process` features concisely, as shown below.

```
#include "ace/OS.h"
#include "ace/Process.h"
```

```
int main (int argc, char *argv[])
{
  ACE_Process_Options options;
  char *n_env = 0;
  int n;

  if (argc == 1) { // Top-level process.
    n_env = ACE_OS::getenv ("FACTORIAL");
    n = n_env == 0 ? 10 : atoi (n_env);
    options.command_line ("%s %d", argv[0], n - 1);
  }
  else if (atoi (argv[1]) == 1) return 1; // Base case.
  else {
    n = atoi (argv[1]);
    options.command_line ("%s %d", argv[0], n - 1);
  }

  ACE_Process child;
  child.spawn (options); // Make the ''recursive'' call.
  child.wait ();
  return n * child.exit_code (); // Compute n factorial.
}
```

The call to `ACE_Process::wait()` will work regardless of whether the spawned process has finished before the call or not. If it has finished, the call completes immediately; if not, the method waits until the child process exits. This method is portable to all operating systems that support multiple processes.

The example above presents the most basic and portable use of `ACE_Process_Options`: to specify the command line for a spawned program. The next section discusses why we need a separate options class and shows its range of capabilities.

8.3 The ACE_Process_Options Class

Motivation

Operating systems provide a variety of methods for setting the properties of newly-created processes. A new process's properties affect its relationship to other processes and its execution environment. Some of the common properties include

- **Program image.** Which program should the new process execute?

- **Open I/O handles.** Should the child process inherit open I/O handles or other OS objects? Should it close some or all of its inherited open handles?

- **Access to display.** Should the child process have access to a terminal or to the user's display?

- **Working directory.** Should the child process run in the same directory as its parent or in a different directory?

- **Process relationship.** Should the child process run in the background as an independent *daemon* or as part of a related group?

- **Security attributes.** Should the child process's security attributes or default file protection settings be changed to expand or restrict its abilities?

These alternatives involve capabilities and APIs that are often unportable, even across similar platforms. A great deal of experience and platform-specific knowledge is needed to assure that each application's process properties are expressed correctly. The ACE_Process_Options class captures this knowledge portably.

Class Capabilities

The ACE_Process_Options class unifies how process properties are communicated to the ACE_Process and ACE_Process_Manager classes, which use these properties to select and influence the underlying OS process creation and environment mechanisms. ACE_Process_Options provides the following capabilities:

- It enables an application to specify desired process control information.

- It allows process control items to be expanded as platforms change.

- It provides a decoupling mechanism that enables ACE to offer these capabilities without varying the process creation interface.

The interface of the ACE_Process_Options class is shown in Figure 8.3 and its key platform-independent methods are outlined in the following table:

Method	Description
command_line()	Uses a printf-style format string to specify the command and its arguments to use when starting a new program in the spawned process.
setenv()	Specifies environment variables to be added to the environment in the spawned process.
working_directory()	Specifies a new directory that the spawned process will change to before starting a new program image.
set_handles()	Sets specific file handles that the spawned process will use for its STDIN, STDOUT, and STDERR.
pass_handle()	Indicates a handle that should be passed to the spawned process.

```
                        ACE_Process_Options

+ command_line (format : const char *, . . .) : int
+ setenv (format : const char *, ...) : int
+ working_directory (dir : const char *)
+ set_handles (in : ACE_HANDLE, out : ACE_HANDLE : err : ACE_HANDLE)
     : int
+ pass_handle (h : ACE_HANDLE) : int

+ creation_flags (flags : u_long)
+ avoid_zombies (on_off : int)
+ setruid (id : uid_t)
+ seteuid (id : uid_t)

+ set_process_attributes () : LPSECURITY_ATTRIBUTES
```

Figure 8.3: **The** ACE_Process_Options **Class Diagram**

Section 8.2 on page 161 explained why ACE_Process offers

1. Methods that are portable to all operating systems that support processes

2. Methods that work only on certain platforms

The ACE_Process_Options class also uses this approach. Its methods listed above offer a portable set of properties for all multiprocess platforms. The methods listed below access platform-specific properties:

Method	Description
creation_flags()	Specifies whether or not to run a new program image in the spawned process (POSIX).
avoid_zombies()	Allows ACE_Process to take steps to ensure that the spawned process does not end up a *zombie* (defunct) process when it exits (POSIX).
setruid() seteuid()	Set the real and effective user ID, respectively, for the spawned process (POSIX).
set_process_attributes()	Allows access to process attribute settings for the spawned process (Win32).

These methods allow multiprocessing applications to take advantage of nonportable capabilities, without having to rewrite process property management code for each platform.

Example

This section generalizes the example code from Section 8.2 as follows:

- It uses the WORKING_DIR environment variable to set the program's working directory, which is where the factorial.log file resides.
- It passes the program name to child processes via an environment variable.
- It prints diagnostic messages to the factorial.log file that contain the program name and process ID.

```
#include "ace/OS.h"
#include "ace/ACE.h"
#include "ace/Process.h"

int main (int argc, char *argv[])
{
  ACE_Process_Options options;
  FILE *fp = 0;
  char *n_env = 0;
  int n;

  if (argc == 1) { // Top-level process.
    n_env = ACE_OS::getenv ("FACTORIAL");
    n = n_env == 0 ? 0 : atoi (n_env);
    options.command_line ("%s %d", argv[0], n == 0 ? 10 : n);
    const char *working_dir = ACE_OS::getenv ("WORKING_DIR");
    if (working_dir) options.working_directory (working_dir);
    fp = fopen ("factorial.log", "a");
```

```
      options.setenv ("PROGRAM=%s", ACE::basename (argv[0]));
   }
   else {
     fp = fopen ("factorial.log", "a");
     if (atoi (argv[1]) == 1) {
       fprintf (fp, "[%s|%d]: base case\n",
                ACE_OS::getenv ("PROGRAM"), ACE_OS::getpid ());
       fclose (fp);
       return 1; // Base case.
     } else {
       n = atoi (argv[1]);
       options.command_line ("%s %d", argv[0], n - 1);
     }
   }

   ACE_Process child;
   child.spawn (options); // Make the ``recursive'' call.
   child.wait ();
   int factorial = n * child.exit_code (); // Compute n factorial.
   fprintf (fp, "[%s|%d]: %d! == %d\n",
            ACE_OS::getenv ("PROGRAM"), ACE_OS::getpid (),
            n, factorial);
   fclose (fp);
   return factorial;
}
```

Although the system functions called by the ACE_Process_Options and ACE_Process code vary considerably for different OS platforms, such as Win32 and POSIX, the code above will compile and run portably and correctly on all of them.

8.4   The ACE_Process_Manager Class

Motivation

Complex networked applications often require groups of processes to coordinate to provide a particular service. For example, a multistage workflow automation application may spawn multiple processes to work on different parts of a large problem. One master process may wait for the entire group of worker processes to exit before proceeding with the next stage in the workflow. This is such a common paradigm that ACE provides the ACE_Process_Manager class.

```
                        ACE_Process_Manager
─────────────────────────────────────────────────────────────
- process_table_ : ACE_Process * []
- current_count_ : size_t
─────────────────────────────────────────────────────────────
+ open (start_size : size_t) : int
+ close () : int
+ spawn (proc : ACE_Process *, opt : ACE_Process_Options) : pid_t
+ spawn_n (n : size_t, opts : ACE_Process_Options, pids : pid_t [])
        : int
+ wait (timeout : const ACE_Time_Value) : int
+ wait (pid : pid_t, timeout : const ACE_Time_Value,
        status : ACE_exitcode * = 0) : pid_t
+ instance () : ACE Process Manager *
```

Figure 8.4: **The** ACE_Process_Manager **Class Diagram**

Class Capabilities

The ACE_Process_Manager class uses the Wrapper Facade pattern to combine the portability and power of ACE_Process with the ability to manage groups of processes as a unit. This class has the following capabilities:

- It provides internal record keeping to manage and monitor groups of processes that are spawned by the ACE_Process class.
- It allows one process to spawn a group of process and wait for them to exit before proceeding with its own processing.

The interface of the ACE_Process_Manager class is shown in Figure 8.4 and its key methods are outlined in the following table:

Method	Description
open()	Initializes an ACE_Process_Manager.
close()	Releases all resources (do not wait for processes to exit).
spawn()	Spawns a process and adds it to a process group to be managed.
spawn_n()	Spawns n new processes, all of which belong to the same process group.
wait()	Waits for some or all of the processes in a process group to exit.
instance()	A static method that returns a pointer to the ACE_Process_ Manager singleton.

The ACE_Process_Manager can be used in two ways:

- **As a singleton** [GHJV95] via its instance() method.

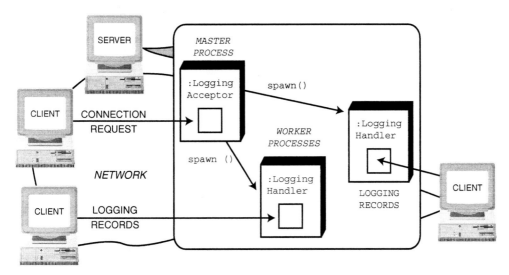

Figure 8.5: **Architecture of the Multiprocessing Logging Server**

- **By instantiating one or more instances.** This capability can be used to support multiple process groups within a process.

Example

The example in Section 7.4 illustrated the design and implementation of a reactive logging server that alleviated the drawbacks of a purely iterative server design. Yet another server model for handling client requests is to spawn a new process to handle each client. Process-based concurrency models are often useful when multithreaded solutions are either:

- **Not possible,** for example, on older UNIX systems that lack efficient thread implementations or that lack threading support altogether, or

- **Not desired,** for example, due to nonreentrant third-party library restrictions or due to reliability requirements for hardware-supported time and space partitioning.

Section 5.2 describes other pros and cons of implementing servers with multiple processes rather than multiple threads.

The structure of our multiprocess-based logging server is shown in Figure 8.5. This revision of the logging server uses a process-per-connection concurrency model. It's similar in many ways to the first version in Section 4.4.3 that used an iterative server design. The main difference here is that a master process spawns a new worker process for each accepted connection to the logging service port. The master process then continues to accept new connections. Each worker process handles all logging requests sent by a client across one connection; the process exits when this connection closes.

A process-per-connection approach has two primary benefits:

1. It "ruggedizes" the logging server against problems where one service instance corrupts others. This could happen, for example, because of internal bugs or by a malicious client finding a way to exploit a buffer overrun vulnerability.

2. It's a straightforward next step to extend the logging server to allow each process to verify or control per-user or per-session security and authentication information. For example, the start of each user-specific logging session could include a user/password exchange. By using a process-based server, rather than a reactive or multithreaded server, handling of user-specific information in each process would not be accidentally (or maliciously!) confused with another user's since each process has its own address space and access privileges.

The process-per-connection server shown below works correctly on both POSIX and Win32 platforms. Given the platform differences explained in Section 8.2 and Sidebar 16 on page 164, this is an impressive achievement. Due to the clean separation of concerns in our example logging server's design and ACE's intelligent use of wrapper facades, the differences required for the server code are minimal and well contained. In particular, there's a conspicuous lack of conditionally compiled application code.

Due to differing process creation models, however, we must first decide how to run the POSIX process. Win32 forces a program image to run in a new process, whereas POSIX does not. On Win32, we keep all of the server logic localized in one program and execute this program image in both the worker and master processes using different command-line arguments. On POSIX platforms, we can either:

- Use the same model as Win32 and run a new program image or
- Enhance performance by not invoking an `exec*()` function call after `fork()` returns.

To gain a performance advantage and to show how easy ACE makes it to do both ways correctly, we won't run a new program image in the worker processes on POSIX.

The process-per-connection logging server code is not particularly involved even though it operates differently on POSIX and Win32. However, the explanations of the event sequences and the details embodied in the ACE wrapper facades that facilitate this simplicity are rather subtle. To make it easier to absorb, we separate the explanation of the `Process_Per_Connection_Logging_Server` class, the example's process management, and the `Logging_Process` class.

The Process_Per_Connection_Logging_Server class. As with the iterative logging server in Section 4.4.3, we define a class representing our server. We start by including the necessary ACE header files:

```
#include "ace/Log_Record.h"
#include "ace/Process.h"
#include "ace/Process_Manager.h"
#include "ace/Signal.h"
#include "Logging_Server.h"
```

We derive the `Process_Per_Connection_Logging_Server` class from the `Logging_Server` class defined in Section 4.4.1. We override the `run()` method to accommodate the two different ways the program can be executed on Win32: as the master process to accept connections and spawn worker processes and as a worker process to service a logging client. The difference is expressed via command-line arguments:

- The master process is started with an optional port number on the command line, just like our other implementations of the networked logging server.
- The worker process is started with two arguments: (1) +H (the "handle" option that ACE adds for a passed handle) and (2) the numeric value of the socket handle inherited from the master process.

Figures 8.6 and 8.7 depict the master and worker process interactions for POSIX and Win32, respectively.

We'll see how command-line parameters are actually passed when we study the `Logging_Process` class, beginning on page 180. But first, we examine our server's class definition:

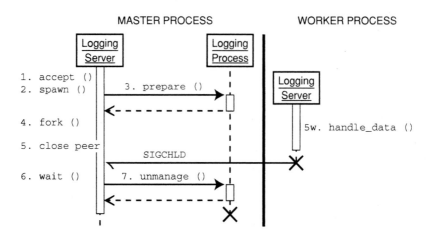

Figure 8.6: **Master/Worker Process Creation Sequence for POSIX**

```
class Process_Per_Connection_Logging_Server
  : public Logging_Server
{
protected:
  char prog_name_[MAXPATHLEN + 1];
```

The `prog_name_` data member receives the server program's name from its `argv[0]` command-line argument. We use this name to spawn worker processes that handle new connections. The `run()` method examines the command line's argument count to decide if the server should run as the master or a worker. If there are two arguments, this is a worker process; otherwise, it's the master process.

```
virtual int run (int argc, char *argv[]) {
  strncpy (prog_name_, argv[0], MAXPATHLEN);
  prog_name_[MAXPATHLEN] = '\0'; // Ensure NUL-termination.
  if (argc == 3)
    return run_worker (argc, argv); // Only on Win32.
  else
    return run_master (argc, argv);
}
```

The `run_master()` method is similar to the `Logging_Server::run()` method; for example, it opens the logging server's listen port and calls `handle_connections()` to accept new client connections. It does not, however, call the `handle_data()` hook method, which is always called in

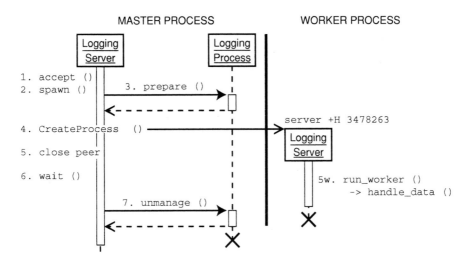

Figure 8.7: **Master/Worker Process Creation Sequence for Win32**

the worker process. The master server spawns a new worker process to handle each client's log records, as shown in Figure 8.5.

```
int run_master (int argc, char *argv[]) {
  u_short logger_port = 0;
  if (argc == 2) logger_port = atoi (argv[1]);
  if (open (logger_port) == -1) return -1;

  for (;;)
    if (handle_connections () == -1) return -1;

  return 0;
}
```

We inherit the open() method implementation from the Logging_Server base class, which initializes the acceptor endpoint to listen passively on a designated port. Since the wait_for_multiple_events() implementation is a no-op, we simply omit it here and call handle_connections() directly to run the master event loop.

The run_worker() method is only executed on Win32. When the worker process is spawned, the master process requests the socket handle be passed to the worker process on the command line. The run_worker() method converts the command-line argument back to a handle, builds an ACE_SOCK_Stream object with the handle, and calls handle_data() to process the client's log records. Since the incoming data type is fixed, it

Sidebar 17: Portable Casting on All C+ Compilers

Most programmers who learned C before C++ are familiar with the cast operator, (type) expression. It's a powerful feature, but is easily misused because it violates type safety and can introduce errors, especially when porting software to new platforms. Although the C++ standard introduced several keywords to allow casting without losing all type meaning, they're not implemented in compilers that predate this feature. ACE therefore supplies a set of macros that allow code to be written portably. They take advantage of the new casts where available and use old C-style casts where needed. The most commonly used casts supplied with ACE are listed in the table below:

ACE Cast Macro	C++ Cast Used if Available
`ACE_const_cast(TYPE,EXPR)`	`const_cast<TYPE>(EXPR)`
`ACE_static_cast(TYPE,EXPR)`	`static_cast<TYPE>(EXPR)`
`ACE_dynamic_cast(TYPE,EXPR)`	`dynamic_cast<TYPE>(EXPR)`
`ACE_reinterpret_cast(TYPE,EXPR)`	`reinterpret_cast<TYPE>(EXPR)`

must be converted using a cast. To do so as safely as a platform's C++ compiler allows, ACE provides a set of portable casting macros (including `ACE_static_cast` used below), that is discussed in Sidebar 17.

```
int run_worker (int argc, char *argv[]) {
  ACE_HANDLE socket_handle =
    ACE_reinterpret_cast (ACE_HANDLE, atoi (argv[2]));
  ACE_SOCK_Stream logging_peer (socket_handle);

  handle_data (&logging_peer);
  logging_peer.close ();
  return 0;
}
```

The master server process listens passively for new client logging connections. As in our previous logging servers, the `handle_connections()` method accepts new connections. In the process-per-connection logging server, however, `handle_connections()` spawns a new worker process to handle each new client connection. Figure 8.6 on page 174 illustrates the sequence of events that occur when `handle_connections()` accepts a new connection and spawns a worker process on POSIX. Figure 8.7 on page 175 shows the same sequence on Win32 (in both figures, the name

Process_Per_Connection_Logging_Server has been shortened to Logging Server to fit in the available space). The figures and explanation both refer to the Logging_Process class, which is described on page 180. Sidebar 18 on page 178 describes the steps in these figures and the following C++ code segments illustrate how these steps are programmed using ACE_Process_Manager.

The implementation of the handle_connections() method of Process_Per_Connection_Logging_Server is shown below:

```
1 virtual int handle_connections () {
2   ACE_SOCK_Stream logging_peer;
3   if (acceptor ().accept (logging_peer) == -1)
4     return -1;
5
6   Logging_Process *logger =
7     new Logging_Process (prog_name_, logging_peer);
8   ACE_Process_Options options;
9   pid_t pid = ACE_Process_Manager::instance ()->spawn
10     (logger, options);
11   if (pid == 0) {
12     acceptor().close ();
13     handle_data (&logging_peer);
14     delete logger;
15     ACE_OS::exit (0);
16   }
17   logging_peer.close ();
18   if (pid == -1)
19     ACE_ERROR_RETURN ((LM_ERROR, "%p\n", "spawn()"), -1);
20
21   return ACE_Process_Manager::instance ()->wait
22     (0, ACE_Time_Value::zero);
23 }
```

We dissect the handle_connections() method implementation below, referring to the steps in Figures 8.6 and 8.7 on page 174 that are explained in Sidebar 18.

Lines 2–4 (Step 1) Call acceptor().accept(); the call blocks until a client connects.

Lines 6–10 (Steps 2–4) Spawn a new process to handle the accepted client connection. The work to set the options properly for each platform is done in the Logging_Process::prepare() method shown on page 180. ACE_Process::spawn() calls the proper platform mechanism to create the new process.

Sidebar 18: How Worker Processes Are Spawned

The numbered steps depicted in Figures 8.6 and 8.7 are similar. They occur in the `handle_connections()` method and are outlined below:

1. Accept a new logging client connection.

2. Call `ACE_Process_Manager::spawn()` to begin spawning the new worker process. It will call `ACE_Process::spawn()`.

3. `ACE_Process::spawn()` calls back to the `Logging_Process::prepare()` method to set up the new process's attributes.

4. The `ACE_Process::spawn()` method calls the platform's process creation mechanism. For example, on POSIX the `fork()` function creates the worker process as an exact duplicate of the master process. The new process begins executing in the `handle_connections()` method, at the point where `fork()` returned. On Win32, however, the `CreateProcess()` function creates a new process that's not duplicated from the master process. The new process inherits the socket handle for the new client as shown in the `Logging_Process::prepare()` method on page 181. The new process runs the same program image as the master process, but with the new handle's value passed on the command line.

5. The logging peer's socket handle is closed in the master, whereas the worker's copy remains open to service the logging client.

5w. In the worker process, the `handle_data()` hook method is called. On POSIX, it's called directly from the `handle_connections()` method. On Win32, the `Process_Per_Connection_Logging_Server::run()` method notices the handle on the command-line and calls the `run_worker()` method, which calls `handle_data()`. The worker process exits when the client's connection is closed.

6. The master process periodically calls `ACE_Process_Manager::wait()` to see if the worker process has exited.

7. When the worker process exits, `ACE_Process_Manager::wait()` calls `Logging_Process::unmanage()`. This gives the master process an opportunity to release any resources associated with the worker process. The `Logging_Process` object then deletes itself.

Lines 11–15 (POSIX Step 5w[1]) A 0 return value from `spawn()` is impossible on Win32 since it will either return the new process's PID or −1 on error. These lines are therefore always executed in the context of a `fork()`'d POSIX process. The worker process closes its inherited `acceptor` object since the worker uses only the client's established connection and doesn't accept new connections. The `handle_data()` method is called to process all of the client's log records, then the `Logging_Process` object is freed, and the worker process exits. The master process will notice a worker process has exited when it next calls `ACE_Process_Manager::wait()` on line 21.

Line 17 If the `spawn()` call returned in the parent (which is always the case for Win32) the `logging_peer` object is no longer needed, so it's closed. The actual TCP connection is not closed because the following platform-specific behavior is encapsulated in the ACE process wrapper facades:

- On POSIX, the worker process inherited a copy of the entire object, including the open handle. The OS reference counts the handles, so the connection won't actually be torn down until both the parent and worker processes close their respective copies of the handle.
- On Windows NT/2000, the handles are managed similarly to POSIX; that is, the connection is torn down only after both processes close the handle.
- On Windows 95/98, handles are not reference counted automatically. However, `ACE_Process_Options::pass_handle()`, called from the `Logging_Process::prepare()` method, duplicated the socket handle contained in `logging_peer`. The parent can therefore close its handle safely without affecting the connection.

As usual, the ACE wrapper facades shield application developers from needing to understand these subtle nuances for each OS platform!

Lines 21–22 (Steps 6 and 7) The `ACE_Process_Manager::wait()` method checks to see if any worker processes have exited, reaping their status and cleaning up any handles they'd opened.

The `handle_data()` method shown below is identical for all platforms. It puts the client socket into blocking mode, opens the log file to hold the log records, and processes logging records until the logging client closes the socket or an error occurs. Lastly, the log file is closed.

---

[1]Step 5w on Win32 is executed by the `run_worker()` method shown on page 176.

```
virtual int handle_data (ACE_SOCK_Stream *logging_peer) {
  // Ensure blocking <recv>s.
  logging_peer->disable (ACE_NONBLOCK);
  ACE_FILE_IO log_file;
  make_log_file (log_file, logging_peer);
  Logging_Handler logging_handler (log_file,
                                   *logging_peer);

  while (logging_handler.log_record () != -1)
    continue;

  log_file.close ();
  return 0;
}
```

The Logging_Process class.   To set up the new worker process properly,
we define a Logging_Process class that's derived from the ACE_Process
class described in Section 8.2. Since setup requirements often vary between platforms and applications, ACE_Process provides the prepare()
and unmanage() hook methods. Our Logging_Process class uses the
prepare() method to pass the new logging client's socket handle to the
worker process. It's also the location where we localize any changes if we
need to revisit the decision not to run a new program image on POSIX.

```
class Logging_Process : public ACE_Process
{
private:
  Logging_Process (); // Force desired constructor to be used.

  char prog_name_[MAXPATHLEN + 1];
  ACE_SOCK_Stream logging_peer_;

public:
  Logging_Process (const char *prog_name,
                   const ACE_SOCK_Stream &logging_peer)
    : logging_peer_ (logging_peer.get_handle ())
  { strcpy (prog_name_, prog_name); }
```

The parameters needed to set up the new worker process are passed to the
Logging_Process class's constructor. These include the command name
used to spawn the new process and the logging client's ACE_SOCK_Stream
to be used by the worker process. Both these parameters are used in
the following prepare() hook method, which is called by ACE_Process::
spawn() before the new process is spawned.

```
virtual int prepare (ACE_Process_Options &options) {
  if (options.pass_handle (logging_peer_.get_handle ()) == -1)
    ACE_ERROR_RETURN ((LM_ERROR, "%p\n", "pass_handle()"), -1);
  options.command_line ("%s", prog_name_);
  options.avoid_zombies (1);
  options.creation_flags (ACE_Process_Options::NO_EXEC);
  return 0;
}
```

The `prepare()` method is illustrated as Step 3 in Figures 8.6 and 8.7 on page 174. Its only argument is a reference to the `ACE_Process_Options` object that `ACE_Process::spawn()` is using to spawn the new process. This gives `prepare()` an opportunity to modify or add to the options as needed. We use `prepare()` to set the options as follows:

- **Pass the logging client's socket handle.** The internals of `ACE_Process` and `ACE_Process_Options` perform all platform-specific details of getting the socket handle to the worker process correctly, including duplicating it on Windows 95/98 and remembering to close the duplicated handle when the process exits. We use the `pass_handle()` method to pass the handle value to the worker process command line, which indicates that a logging client needs service.

- **Set the program name.** This is needed both for a POSIX `fork()` call and to run the new program image when needed.

- **Avoid zombie processes.** This flag is needed only for POSIX and is ignored for Win32.

- **Set the** NO_EXEC **flag** so that POSIX systems simply `fork()` a new worker process and do not `exec()` a new program image. This flag is also ignored on Win32.

Although some methods have no effect on Win32, we call them anyway so the procedure for setting up the worker process is portable to all ACE platforms that support multiple processes. For a discussion of why this is the correct design (and when it isn't), see Section A.5 on page 248.

`ACE_Process_Manager` encapsulates platform-specific knowledge that determines when a process exits and calls the `unmanage()` hook method on any process object whose underlying process has exited. The `Logging_Process::unmanage()` is illustrated as Step 7 in Figures 8.6 and 8.7 on page 174 and is shown below:

```
virtual void unmanage () {
  delete this;
}
```

It simply cleans up the `Logging_Process` object that was allocated dynamically when the logging client connection was accepted. The logging peer socket handle may have been duplicated, however, when passed to the worker process on Windows 95/98. By encapsulating behavior and state in the `ACE_Process` class, that handle will be closed in the `ACE_Process` destructor, so our cleanup code is also portable to all platforms that ACE supports.

Finally, we show the `main()` program, which is a slight extension of our earlier servers.

```
static void sigterm_handler (int /* signum */) { /* No-op. */ }

int main (int argc, char *argv[])
{
  // Register to receive the <SIGTERM> signal.
  ACE_Sig_Action sa (sigterm_handler, SIGTERM);

  Process_Per_Connection_Logging_Server server;

  if (server.run (argc, argv) == -1 && errno != EINTR)
    ACE_ERROR_RETURN ((LM_ERROR, "%p\n", "server.run()"), 1);

  // Barrier synchronization.
  return ACE_Process_Manager::instance ()->wait ();
}
```

The `ACE_Sig_Action` class registers the process to handle the SIGTERM signal, which administrators can use to shutdown the parent server process. Before exiting, the parent calls `ACE_Process_Manager::wait()` to synchronize on the exits of all worker logging processes before shutting itself down. This *barrier synchronization* capability could be useful if the parent process needed to write a final time stamp to the logging output device or file.

8.5 Summary

Many multiprocessing operating systems were developed when proprietary systems were in vogue, so each developed its own specific mechanisms for process management. Since maintaining version-to-version OS compatibility is important, many of these proprietary process mechanisms and

APIs remain to this day. This chapter showed how to use the ACE process management capabilities, which allow multiprocessing servers to be programmed portably across a range of platforms. We applied the `ACE_Process_Manager` to a new logging server implementation that grouped a set of spawned processes together. The grouping allowed the master process to wait for all the worker processes to exit before shutting itself down.

Due to inherent differences in OS process management semantics, developers of networked applications must evaluate their system's concurrency requirements carefully. Whereas previous chapters focused largely on alleviating accidental complexities introduced by low-level APIs, this chapter expanded on the challenges of multiplatform software development. It showed how the portable ACE wrapper facades make multiprocessing applications much easier to write, while also making it clear that the capabilities of an application's current and future platforms must be considered carefully when evaluating multiprocessing concurrency designs. For example, the ACE process wrapper facades can shield applications from many OS details, but they cannot provide process abstractions on platforms that lack them altogether.

CHAPTER 9

The ACE Threading Wrapper Facades

CHAPTER SYNOPSIS

This chapter describes the ACE wrapper facades that encapsulate OS multithreading mechanisms with portable C++ classes. We apply these ACE threading wrapper facades to illustrate a series of increasingly flexible and efficient enhancements to our networked logging service.

9.1 Overview

Many networked applications lend themselves naturally to multithreading because processing tasks can be separated from I/O tasks. Multithreading is particularly convenient in servers that manage connection-oriented or connectionless network associations for many clients simultaneously. Today's increasingly powerful OS support for multithreading helps networked applications to:

- **Leverage hardware advances,** such as symmetric multiprocessing that enables true execution *parallelism,*

- **Increase performance** by overlapping computation and communication,

- **Improve response time** for GUIs and network servers to ensure that time-sensitive tasks are scheduled as needed, and

- **Simplify program structure** by enabling applications to use intuitive synchronous programming mechanisms, rather than more complex asynchronous programming mechanisms.

This chapter describes the following ACE classes that networked applications can use to spawn and manage one or more threads of control within a process:

ACE Class	Description
`ACE_Thread_Manager`	Allows applications to portably create and manage the lifetime, synchronization, and properties of threads.
`ACE_Sched_Params`	A portable encapsulation of OS scheduling class features that's used in conjunction with the `ACE_OS::sched_params()` wrapper method to control various properties of real-time threads.
`ACE_TSS`	Encapsulates thread-specific storage mechanisms to allow objects that are "physically" private to a thread to be accessed as though they were "logically" global to a program.

These wrapper facades provide the following benefits:

- **Ensure portability across heterogeneous OS platforms.** Operating systems have diverse multithreading syntax and semantics, which ACE hides via its wrapper facades. For example, the `ACE_Thread_Manager` class ensures detached/joinable threads behave the same regardless of the underlying OS threading mechanisms.

- **Manage a group of threads as a cohesive collection.** Concurrent networked applications often require multiple threads to start and end as a unit. The `ACE_Thread_Manager` class provides a thread group capability that allows other threads to wait for an entire group of threads to exit before proceeding with their processing.

- **Influence thread scheduling policies and priorities.** Many networked applications require tight control over the priorities of their threads. Real-time and general-purpose operating systems often differ in their scheduling capabilities, and multiplatform networked applications need a way to manage the disparate scheduling properties portably. The `ACE_Sched_Params` class is designed to offer access to run-time scheduling information in a uniform, portable, and easy-to-use manner.

- **Efficiently use and manage thread-specific storage (TSS).** TSS is a mechanism that enables multiple objects and methods to manage information that's specific to each thread. ACE's TSS wrapper facade class overcomes syntax differences, as well as capability differences, between platforms.

This chapter motivates and describes the capabilities of the ACE multithreading classes. We present examples of each class to illustrate how they can simplify and optimize various aspects of our networked logging service.

9.2 The ACE_Thread_Manager Class

Motivation

Different operating systems use different APIs to create, manage, and synchronize the completion of threads. Today's multithreading mechanisms suffer from accidental complexities similar to those discussed in previous chapters. They also introduce the following two types of variability that make writing portable applications hard:

- **Syntactic**—Native OS threading APIs are often non-portable due to syntactic differences, even if they provide the same capabilities. For example, the Win32 `CreateThread()` and the Pthreads `pthread_create()` functions provide similar thread creation capabilities, even though their APIs differ syntactically.

- **Semantic**—Wrapper facades that export a syntactically uniform C++ programming interface don't necessarily address semantic variations across OS multithreading mechanisms. For example, both Pthreads and UI threads support detached threads, whereas Win32 does not, and VxWorks supports only detached threads.

One particularly vexing aspect of multithreaded applications is determining how to cancel threads portably. Some OS platforms provide native support for canceling threads, for example:

- Pthreads defines a powerful set of APIs that allow threads to be canceled asynchronously or cooperatively via the `pthread_cancel()` and `pthread_testcancel()` functions.

- It's also possible to cancel threads on some UNIX platforms via signals, for example, via the Pthreads `pthread_kill()` and UI threads `thr_kill()` functions.

- The Win32 `TerminateThread()` function offers asynchronous cancelation.

Unfortunately, the native OS thread cancelation mechanisms outlined above are nonportable and error prone. For example, UNIX signals and the Win32 `TerminateThread()` function can stop a thread dead in its tracks, preventing it from releasing any resources it's holding. The Pthreads asynchronous thread cancelation mechanisms provide better support for cleaning up resources held by a thread, but they are still hard to understand and program correctly, and aren't portable to non-Pthreads platforms.

Since it's tedious and error prone to address all of these portability issues in each application, ACE provides the `ACE_Thread_Manager` class.

Class Capabilities

The `ACE_Thread_Manager` class uses the Wrapper Facade pattern to guide the encapsulation of the syntactic and semantic variation among different OS multithreading APIs. This class provides the following portable capabilities:

- Spawns one thread, or multiple threads at once, each running an application-designated function concurrently

- Alters the most common thread attributes, for example, scheduling priority and stack size, for each of the spawned threads

- Spawns and manages a set of threads as a cohesive collection, called a thread group

- Manages the threads in an `ACE_Task`, which we present in [SH]

- Facilitates *cooperative cancelation* of threads, and

- Waits for one or more threads to exit.

The interface of the `ACE_Thread_Manager` class is shown in Figure 9.1 and its key platform-independent methods are outlined in the following table:

Method	Description
spawn()	Creates a new thread of control, passing it the function and function parameter to run as the thread's entry point.
spawn_n()	Creates n new threads belonging to the same thread group. Other threads can wait for this entire group of threads to exit.
wait()	Blocks until all threads in the thread manager have exited and reaps the exit status of any joinable threads.
join()	Waits for a particular thread to exit and reaps its exit status.
cancel_all()	Requests all threads managed by an ACE_Thread_Manager object to stop.
testcancel()	Asks if the designated thread has been requested to stop.
exit()	Exits a thread and releases the thread's resources.
close()	Closes down and releases resources for all managed threads.
instance()	A static method that returns a pointer to the ACE_Thread_Manager singleton.

```
ACE_Thread_Manager

# grp_id_ : int

+ spawn (func : ACE_THR_FUNC, args : void * = 0,
         flags : long = THR_NEW_LWP | THR_JOINABLE,
         id: ACE_thread_t * = 0, handle : ACE_hthread_t * = 0,
         priority : long = ACE_DEFAULT_THREAD_PRIORITY,
         grp_id : int = -1, stack : void * = 0,
         stack_size : size_t = 0) : int
+ spawn_n (n : size_t, func : ACE_THR_FUNC, args : void * = 0,
          flags : long = THR_NEW_LWP | THR_JOINABLE,
          priority : long = ACE_DEFAULT__THREAD_PRIORITY,
          grp_id : int = -1, task : ACE_Task_Base * = 0,
          handles : ACE_hthread_t [ ] = 0, stacks : void * [ ] = 0,
          stack_sizes : size_t [ ] = 0) : int
+ wait (timeout : const ACE_Time_Value * = 0,
        abandon_detached_threads : int = 0) : int
+ join (id : ACE_thread_t, status : void ** = 0) : int
+ cancel_all (async_cancel : int = 0) : int
+ testcancel (id : ACE_thread_t ) : int
+ exit (status : void * = 0, do_thread_exit : int = 1) : int
+ close ( ) : int
+ instance ( ) : ACE Thread Manager *

+ suspend (id : ACE_thread_t) : int
+ resume (id : ACE_thread_t) : int
+ kill (id : ACE_thread_t, signum : int) : int
```

Figure 9.1: **The** ACE_Thread_Manager **Class Diagram**

The `ACE_Thread_Manager::spawn()` method can be passed a set of flags to specify the properties of the created thread. This value is a bit-wise inclusive "or" of the flags shown in the following table:

Flag	Description
THR_SCOPE_SYSTEM	The new thread is created with *system* scheduling contention scope, permanently bound to a newly created kernel-thread.
THR_SCOPE_PROCESS	The new thread is created with *process* scheduling contention scope, that is, it runs as a user thread.
THR_NEW_LWP	This flag affects the concurrency attribute of the process. The desired level of concurrency for unbound threads is increased by one, which typically adds a new kernel thread to the pool available to run user threads. On OS platforms that don't support an N:M user/kernel threading model this flag is ignored.
THR_DETACHED	The new thread is created detached, which means that its exit status is not accessible to other threads. Its thread ID and other resources are reclaimed by the OS as soon as the thread terminates. This flag is the opposite of THR_JOINABLE.
THR_JOINABLE	The new thread is created joinable, which means that its exit status can be obtained by other threads via the `ACE_Thread_Manager::join()` method. Its thread ID and other resources are not reclaimed by the OS until another thread joins with it. This flag is the opposite of THR_DETACHED. The default behavior for all ACE thread creation methods is THR_JOINABLE.

The `ACE_Thread_Manager` not only spawns threads with various properties, it also provides a cooperative thread cancelation mechanism that's safe, easy to use, and portable. To use this mechanism, the canceling thread uses `ACE_Thread_Manager::cancel()` to set a flag indicating that a designated thread should cancel itself. The canceled thread is responsible for cooperating in this scheme by periodically calling `ACE_Thread_Manager::testcancel()` to see if it's been requested to cancel itself.

Since threads are not canceled immediately, the ACE cooperative thread cancelation feature is analogous to using the Pthreads *deferred cancelation* policy with the cancelation point being the call to `ACE_Thread_Manager::testcancel()`. ACE cooperative thread cancelation differs from Pthreads deferred cancelation in the following ways:

- Thread cleanup in ACE must be programmed explicitly after the cancelation point
- After a thread has been canceled in ACE, it can elect to finish any in-progress work or even ignore the cancelation request altogether.

Thus, ACE thread cancelation is strictly voluntary, which is the only way to cancel a thread both portably and safely.

As with the `ACE_Process_Manager` described in Section 8.4, the `ACE_Thread_Manager` can be used in two ways:

- **As a singleton** [GHJV95] accessed via its `instance()` method. This method is implemented using the Double-Checked Locking Optimization pattern, as is described in Sidebar 19.
- **By instantiating one or more instances.** This capability can be used to support multiple sets of thread groups within a process. Although this is a legitimate use at any time, it's recommended when developing a *shared library* (DLL) that uses the `ACE_Thread_Manager` class. This practice avoids interfering with the singleton instance that the calling application may be using.

Example

Multithreaded servers are common on operating systems where spawning threads incurs less overhead than spawning processes. The following example uses the `ACE_Thread_Manager` to implement our first multithreaded logging server based on a thread-per-connection concurrency model. As shown in Figure 9.2, the master thread runs continuously and plays the role of a factory that

1. Accepts a connection and creates an `ACE_SOCK_Stream` object dynamically and
2. Spawns a worker thread that uses this object to handle the client's logging session.

The worker thread performs all subsequent log record processing on the `ACE_SOCK_Stream` and destroys it when the connection is closed. This concurrency design is similar to the example in Section 8.4 that spawned a new process for each client connection. This thread-per-connection logging server differs from the process-per-connection implementation in the following ways, however:

Sidebar 19: Serializing Singletons in ACE

The Singleton pattern (GHJV95) ensures that a class has only one instance and provides a global point of access to it. Singletons defined in ACE use the Double-Checked Locking Optimization pattern (SSRB00) to reduce contention and synchronization overhead when critical sections of code must acquire locks in a thread-safe manner just once during program execution. The following code shows how the static `ACE_Thread_Manager::instance()` method uses this pattern:

```
ACE_Thread_Manager *ACE_Thread_Manager::instance () {
  if (ACE_Thread_Manager::thr_mgr_ == 0) {
    ACE_GUARD_RETURN (ACE_Recursive_Thread_Mutex, ace_mon,
                      *ACE_Static_Object_Lock::instance(),
                      0));
    if (ACE_Thread_Manager::thr_mgr_ == 0)
      ACE_Thread_Manager::thr_mgr_ = new ACE_Thread_Manager;
  }
  return ACE_Thread_Manager::thr_mgr_;
}
```

The `ACE_Static_Object_Lock::instance()` returns a preinitialized lock that is created before the `main()` function runs, as described in Sidebar 23 on page 218.

- It spawns a new thread for each connection instead of a new process, so it should be more efficient.
- It's more portable because it works on any platform that supports threads.
- It's considerably simpler because portable multithreaded servers are easier to program than multiprocessed servers.

Section 5.2 provides a more general description of the pros and cons of implementing servers with multiple threads rather than with multiple processes.

We start, as usual, by including the necessary ACE header files:

```
#include "ace/SOCK_Stream.h"
#include "ace/Thread_Manager.h"
#include "Logging_Server.h"
#include "Logging_Handler.h"
```

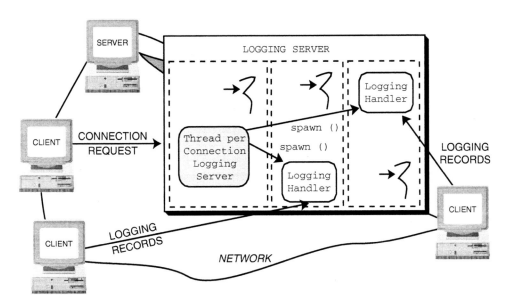

Figure 9.2: **Architecture of the Thread-per-Connection Logging Server**

We define a `Thread_Per_Connection_Logging_Server` class that inherits from `Logging_Server`.

```
class Thread_Per_Connection_Logging_Server : public Logging_Server
{
private:
  class Thread_Args {
  public:
    Thread_Args (Thread_Per_Conenction_Logging_Server *lsp)
      : this_ (lsp) {}

    Thread_Per_Connection_Logging_Server *this_;
    ACE_SOCK_Stream logging_peer_;
  };

  // Passed as a parameter to <ACE_Thread_Manager::spawn>.
  static void *run_svc (void *arg);

protected:
  // Other methods shown below...
};
```

As with `Process_Per_Connection_Logging_Server` in Section 8.4, we inherit and reuse the `open()` and `wait_for_multiple_events()` methods.

Sidebar 20: Traps and Pitfalls of Mixing Threads and Objects

The life cycle of objects passed as parameters to thread entry point functions must be managed carefully. Many programmers confuse a thread and an object by saying things like "this object runs in a thread." It's critical to make the following distinction:

- A thread is a unit of execution.
- An object is a chunk of memory and associated methods.

Thus, there's no implicit connection between a thread and any object that the thread accesses during execution. It's essential therefore to make sure that no thread can access an object after it's been deleted.

For example, if the `Thread_Args` object was constructed/destroyed in the scope of the `for` loop, the thread would have this object over-written by a subsequent client connection. To avoid these problems, we therefore allocate `Thread_Args` objects dynamically and let the `run_svc()` function delete them before returning.

The `handle_connections()` method accepts a connection into the `ACE_SOCK_Stream` data member of the `thread_args` object. (Sidebar 20 explains why we allocate `thread_args` dynamically). We then use the singleton `ACE_Thread_Manager` to spawn a new thread that handles the newly connected client.

```cpp
virtual int handle_connections () {
  auto_ptr<Thread_Args> thread_args (new Thread_Args (this));

  if (acceptor ().accept (thread_args->logging_peer_) == -1)
    return -1;
  if (ACE_Thread_Manager::instance ()->spawn (
      // Pointer-to-function entry point.
      Thread_Per_Connection_Logging_Server::run_svc,
      // <run_svc> parameter.
      ACE_static_cast (void *, thread_args.get ()),
      THR_DETACHED | THR_SCOPE_SYSTEM) == -1)
    return -1;
  thread_args.release ();    // Spawned thread now owns memory
  return 0;
}
```

The static `run_svc()` method is the entry point function of each new thread. The underlying OS thread creation function will pass the `thread_args` pointer to `run_svc()`, which assumes control of the `logging_peer`'s lifetime. Since we don't rendezvous with the thread to collect its exit status, we pass the THR_DETACHED flag, which instructs the `ACE_Thread_Manager` and underlying OS threading implementation to free up resources as soon as a thread exits. All threads spawned by the `ACE_Thread_Manager` singleton can be managed as a whole. We can therefore wait for them to finish even though they weren't designated as joinable via the THR_JOINABLE flag when they were spawned. Sidebar 21 illustrates how threads are spawned using these flags.

Sidebar 21: How Threads are Spawned in ACE

The figure below illustrates the sequence of calls that occur when ACE_ Thread_Manager::spawn() is invoked on a platform configuration that uses the UI Threads thr_create() system function:

```
1.  ACE_Thread_Manager::spawn
        (run_svc,
        thread_args,
        THR_DETACHED | THR_SCOPE_SYSTEM);
2.  thr_create
        (0, 0,
        run_svc, thread_args,
        THR_DETACHED | THR_SCOPE_SYSTEM, &thread_id);
```

```
                                    RUN-TIME
                                    THREAD STACK


                                    3.  run_svc (thread_args)
                                        { /* ... */ }
```

Regardless of OS, the following steps occur to spawn a thread:

1. The OS creates a thread execution context
2. The OS allocates memory for the thread's stack
3. The new thread's register set is prepared so that when it's scheduled into execution, it will call the thread entry point function supplied as a parameter to spawn() and
4. The thread is marked runnable so the OS can start executing it

---

The `run_svc()` method shown below serves as the entry point for each new thread created to process a client log records.

```
void *Thread_Per_Connection_Logging_Server::run_svc (void *arg)
{
  auto_ptr<Thread_Args>
      thread_args (ACE_static_cast (Thread_Args *, arg));

  thread_args->this_->handle_data (&thread_args->logging_peer_);
  thread_args->logging_peer_.close ();
  return 0;     // Return value is ignored.
}
```

As shown in Sidebar 21 on page 195, the ACE_Thread_Manager::spawn()
method is passed the Thread_Args pointer used by run_svc(). This
pointer must be cast to a void * to conform to the ACE threading API,
which is portable across operating systems. After the run_svc() function is invoked by the OS thread library, it casts the pointer back to a
Thread_Args *. The ACE ACE_static_cast() macro (see Sidebar 17 on
page 176) makes it easy to cast the pointer as safely as the compiler allows. Note that since we spawned run_svc() in a detached thread its
return value is ignored.

The static run_svc() method uses the data members in the Thread_
Args parameter to forward control back to the following handle_data()
method so that log record processing can continue.

```
protected:
  virtual int handle_data (ACE_SOCK_Stream *client) {
    ACE_FILE_IO log_file;
    // Client's hostname is used as the logfile name.
    make_log_file (log_file, client);

    // Place the connection into blocking mode.
    client->disable (ACE_NONBLOCK);

    Logging_Handler logging_handler (log_file, *client);
    ACE_Thread_Manager *tm = ACE_Thread_Manager::instance ();
    ACE_thread_t me = ACE_OS::thr_self ();

    // Keep handling log records until client closes connection
    // or this thread is asked to cancel itself.
    while (!tm->testcancel (me)
           && logging_handler.log_record () != -1)
      continue;

    log_file.close ();
    return 0;
  }
```

This version of handle_data() is similar to the process-per-connection example on page 179. In this version, however, the handle_data() thread that's processing client log records can be asked to cancel itself, which is an example of *cooperative cancelation*. To cooperate, each handle_data() thread calls ACE_Thread_Manager::testcancel() before handling a log record to see if the main thread has requested a cancelation.

One shortcoming of the placement of the testcancel() call and the design of the Logging_Handler::log_record() method is that the thread won't notice the cancel request until after the next log record is received. If clients send log records fairly often this may not be a problem. The ACE Reactor and Task frameworks described in [SH02] can be used to avoid this shortcoming.

Finally, the main() program executes the logging server's event loop within its run() template method. Note that run() no longer calls handle_data() because run_svc() calls it from each spawned thread.

```
int main (int argc, char *argv[])
{
  // Register to receive the <SIGTERM> signal.
  ACE_Sig_Action sa (sigterm_handler, SIGTERM);

  Thread_Per_Connection_Logging_Server server;
  if (server.run (argc, argv) == -1)
    ACE_ERROR_RETURN ((LM_ERROR, "%p\n", "server.run()"), 1);

  // Cooperative thread cancelation.
  ACE_Thread_Manager::instance ()->cancel_all ();

  // Barrier synchronization, wait no more than a minute.
  ACE_Time_Value timeout (ACE_OS::gettimeofday ());
  timeout += 60;
  return ACE_Thread_Manager::instance ()->wait (&timeout);
}
```

The thread-per-connection implementation of the logging server catches the SIGTERM signal to allow a system administrator to shut it down. Rather than wait an unlimited time for all logging clients to terminate their sessions, however, the main thread uses the ACE_Thread_Manager cooperative cancelation mechanism to request all service threads spawned by the ACE_Thread_Manager singleton to shut down.

The wait() call at the end of main() allows the logging server to wait up to a minute to synchronize on the completion of all the canceled threads. This is an example of *barrier synchronization* and it prevents problems from occurring on OS platforms where undesirable behavior occurs if the main thread exits while other threads are still running. By bounding our waiting time via the `timeout` argument, however, we ensure that the logging server doesn't hang indefinitely.

9.3   The ACE_Sched_Params Class

Motivation

All threads spawned by the `Thread_Per_Connection_Logging_Server` class run at the same priority, which by default is the value of the predefined macro `ACE_DEFAULT_THREAD_PRIORITY`. Certain types of networked applications, particularly those with real-time requirements, need more control over their thread priorities. It's possible to specify the priority of a newly created thread in ACE by passing a parameter to the `ACE_Thread_Manager::spawn()` or `spawn_n()` methods. There are two problems with this approach, however:

- **Nonportable**—Different OS plaforms represent priorities in different ways, for example, in some operating systems, higher priorities have higher numeric values, whereas in other operating systems, they have lower numeric values.

- **Non-real-time**—Most operating systems require additional (and non-standard) steps to make a thread run in the real-time scheduling class described in Section 5.5.

Addressing these problems in each application is tedious and error prone, which is why ACE provides the `ACE_Sched_Params` wrapper facade class and the `ACE_OS::sched_params()` wrapper method.

Class Capabilities

The `ACE_Sched_Params` class uses the Wrapper Facade pattern to guide the encapsulation of the OS scheduling class APIs discussed in Section 5.5. This class can be used with the `ACE_OS::sched_params()` method to provide the following capabilities:

- A portable means to specify scheduling policies, such as first in, first out (FIFO) and round-robin

- A way to specify a time-slice quantum for the round-robin scheduling policy

- A way to specify the scope in which the policy applies, for example, to the current process or the current thread, and

- A consistent representation of scheduling priorities, which is necessary since higher scheduling priorities are indicated by lower priority values on some OS platforms.

The `ACE_OS::sched_params()` method encapsulates the OS-specific function(s) that manipulate the scheduling class and `ACE_Sched_Params` provides the values used by this method.

The interface of the `ACE_Sched_Params` class is shown in Figure 9.3 and its key methods are outlined in the following table:

Method	Description
`ACE_Sched_Params()`	Sets the scheduling policy, priority, scope, and quantum for a real-time thread.
`priority_min()`	Returns the minimum priority for a given scheduling policy and scope.
`priority_max()`	Returns the maximum priority for a given scheduling policy and scope.
`next_priority()`	Given a policy, priority, and scope, returns the next higher priority, where "higher" refers to scheduling priority, not to the priority value itself. If the priority is already the highest priority for the specified policy, then it's returned.
`previous_priority()`	Given a policy, priority, and scope, returns the previous lower priority, where "lower" refers to scheduling priority, not to the priority value itself. If the priority is already the lowest priority for the specified policy, then it's returned.

The `ACE_OS::sched_params()` method is usually called from `main()` before any threads have been spawned. Since spawned threads inherit their parent's scheduling class and priority, this call sets the default base priority. Individual thread priorities can be designated when created by the `ACE_Thread_Manager::spawn()` method or adjusted via `ACE_OS::thr_prio()`.

```
                          ACE_Sched_Params
─────────────────────────────────────────────────────────────────
 - policy_ : int
 - priority_ : int
 - scope_ : int
 - quantum_ : ACE_Time_Value
─────────────────────────────────────────────────────────────────
 + ACE_Sched_Params (policy : int, priority : int,
                     scope : int = ACE_SCOPE_THREAD,
                     quantum : ACE_Time_Value = ACE_Time_Value::zero)
 + priority min (policy : int, scope : int = ACE SCOPE THREAD) : int
 + priority max (policy: int, scope : int = ACE SCOPE THREAD) : int
 + next priority (policy : int, int priority,
                  scope : int = ACE SCOPE THREAD) : int
 + previous priority (policy : int, priority : int,
                      scope : int = ACE SCOPE THREAD) : int
```

Figure 9.3: **The** ACE_Sched_Params **Class Diagram**

Example

To show how ACE can be used to program OS real-time scheduling class features portably, we'll modify our thread-per-connection logging server example from Section 9.2. After a careful empirical analysis of our networked logging service deployments, we decided to give preference to connected clients, rather than to new connection requests. The thread that accepts connections will therefore run at a lower real-time priority than the threads we'll spawn to receive and process log records.

In the RT_Thread_Per_Connection_Logging_Server.h file, we inherit from the Thread_Per_Connection_Logging_Server class to create a networked logging server whose threads will run in the real-time OS scheduling class.

```
class RT_Thread_Per_Connection_Logging_Server
  : public Thread_Per_Connection_Logging_Server
{
public:
```

We next override the open() hook method to enable FIFO scheduling for all threads spawned in the process. By default, spawned threads will run at the minimum real-time thread priority. If the application lacks sufficient permissions, we fall back to running in the time-shared scheduling class.

```
virtual int open (u_short port) {
  ACE_Sched_Params fifo_sched_params
    (ACE_SCHED_FIFO,
     ACE_Sched_Params::priority_min (ACE_SCHED_FIFO),
     ACE_SCOPE_PROCESS);

  if (ACE_OS::sched_params (fifo_sched_params) == -1) {
    if (errno == EPERM || errno == ENOTSUP)
      ACE_DEBUG ((LM_DEBUG,
                  "Warning: user's not superuser, so "
                  "we'll run in the time-shared class\n"));
    else
      ACE_ERROR_RETURN ((LM_ERROR,
                         "%p\n", "ACE_OS::sched_params()"), -1);
  }
  // Initialize the parent classes.
  return Thread_Per_Connection_Logging_Server::open (port);
}
```

Finally, we override the `handle_data()` method so that it increases the priority of each thread that processes log records from connected clients.

```
virtual int handle_data (ACE_SOCK_Stream *logging_client) {
  int prio =
    ACE_Sched_Params::next_priority
      (ACE_SCHED_FIFO,
       ACE_Sched_Params::priority_min (ACE_SCHED_FIFO),
       ACE_SCOPE_THREAD);
  ACE_OS::thr_setprio (prio);
  return Thread_Per_Connection_Logging_Server::handle_data
         (logging_client);
}
```

Our use of object-oriented design, C++ features, and ACE wrapper facades allows us to add real-time scheduling class behavior to our thread-per-connection logging server without changing any existing classes or writing any platform-specific code. The `main()` function is like the one from Section 9.2, with an instance of our `RT_Thread_Per_Connection_Logging_Server` class in place of `Thread_Per_Connection_Logging_Server`.

9.4   The ACE_TSS Class

Motivation

Although C++ global variables are sometimes useful, their potential for harmful side-effects and undefined initialization semantics [LGS00] can cause subtle problems. These problems are exacerbated in multithreaded applications. In particular, when multiple threads access unsynchronized global variables simultaneously, information can get lost or the wrong information can be used.

Consider the C errno variable for example. Serializing access to a single, per-process errno is pointless since it can be changed concurrently, for example, between when it's set in a system function and tested in application code. Therefore, the synchronization mechanisms outlined in Section 6.4 aren't relevant. Each thread needs its own copy of errno, which is what OS thread-specific storage (TSS) mechanisms provide. By using the TSS mechanism, no thread can see another thread's instance of errno.

Unfortunately, the native TSS C APIs provided by operating systems have the following problems:

- **Error prone**—Most TSS C APIs store pointers to thread-specific objects as void*'s, which is the most sensible approach for a general-use API. It's also, however, another source of accidental complexity because the error prone void pointers eliminate type safety. They must also be cast to the actual type, introducing a source of programmer error.

- **Nonportable**—In addition to API differences, TSS features and usage differ across platforms as well. For example, Win32, unlike Pthreads and UI threads, don't provide a reliable way to deallocate thread-specific objects when a thread exits. In UI threads, conversely, there's no API to delete a key. These diverse semantics make it challenging to write code that runs portably and robustly across OS platforms.

Addressing these problems in each application is tedious and error prone, which is why ACE provides the ACE_TSS class.

Class Capabilities

The ACE_TSS class implements the *Thread-Specific Storage pattern*, which encapsulates and enhances the native OS TSS APIs [SSRB00]. This class provides the following capabilities:

- It supports data that are "physically" thread specific, that is, private to a thread, but allows them to be accessed as though they were "logically" global to a program.

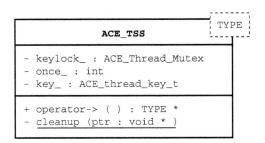

Figure 9.4: **The** ACE_TSS **Class Diagram**

- It uses the C++ delegation operator, operator->(), to provide thread-specific *smart pointers* [Mey96].
- It encapsulates the management of the keys associated with TSS objects.
- For platforms that lack adequate TSS support natively, such as VxWorks, ACE_TSS emulates TSS efficiently.

The interface for the ACE_TSS class is shown in Figure 9.4, and its key methods are shown below:

Method	Description
operator->()	Get the thread-specific object associated with the TSS key.
cleanup()	A static method that deletes a TSS object when a thread exits.

The ACE_TSS template is a proxy that transforms ordinary C++ classes into type-safe classes whose instances reside in thread-specific storage. It combines the operator->() delegation method with other C++ features, such as templates, *inlining*, and overloading. In addition, it uses common synchronization patterns and idioms [SSRB00], such as Double-Checked Locking Optimization and Scoped Locking, as shown in the implementation of operator->() below:

```
template <class TYPE> TYPE *
ACE_TSS<TYPE>::operator-> () {
  if (once_ == 0) {
    // Ensure that we're serialized.
    ACE_GUARD_RETURN (ACE_Thread_Mutex, guard, keylock_, 0);

    if (once_ == 0) {
      ACE_OS::thr_keycreate (&key_, &ACE_TSS<TYPE>::cleanup);
```

```
      once_ = 1;
    }
  }
  TYPE *ts_obj = 0;

  // Initialize <ts_obj> from thread-specific storage.
  ACE_OS::thr_getspecific (key_, (void **) &ts_obj);

  // Check if this method's been called in this thread.
  if (ts_obj == 0) {
    // Allocate memory off the heap and store it in a pointer.
    ts_obj = new TYPE;

    // Store the dynamically allocated pointer in TSS.
    ACE_OS::thr_setspecific (key_, ts_obj);
  }
  return ts_obj;
}
```

More issues to consider when implementing a C++ thread-specific storage proxy are shown in the Thread-Specific Storage pattern in [SSRB00].

Example

This example illustrates how ACE_TSS can be applied to our thread-per-connection logging server example from Section 9.2. In this implementation, each thread gets its own request count that resides in thread-specific storage. This design allows us to alleviate race conditions on the request count without requiring a mutex. It also allows us to use thread-specific storage without incurring all the accidental complexity associated with the error prone and nonportable native C APIs.

We start by defining a simple class that keeps track of request counts:

```
class Request_Count {
public:
  Request_Count (): count_ (0) {}
  void increment () { ++count_; }
  int value () const { return count_; }

private:
  int count_;
};
```

Note how Request_Count knows nothing about thread-specific storage. We then use this class as the type parameter to the ACE_TSS template, as follows:

```
static ACE_TSS<Request_Count> request_count;
```

Each thread now has a separate copy of `Request_Count`, which is accessed via `request_count`. Although this object appears to be "logically global," that is, it's accessed just like any other object at file scope, its state is "physically local" to the thread in which it's used. We show how simple it is to integrate `request_count` into the `handle_data()` method:

```
virtual int handle_data (ACE_SOCK_Stream *) {
  while (logging_handler_.log_record () != -1)
    // Keep track of number of requests.
    request_count->increment ();

  ACE_DEBUG ((LM_DEBUG, "request_count = %d\n",
             request_count->value ()));
}
```

By using the `ACE_TSS` wrapper facade, we needn't lock the `increment()` and `value()` calls, which eliminates contention and race conditions.

9.5 Summary

Different operating systems not only provide multithreading APIs that differ syntactically, but the semantics of these APIs also vary in subtle ways. To alleviate this complexity, the ACE threading wrapper facades implement a portable set of capabilities that export uniform multithreading syntax and semantics. This section presented several more revisions of our logging server example, where we showed how to handle multiple client sessions using multiple threads rather than multiple processes, as well as how to control the real-time scheduling properties of server threads.

ACE also provides the `ACE_Task` concurrency framework that allows developers to use threading in a powerful and extensible object-oriented fashion. Moreover, the `ACE_Task` concurrency framework not only provides a facility for spawning threads in the context of an object, but also a flexible and powerful queueing mechanism for transferring data and objects between tasks in message-oriented and task-oriented architectures. As described in [SH], the `ACE_Task` framework can be applied to implement the following common concurrency patterns [SSRB00]:

- The *Active Object pattern*, which decouples method execution from method invocation. Its purpose is to enhance concurrency and simplify synchronized access to objects that reside in their own threads.

- The *Half-Sync/Half-Async pattern*, which decouples synchronous and asynchronous processing in concurrent systems to simplify programming without reducing performance unduly. This pattern introduces two communicating layers: one for synchronous and one for asynchronous service processing. A queueing layer mediates communication between the synchronous and asynchronous layers.

CHAPTER 10

The ACE Synchronization Wrapper Facades

CHAPTER SYNOPSIS

This chapter describes the ACE wrapper facades that encapsulate OS synchronization mechanisms with portable C++ classes. We show a series of related examples to illustrate how these classes can be applied in practice. In addition, we describe how the core ACE synchronization wrapper facades can be combined to emulate synchronization mechanisms that aren't supported natively.

10.1 Overview

Hardware characteristics can affect the behavior of OS threading mechanisms significantly. For example, multiple threads can run in parallel on separate processors. On a uniprocessor, only one thread is active at any point in time, though threads may be scheduled in and out of execution, giving the appearance of running in parallel. In both of these scenarios, however, developers must use synchronization mechanisms to avoid race conditions and to ensure that their applications coordinate their access to shared resources.

Different operating systems provide different synchronization mechanisms with different semantics using different APIs. Some of these APIs conform to international standards, such as Pthreads [IEE96]. Other APIs conform to *de facto* standards, such as Win32 [Sol98]. This chapter describes the following ACE classes that networked applications can use to synchronize threads and/or processes portably:

ACE Class	Description
ACE_Guard ACE_Read_Guard ACE_Write_Guard	Apply the Scoped Locking idiom [SSRB00] to ensure a lock is acquired and released automatically when a block of C++ code is entered and exited, respectively.
ACE_Thread_Mutex ACE_Process_Mutex ACE_Null_Mutex	Provide a simple and efficient mechanism that concurrent applications can use to serialize access to shared resources.
ACE_RW_Thread_Mutex ACE_RW_Process_Mutex	Allow efficient, concurrent access to resources whose contents are searched much more often than they are changed.
ACE_Thread_Semaphore ACE_Process_Semaphore ACE_Null_Semaphore	Implement a counting semaphore, which is a general mechanism for synchronizing multiple threads of control.
ACE_Condition_Thread_Mutex ACE_Null_Condition	Allow threads to coordinate and schedule their processing efficiently.

These wrapper facades provide the following benefits:

- **Improve type safety** by
  - Automating the initialization of synchronization objects, for example, when they appear as data members in C++ classes.
  - Preventing incorrect usage, for example, copying one mutex to another.
  - Ensuring that locks are acquired and released automatically as scopes are entered and exited, even if exceptions or errors occur.

- **Ensure portability across heterogeneous OS platforms.** For example, ACE provides portable implementations of readers/writer locks and condition variables on platforms that don't support these synchronization mechanisms natively.

- **Enhance abstraction and modularity without compromising efficiency.** Using C++ language features, such as inline functions and templates, ensures that the ACE synchronization wrapper facades incur little or no additional time and space overhead.

- **Export a uniform synchronization interface** that enables applications to acquire and release various types of locks. For example, the

```
┌─────────────────────────────────────────────────┐
│                   ACE_LOCK*                       │
├─────────────────────────────────────────────────┤
│                                                   │
├─────────────────────────────────────────────────┤
│ + remove ( ) : int                                │
│ + acquire ( ) : int                               │
│ + tryacquire ( ) : int                            │
│ + release ( ) : int                               │
│ + acquire_read ( ) : int                          │
│ + acquire_write ( ) : int                         │
│ + tryacquire_read ( ) : int                       │
│ + tryacquire_write ( ) : int                      │
│ + tryacquire_write_upgrade ( ) : int              │
└─────────────────────────────────────────────────┘
```

Figure 10.1: **The** ACE_LOCK* **Pseudo-class**

ACE mutex, readers/writer, semaphore, and file lock mechanisms all support the ACE_LOCK* interface shown in Figure 10.1. ACE_LOCK* is a "pseudo-class," that is, it's not a real C++ class in ACE. We just use it to illustrate the uniformity of the signatures supported by many of the ACE synchronization classes, such as ACE_Thread_Mutex, ACE_Process_Mutex, and ACE_Thread_Semaphore.

- **Reduce the amount of obtrusive changes** needed to make code thread-safe. The uniformity of the ACE synchronization interfaces enables a single ACE_Guard template class to ensure that most types of locks can be acquired and released as scopes are entered and exited, respectively.

This chapter motivates and describes the capabilities of the core ACE synchronization wrapper facade classes. We present examples of each class to illustrate how they can simplify common synchronization issues encountered by concurrent networked applications.

10.2 The ACE_Guard Classes

Motivation

The uniformity of ACE's synchronization wrapper facade interfaces makes it easy to use them correctly, which helps to overcome several accidental complexities of cross-platform network programming. A separate issue that often occurs is related to lock scoping. Improper lock acquisition and release can result in system deadlock or inadvertent race conditions. When

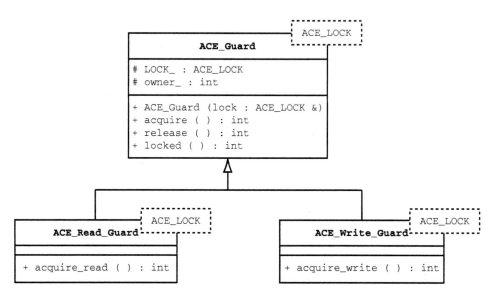

Figure 10.2: **The** ACE_Guard **Family Class Diagrams**

acquiring and releasing locks explicitly, it can be hard to ensure that all paths through the code release the lock, especially when C++ exceptions are thrown. ACE provides the ACE_Guard class and its associated subclasses to help assure that locks are acquired and released properly.

Class Capabilities

The ACE_Guard, ACE_Read_Guard, and ACE_Write_Guard classes implement the *Scoped Locking idiom* [SSRB00], which leverages the semantics of C++ class constructors and destructors to ensure a lock is acquired and released automatically upon entry to and exit from a block of C++ code, respectively. Figure 10.2 shows the interface of these classes and their relationships to each other.

The following C++ source code segment from the ACE_Guard class shows how it implements the Scoped Locking idiom:

```
template <class LOCK>
class ACE_Guard
{
public:
  // Implicitly and automatically acquire the lock.
  ACE_Guard (LOCK &lock): lock_ (&lock) { acquire (); }
```

```
// Implicitly release the lock.
~ACE_Guard () { release (); }

// Explicitly acquire the lock.
int acquire () {
  return owner_ = lock_->acquire ();
}

// Explicitly release the lock.
int release () {
  if (owner_ == -1)
    return -1;
  else {
    owner_ = -1
    return lock_->release ();
  }
}

int locked () const { return owner_ != -1; }
// ... Other methods omitted
protected:
  // Used by subclasses to store pointer.
  ACE_Guard (LOCK *lock): lock_ (lock) {}

  // Pointer to the LOCK we're guarding.
  LOCK *lock_;

  // Keeps track of whether we acquired the lock or failed.
  int owner_;
};
```

An instance of ACE_Guard defines a scope of code over which a lock is acquired and then released automatically when the guard object is created and destroyed. ACE_Guard is a class template that works for any LOCK class whose public methods match the signatures contained in the ACE_ LOCK* pseudo-class shown in Figure 10.1 on page 209. As illustrated later, this includes most of the ACE synchronization wrapper facades presented in this chapter.

The ACE_Read_Guard and ACE_Write_Guard template classes have the same interface as the ACE_Guard class. However, their acquire() methods acquire read locks and write locks, respectively, via the acquire_read() and acquire_write() methods defined on the LOCK template parameter, as shown below:

```
template <class LOCK>
class ACE_Write_Guard : public ACE_Guard<LOCK>
{
public:
  // Automatically acquire the lock for writing.
  ACE_Write_Guard (LOCK &lock): ACE_Guard (&lock)
  { owner_ = lock_.acquire_write (); }

  // ... Same operations as <ACE_Guard>.
};

template <class LOCK>
class ACE_Read_Guard : public ACE_Guard<LOCK>
{
public:
  // Automatically acquire the lock for reading.
  ACE_Read_Guard (LOCK &lock): ACE_Guard (&lock)
  { owner_ = lock_.acquire_read (); }

  // ... Same operations as <ACE_Guard>.
};
```

The `Atomic_Op` implementation on page 220 illustrates the use of the `ACE_Write_Guard` and `ACE_Read_Guard` classes.

10.3 The ACE Mutex Classes

Motivation

Most operating systems provide some form of mutex mechanism that concurrent applications can use to serialize access to shared resources. As with most of the other platform-specific capabilities we've seen in this book, there are subtle variations in syntax and semantics between different OS platforms. Mutexes also have different initialization requirements. The ACE mutex wrapper facades were designed to overcome all these problems in a convenient way.

Class Capabilities

ACE uses the Wrapper Facade pattern to guide the encapsulation of native OS mutex synchronization mechanisms with the `ACE_Process_Mutex` and `ACE_Thread_Mutex` classes, which implement nonrecursive mutex semantics portably at system scope and process scope, respectively.[1] They can therefore be used to serialize thread access to critical sections across processes or in one process. The interface for the `ACE_Thread_Mutex` class is identical to the `ACE_LOCK*` pseudo-class shown in Figure 10.1 on page 209. The following C++ class fragment illustrates how the `ACE_Thread_Mutex` can be implemented using Pthreads:

```
class ACE_Thread_Mutex
{
public:
  ACE_Thread_Mutex (const char * = 0, ACE_mutexattr_t *attrs = 0)
  { pthread_mutex_init (&lock_, attrs); }
  ~ACE_Thread_Mutex () { pthread_mutex_destroy (&lock_); }
  int acquire () { return pthread_mutex_lock (&lock_); }
  int acquire (ACE_Time_Value *timeout) {
    return pthread_mutex_timedlock
      (&lock_, timeout == 0 ? 0 : *timeout);
  }
  int release () { return pthread_mutex_unlock (&lock_); }
  // ... Other methods omitted ...
private:
  pthread_mutex_t lock_; // Pthreads mutex mechanism.
};
```

All calls to the `acquire()` method of an `ACE_Thread_Mutex` object will block until the thread that currently owns the lock has left its critical section. To leave a critical section, a thread must invoke the `release()` method on the mutex object it owns, thereby enabling another thread blocked on the mutex to enter its critical section.

On the Win32 platform, the `ACE_Thread_Mutex` class is implemented with a `CRITICAL_SECTION`, which is a lightweight Win32 lock that serializes threads within a single process. In contrast, the `ACE_Process_Mutex` implementation uses the `HANDLE`-based mutex on Win32, which can work within or between processes on the same machine:

```
class ACE_Process_Mutex
{
public:
  ACE_Process_Mutex (const char *name, ACE_mutexattr_t *)
  { lock_ = CreateMutex (0, FALSE, name); }
  ~Thread_Mutex () { CloseHandle (lock_); }
```

---

[1]Process-scoped recursive mutexes are implemented in the `ACE_Recursive_Thread_Mutex` class, which is shown in Section 10.6 on page 229.

```
  int acquire ()
  { return WaitForSingleObject (lock_, INFINITE); }
  int acquire (ACE_Time_Value *timeout) {
    return WaitForSingleObject
      (lock_, timeout == 0 ? INFINITE : timeout->msec ());
  }
  int release () { return ReleaseMutex (lock_); }
  // ... Other methods omitted ...
private:
  HANDLE lock_; // Win32 serialization mechanism.
};
```

The `ACE_Thread_Mutex` class is implemented using the native process-scoped mutex mechanisms on all OS platforms. Depending on the characteristics of the OS platform, however, the `ACE_Process_Mutex` can be implemented with different mechanisms, for example:

- A native mutex is used on Win32, as shown above.
- Some UNIX threading implementations, such as Pthreads and UI threads, require that interprocess mutexes be allocated from shared memory. On these platforms, ACE prefers to use a UNIX System V semaphore if available, since that provides a more reliable mechanism for recovering system resources than the native interprocess mutexes.
- Some applications require more semaphores than the System V IPC kernel parameters allow, or they require the ability to do a timed `acquire()` operation. In such cases, ACE can be configured to use a native mutex in shared memory, which puts more responsibility on the application developer to ensure proper cleanup.

Regardless of which underlying mechanism ACE uses, the class interface is identical, which allows application developers to experiment with different configurations without changing their source code.

The `ACE_Null_Mutex` is another type of mutex supported by ACE. Part of its interface and implementation are shown below:

```
class ACE_Null_Mutex
{
public:
  ACE_Null_Mutex (const char * = 0, ACE_mutexattr_t * = 0) {}
  int acquire () { return 0; }
  int release () { return 0; }
  // ...
};
```

The ACE_Null_Mutex class implements all of its methods as "no-op" inline functions, which can be removed completely by a compiler optimizer. This class provides a zero-overhead implementation of the pseudo ACE_LOCK* interface shared by the other ACE C++ wrapper facades for threading and synchronization.

ACE_Null_Mutex is an example of the Null Object pattern [Woo97]. It can be used in conjunction with the Strategized Locking pattern [SSRB00] so that applications can parameterize the type of synchronization they require without changing application code. This capability is useful for cases where mutual exclusion isn't needed, for example, when an application configuration runs in a single thread and/or never contends with other threads for access to resources.

Example

The following code illustrates how the ACE_Thread_Mutex can be applied to address some of the problems with the UNIX International mutex solution shown on page 135 in Section 6.5.

```
#include "ace/Synch.h"

typedef u_long COUNTER;
static COUNTER request_count; // File scope global variable.

// Mutex protecting request_count (constructor initializes).
static ACE_Thread_Mutex m;

// ...
  virtual int handle_data (ACE_SOCK_Stream *) {
    while (logging_handler_.log_record () != -1) {
      // Try to acquire the lock.
      if (m.acquire () == -1) return 0;
      ++request_count;    // Count # of requests
      m.release (); // Release lock.
    }

    m.acquire ();
    int count = request_count;
    m.release ();
    ACE_DEBUG ((LM_DEBUG, "request_count = %d\n", count));
    logging_handler_.close ();
    return 0;
  }
```

The use of the ACE_Thread_Mutex C++ wrapper class cleans up the original code somewhat, improves portability, and initializes the underlying mutex object automatically when it's instantiated.

Sidebar 22: Overview of the ACE_GUARD Macros

ACE defines a set of macros that simplify the use of the ACE_Guard, ACE_Write_Guard, and ACE_Read_Guard classes. These macros test for deadlock and detect when operations on the underlying locks fail. As shown below, they check to make sure that the lock is actually locked before proceeding:

```
# define ACE_GUARD(MUTEX,OBJ,LOCK) \
  ACE_Guard< MUTEX > OBJ (LOCK); \
    if (OBJ.locked () == 0) return;
# define ACE_GUARD_RETURN(MUTEX,OBJ,LOCK,RETURN) \
  ACE_Guard< MUTEX > OBJ (LOCK); \
    if (OBJ.locked () == 0) return RETURN;
# define ACE_WRITE_GUARD(MUTEX,OBJ,LOCK) \
  ACE_Write_Guard< MUTEX > OBJ (LOCK); \
    if (OBJ.locked () == 0) return;
# define ACE_WRITE_GUARD_RETURN(MUTEX,OBJ,LOCK,RETURN) \
  ACE_Write_Guard< MUTEX > OBJ (LOCK); \
    if (OBJ.locked () == 0) return RETURN;
# define ACE_READ_GUARD(MUTEX,OBJ,LOCK) \
  ACE_Read_Guard< MUTEX > OBJ (LOCK); \
    if (OBJ.locked () == 0) return;
# define ACE_READ_GUARD_RETURN(MUTEX,OBJ,LOCK,RETURN) \
  ACE_Read_Guard< MUTEX > OBJ (LOCK); \
    if (OBJ.locked () == 0) return RETURN;
```

The ACE concurrency wrapper facades don't solve all the problems identified in Section 6.5, however. For example, programmers must still release the mutex manually, which can yield bugs due to programmer negligence or due to the occurrence of C++ exceptions. Moreover, it is tedious and error prone for programmers to check explicitly whether the mutex was actually acquired. For instance, you'll notice that we neglected to check if the ACE_Thread_Mutex::acquire() method succeeded before assigning request_count to count. We can simplify this example by applying the Scoped Locking idiom [SSRB00] via the ACE_GUARD* macros described in Sidebar 22.

```
virtual int handle_data (ACE_SOCK_Stream *) {
  while (logging_handler_.log_record () != -1) {
    // Acquire lock in constructor.
    ACE_GUARD_RETURN (ACE_Thread_Mutex, guard, m, -1);
    ++request_count;    // Count # of requests
    // Release lock in destructor.
  }

  int count;
  {
    ACE_GUARD_RETURN (ACE_Thread_Mutex, guard, m, -1);
    count = request_count;
  }
  ACE_DEBUG ((LM_DEBUG, "request_count = %d\n", count));
}
```

By making a slight change to the code, we've now ensured that the ACE_
Thread_Mutex is acquired and released automatically. We've also ensured
that we'll handle mutex failures properly.

Although we've addressed many issues outlined in Section 6.5, the following two problems still remain:

- **The solution is still obtrusive,** that is, we must insert the ACE_
  GUARD macros manually within a new statement scope delimited by
  curly braces. Section 10.4 shows how to eliminate this obtrusiveness.

- **The solution is also error prone,** that is, the static ACE_Thread_
  Mutex global object m must be initialized properly before the handle_
  data () method is called. It's surprisingly hard to ensure this since
  C++ doesn't guarantee the order of initialization of global and static
  objects in different files. Sidebar 23 describes how ACE addresses
  this problem via its ACE_Object_Manager class.

The ACE_Object_Manager class provides a global recursive mutex that
we could use in our logging server example:

```
// ...
while (logging_handler_.log_record () != -1) {
  // Acquire lock in constructor.
  ACE_GUARD_RETURN (ACE_Recursive_Thread_Mutex, guard,
                    ACE_Static_Object_Lock::instance (),
                    -1);
  ++request_count;    // Count # of requests
  // Release lock in destructor.
}
// ...
```

Sidebar 23: The ACE_Object_Manager Class

To ensure consistent initialization order of global and static objects, ACE provides the `ACE_Object_Manager` class, which implements the Object Lifetime Manager pattern (LGS00). This pattern governs the entire lifetime of objects, from creating them prior to their first use to ensuring they are destroyed properly at program termination. The `ACE_Object_Manager` class provides the following capabilities that help replace static object creation/destruction with automatic dynamic object preallocation/deallocation:

- It manages object cleanup (typically singletons) at program termination. In addition to managing the cleanup of the ACE library, it provides an interface for applications to register objects to be cleaned up.
- It shuts down ACE library services at program termination so that they can reclaim their storage. This works by creating a static instance whose destructor gets called along with those of all other static objects. Hooks are provided for application code to register objects and arrays for cleanup when the program terminates. The order of these cleanup calls is in the reverse (LIFO) order of their registration; that is, the last object/array to register gets cleaned up first.
- It preinitializes certain objects, such as `ACE_Static_Object_Lock`, so that they will be created before the `main()` function runs.

Since the `ACE_Static_Object_Lock` instance is controlled by the `ACE_Object_Manager` it's guaranteed to be initialized when a program starts and will be destroyed properly when the program exits.

10.4 The ACE Readers/Writer Lock Classes

Motivation

Readers/writer locks allow efficient concurrent access to resources whose contents are searched much more often than they are changed. Many operating systems support readers/writer semantics in their file-locking

APIs. Involving the file system in synchronization activities is unnecessarily inefficient, however, and can block under unpredictable situations, such as when using network-mounted storage for the lock file. Moreover, file-locking mechanisms work only at the system-scope level, rather than at process scope.

Surprisingly few operating systems provide readers/writer lock implementations at the process-scope level. For example, Pthreads (without UNIX98 extensions), Win32 threads, and many real-time operating systems don't support them natively. UI threads support readers/writer locks via the `rwlock_t` type. Addressing these portability variations in each application is tedious and error prone, which is why ACE provides the readers/writer lock wrapper facades.

Class Capabilities

ACE encapsulates the native OS readers/writer lock mechanisms with the `ACE_RW_Thread_Mutex` and `ACE_RW_Process_Mutex` classes. These classes apply the Wrapper Facade pattern to implement the semantics of process- and system-scoped readers/writer locks portably. The interface for these classes is identical to the signatures of `ACE_LOCK*` pseudo-class shown in shown in Figure 10.1 on page 209.

If a platform supports process-scoped readers/writer locks, the `ACE_RW_Thread_Mutex` class simply encapsulates the native synchronization variable. On OS platforms that lack native readers/writer locks, however, ACE provides readers/writer implementations using existing low-level synchronization mechanisms, such as mutexes, condition variables, or semaphores. The ACE readers/writer implementation gives preference to writers. Thus, if there are multiple readers and a single writer waiting on the lock, the writer will acquire it first.

Example

Although the `ACE_Guard`-based implementation of `handle_data()` in the example on page 216 solved several problems, it still required obtrusive code changes, that is, adding the `ACE_GUARD_RETURN` inside the loop. A less error prone and obtrusive solution leverages

- C++ operator overloading
- `ACE_RW_Thread_Mutex`

- The Scoped Locking idiom, through use of the ACE_WRITE_GUARD and ACE_READ_GUARD macros

We use these capabilities below to create an Atomic_Op class that supports thread-safe arithmetic operations:

```
class Atomic_Op
{
public:
  // Initialize <count_> to <count>.
  Atomic_Op (long count = 0)
    : count_ (count) {}

  // Atomically pre-increment <count_>.
  long operator++ () {
    // Use the <acquire_write> method to acquire a write lock.
    ACE_WRITE_GUARD_RETURN (ACE_RW_Thread_Mutex, guard, lock_,
                            -1);
    return ++count_;
  }

  // Atomically return <count_>.
  operator long () {
    // Use the <acquire_read> method to acquire a read lock.
    ACE_READ_GUARD_RETURN (ACE_RW_Thread_Mutex, guard, lock_,
                           0);
    return count_;
  }

  // ... Other arithmetic operators omitted.

private:
  // Readers/writer lock.
  ACE_RW_Thread_Mutex lock_;

  // Value of the <Atomic_Op> count.
  long count_;
};
```

The Atomic_Op class overloads the standard arithmetic operators, that is, ++, --, +=, etc., on long data types. Since these methods modify the count_ they achieve exclusive access by acquiring a write lock. In contrast, a read lock will suffice for the operator long() since it allows multiple threads to read the count_ concurrently.

By applying the Atomic_Op class, we can now write the following code, which is almost identical to the original nonthread-safe code. Only the typedef of COUNTER has changed:

```
typedef Atomic_Op COUNTER;

static COUNTER request_count; // File scope global variable.

  virtual int handle_data (ACE_SOCK_Stream *) {
    while (logging_handler_.log_record () != -1)
    // Keep track of number of requests.
    ++request_count; // Actually calls <Atomic_Op::operator++>.

    ACE_DEBUG ((LM_DEBUG, "request_count = %d\n",
              // Actually calls <Atomic_Op::operator long>.
              (long) request_count));
  }
```

The calls to both `operator++()` and `operator long()` use the `acquire_write()` and `acquire_read()` methods on the `ACE_RW_Thread_Mutex`, respectively. Thus, arithmetic operations on objects of instantiated `Atomic_Op` classes now increment/decrement counters correctly on a multiprocessor, without changing much existing application code!

The `Atomic_Op` class shown above is actually a simplification of the `ACE_Atomic_Op` class template, a portion of which is defined below:

```
template <class TYPE, class LOCK>
class ACE_Atomic_Op {
public:
  // ... Constructors and arithmetic operators omitted.
private:
  LOCK lock_;
  TYPE type_;
};
```

The `ACE_Atomic_Op` produces a simple, yet remarkably expressive parameterized class abstraction by combining

- The Scoped Locking idiom and Strategized Locking pattern with
- The use of C++ templates and operator overloading.

This template class operates correctly and atomically on the family of types requiring atomic operations. To provide the same thread-safe functionality for other arithmetic types, for example, we can simply instantiate new objects of the `ACE_Atomic_Op` template class as follows:

```
ACE_Atomic_Op<double, ACE_Null_Mutex> double_counter;
ACE_Atomic_Op<Complex, ACE_RW_Thread_Mutex> complex_counter;
```

10.5   The ACE Semaphore Classes

Motivation

Semaphores are a powerful mechanism used to lock and/or synchronize access to shared resources in concurrent applications. A semaphore contains a count that indicates the status of a shared resource. Application designers assign the meaning of the semaphore's count, as well as its initial value. Semaphores can therefore be used to mediate access to a pool of resources.

Since releasing a semaphore increments its count regardless of the presence of waiters, they are useful for keeping track of events that change shared program state. Threads can make decisions based on these events, even if they've already occurred. Although some form of semaphore mechanism is available on most operating systems, the ACE semaphore wrapper facades resolve issues arising from subtle variations in syntax and semantics across a broad range of environments.

Class Capabilities

The `ACE_Thread_Semaphore` and `ACE_Process_Semaphore` classes portably encapsulate process-scoped and system-scoped semaphores, respectively, in accordance with the Wrapper Facade pattern. These class interfaces are largely the same as the `ACE_LOCK*` pseudo-class shown in Figure 10.1 on page 209. The constructor is slightly different, however, since semaphore initialization is more expressive than mutexes and readers/writer locks, allowing the semaphore's initial count to be set. The relevant portion of the `ACE_Thread_Semaphore` API is shown below:

```
class ACE_Thread_Semaphore
{
public:
  // Initialize the semaphore, with an initial value of <count>,
  // a maximum value of <max>, and unlocked by default.
  ACE_Thread_Semaphore (u_int count = 1,
                        const char *name = 0,
                        void *arg = 0,
                        int max = 0x7FFFFFFF);
  // ... same as pseudo <ACE_LOCK> signatures.
};
```

The ACE_Process_Semaphore has the same interface, though it synchronizes threads at the system scope rather than at the process scope.

These two ACE classes encapsulate OS-native semaphore mechanisms whenever possible, emulating them if the OS platform doesn't support semaphores natively. This allows applications to use semaphores and still be ported to new platforms regardless of the native semaphore support, or lack thereof. Section A.5.2 on page 251 shows an emulation of ACE_Thread_Semaphore on platforms that don't support it natively.

The ACE_Null_Semaphore class implements all of its methods as "no-op" inline functions. We implement two of its acquire() methods below:

```
class ACE_Null_Semaphore
{
public:
  int acquire () { return 0; }
  int acquire (ACE_Time_Value *) { errno = ETIME; return -1; }
  // ...
};
```

Note that the timed version of acquire() returns −1 and sets errno to ETIME to ensure that ACE_Null_Semaphore can be interchanged properly in conjunction with the Strategized Locking pattern [SSRB00]. For the non-null ACE semaphores, the blocking version of acquire() is often used to serialize access to a critical section, whereas the timed version is often used to wait for another thread to update some condition or change some shared state. When using an ACE_Null_Semaphore, however, there's no other thread involved to change a state or condition. Otherwise, a null semaphore would be inappropriate. Returning an error value signifies that the state or condition has not been (and can't be) changed, which is consistent with the behavior of the threaded case in which a timeout occurs before the state or condition is changed.

Example

Although semaphores can coordinate the processing of multiple threads, they don't themselves pass any data between threads. Passing data between threads is a common concurrent programming technique, however, so some type of lightweight intraprocess message queueing mechanism can be quite useful. We therefore show a Message_Queue class implementation that provides the following capabilities:

- It allows messages (ACE_Message_Block objects) to be enqueued at the rear of the queue and dequeued from the front of the queue.
- It supports tunable flow control that prevents fast message producer threads from swamping the resources of slower message consumer threads.
- It allows timeouts to be specified on both enqueue and dequeue operations to avoid unlimited blocking when necessary.

We show the key parts of the Message_Queue class implementation below and showcase the use of ACE_Thread_Semaphore. To simplify the design and evolution of this code, we also apply the following patterns and idioms from POSA2 [SSRB00]:

- **Monitor Object**—The public methods of Message_Queue behave as synchronized methods in accordance with the Monitor Object design pattern [SSRB00], which ensures that only one method at a time runs within an object and allows an object's methods to schedule their execution sequences cooperatively.
- **Thread-Safe Interface**—The Message_Queue public methods acquire locks and delegate the actual queueing behavior to the private implementation methods in accordance with the *Thread-Safe Interface pattern*. This design pattern minimizes locking overhead and ensures that intraobject method calls don't "self-deadlock" by trying to reacquire a lock that an object already holds.
- **Scoped Locking**—The ACE_GUARD* macros ensure that any synchronization wrapper facade whose signature conforms to the ACE_LOCK* pseudo-class is acquired and released automatically in accordance with the Scoped Locking idiom [SSRB00].

Most of the patterns from the POSA2 book can be implemented using ACE concurrency and synchronization classes.

We start with the definition of the Message_Queue class:

```
class Message_Queue
{
public:
  // Default high and low water marks.
  enum {
    DEFAULT_LWM = 0,        // 0 is the low water mark.
    DEFAULT_HWM = 16 * 1024 // 16 K is the high water mark.
  };
```

```
    // Initialize.
    Message_Queue (size_t = DEFAULT_HWM, size_t = DEFAULT_LWM);

    // Destroy.
    ~Message_Queue ();

    // Checks if queue is full/empty.
    int is_full () const;
    int is_empty () const;

    // Interface for enqueueing and dequeueing ACE_Message_Blocks.
    int enqueue_tail (ACE_Message_Block *, ACE_Time_Value * = 0);
    int dequeue_head (ACE_Message_Block *&, ACE_Time_Value * = 0);

private:
    // Implementations that enqueue/dequeue ACE_Message_Blocks.
    int enqueue_tail_i (ACE_Message_Block *, ACE_Time_Value * = 0);
    int dequeue_head_i (ACE_Message_Block *&, ACE_Time_Value * = 0);

    // Implement the checks for boundary conditions.
    int is_empty_i () const;
    int is_full_i () const;

    // Lowest number before unblocking occurs.
    int low_water_mark_;
    // Greatest number of bytes before blocking.
    int high_water_mark_;
    // Current number of bytes in the queue.
    int cur_bytes_;
    // Current number of messages in the queue.
    int cur_count_;
    // Number of threads waiting to dequeue a message.
    size_t dequeue_waiters_;
    // Number of threads waiting to enqueue a message.
    size_t enqueue_waiters_;

    // C++ wrapper facades to coordinate concurrent access.
    mutable ACE_Thread_Mutex lock_;
    ACE_Thread_Semaphore notempty_;
    ACE_Thread_Semaphore notfull_;

    // Remaining details of queue implementation omitted....
};
```

The `Message_Queue` constructor shown below creates an empty message list and initializes the `ACE_Thread_Semaphores` to start with a count of 0 (the mutex `lock_` is initialized automatically by its default constructor).

```
Message_Queue::Message_Queue (size_t hwm, size_t lwm)
  : low_water_mark_ (lwm),
    high_water_mark_ (hwm),
    cur_bytes_ (0),
    cur_count_ (0),
    dequeue_waiters_ (0),
    enqueue_waiters_ (0),
    notempty_ (0),
    notfull_ (0)
{ /* Remaining constructor implementation omitted ... */ }
```

The following methods check if a queue is "empty," that is, contains no messages, or "full," that is, contains more than high_water_mark_ bytes in it. These methods, like the others below, are designed in accordance with the Thread-Safe Interface pattern [SSRB00].

We start with the is_empty() and is_full() interface methods:

```
int Message_Queue::is_empty () const {
  ACE_GUARD_RETURN (ACE_Thread_Mutex, guard, lock_, -1);
  return is_empty_i ();
}

int Message_Queue::is_full () const {
  ACE_GUARD_RETURN (ACE_Thread_Mutex, guard, lock_, -1);
  return is_full_i ();
}
```

These methods acquire the lock_ and then forward the call to one of the following implementation methods:

```
int Message_Queue::is_empty_i () const {
  return cur_bytes_ <= 0 && cur_count_ <= 0;
}

int Message_Queue::is_full_i () const {
  return cur_bytes_ >= high_water_mark_;
}
```

These methods assume the lock_ is held and actually perform the work.

The enqueue_tail() method inserts a new item at the end of the queue and returns a count of the number of messages in the queue. As with the dequeue_head() method, if the timeout parameter is 0, the caller will block until action is possible. Otherwise, the caller will block only up to the amount of time in *timeout. A blocked call can return when a signal occurs or if the time specified in timeout elapses, in which case errno is set to EWOULDBLOCK.

```
int Message_Queue::enqueue_tail (ACE_Message_Block *new_mblk,
                                 ACE_Time_Value *timeout)
{
  ACE_GUARD_RETURN (ACE_Thread_Mutex, guard, lock_, -1);
  int result = 0;

  // Wait until the queue is no longer full.
  while (is_full_i () && result != -1) {
    ++enqueue_waiters_;
    guard.release ();
    result = notfull_.acquire (timeout);
    guard.acquire ();
  }

  if (result == -1) {
    if (enqueue_waiters_ > 0)
      --enqueue_waiters_;
    if (errno == ETIME)
      errno = EWOULDBLOCK;
    return -1;
  }

  // Enqueue the message at the tail of the queue.
  int queued_messages = enqueue_tail_i (new_mblk);

  // Tell any blocked threads that the queue has a new item!
  if (dequeue_waiters_ > 0) {
    --dequeue_waiters_;
    notempty_.release ();
  }
  return queued_messages; // guard's destructor releases lock_.
}
```

The `enqueue_tail()` method releases the `notempty_` semaphore when there's at least one thread waiting to dequeue a message. The actual enqueueing logic resides in `enqueue_tail_i()`, which we omit here since it's a low-level implementation detail. Note the potential race condition in the time window between the call to `not_full_.acquire()` and reacquiring the `guard` lock. It's possible for another thread to call `dequeue_head()`, decrementing `enqueue_waiters_` in that small window of time. After the lock is reacquired, therefore, the count is checked to guard against decrementing `enqueue_waiters_` below 0.

The `dequeue_head()` method removes the front item from the queue, passes it back to the caller, and returns a count of the number of items still in the queue, as follows:

```
int Message_Queue::dequeue_head (ACE_Message_Block *&first_item,
                                 ACE_Time_Value *timeout)
{
  ACE_GUARD_RETURN (ACE_Thread_Mutex, guard, lock_, -1);
  int result = 0;

  // Wait until the queue is no longer empty.
  while (is_empty_i () && result != -1) {
    ++dequeue_waiters_;
    guard.release ();
    result = notempty_.acquire (timeout);
    guard.acquire ();
  }

  if (result == -1) {
    if (dequeue_waiters_ > 0)
      --dequeue_waiters_;
    if (errno == ETIME)
      errno = EWOULDBLOCK;
    return -1;
  }

  // Remove the first message from the queue.
  int queued_messages = dequeue_head_i (first_item);

  // Only signal if we've fallen below the low water mark.
  if (cur_bytes_ <= low_water_mark_ && enqueue_waiters_ > 0) {
    enqueue_waiters_--;
    notfull_.release ();
  }
  return queued_messages; // <guard> destructor releases <lock_>
}
```

The Message_Queue class shown above implements a subset of the features in the ACE_Message_Queue and ACE_Message_Queue_Ex, which are presented in [SH]. These ACE message queue classes differ from the Message_Queue implementation shown above in the following ways:

- In addition to FIFO queueing, they also allow messages to be inserted at the front of the queue (i.e., LIFO order) or in priority order.
- They use C++ traits and the Strategized Locking pattern to parameterize their synchronization mechanisms, which allows programmers to trade off strict thread-safe synchronization for greater efficiency in single-threaded queue configurations.
- They provide allocators that enable the memory for messages to be obtained from various sources, such as shared memory, heap memory,

static memory, or thread-specific memory.

- They can be configured to schedule thread execution order via either `ACE_Thread_Semaphore` or `ACE_Condition_Thread_Mutex` to trade off higher efficiency for more features, respectively.
- `ACE_Message_Queue_Ex` is a strongly-typed version of `ACE_Message_Queue` that enqueues and dequeues instances of a `MESSAGE_TYPE` template parameter, rather than an `ACE_Message_Block`.

10.6 The ACE Condition Variable Classes

Motivation

Condition variables allow threads to coordinate and schedule their processing efficiently. Although condition variables are mandated in the Pthreads standard, some widely used OS platforms, such as Win32 and VxWorks, do not implement condition variables natively. Although condition variables can be emulated using other native synchronization mechanisms, such as semaphores and mutexes, it's unnecessarily wasteful and error-prone for application developers to write these emulations. ACE provides the `ACE_Condition_Thread_Mutex` condition variable wrapper facade to alleviate this problem.

Class Capabilities

The `ACE_Condition_Thread_Mutex` uses the Wrapper Facade pattern to guide its encapsulation of process-scoped condition variable semantics. The interface of the `ACE_Condition_Thread_Mutex` class is shown in Figure 10.3 and the following table outlines its key methods:

Methods	Description
`wait()`	Atomically releases the mutex associated with the condition variable and sleeps awaiting a timeout or a subsequent notification from another thread via the `signal()` or `broadcast()` methods.
`signal()`	Notifies one thread waiting on the condition variable.
`broadcast()`	Notifies all threads waiting on the condition variable.

If the `time` parameter to `ACE_Condition_Thread_Mutex::wait()` is non-0 the method will block up to that absolute point of time, which is

```
                    ACE_Condition_Thread_Mutex

- cond_  : ACE_cond_t
- mutex_ : ACE_Thread_Mutex&

+ ACE_Condition_Thread_Mutex (mtx : const ACE_Thread_Mutex&,
                              name : const char *,
                              arg : void *)
+ wait (time : ACE_Time_Value*) : int
+ signal ( ) : int
+ broadcast ( ) : int
```

Figure 10.3: **The** ACE_Condition_Thread_Mutex **Class Diagram**

specified as an ACE_Time_Value. If the time elapses before the condition
variable is notified, the method returns −1 to the caller with an ETIME
errno, signifying that a timeout has occurred. Regardless of how wait()
returns, the mutex associated with the condition variable will always be
locked.

Condition variables are more appropriate than mutexes or semaphores
when complex condition expressions or scheduling behaviors are needed.
For instance, condition variables are often used to implement synchronized message queues that provide "producer/consumer" communication
to pass messages between threads. The condition variables block producer
threads when a message queue is full and block consumer threads when
the queue is empty. Since there's no need to maintain event history, condition variables needn't record when they are signaled.

The ACE_Null_Condition class is a zero-cost implementation that
conforms to the ACE_Condition_Thread_Mutex interface. This class is
similar to the ACE_Null_Mutex class described in Section 10.3; that is, all
its methods are implemented as no-ops in accordance with the Null Object
pattern [Woo97]. The ACE_Null_Condition class is presented below:

```
class ACE_Null_Condition
{
public:
  ACE_Null_Condition (const ACE_Null_Mutex&, int =0, void* =0) {}
  ~ACE_Null_Condition () {}
  int remove () { return 0; }
  int wait (ACE_Time_Value* =0) const {errno = ETIME; return -1;}
  int signal () const { return 0; }
  int broadcast () const { return 0; }
};
```

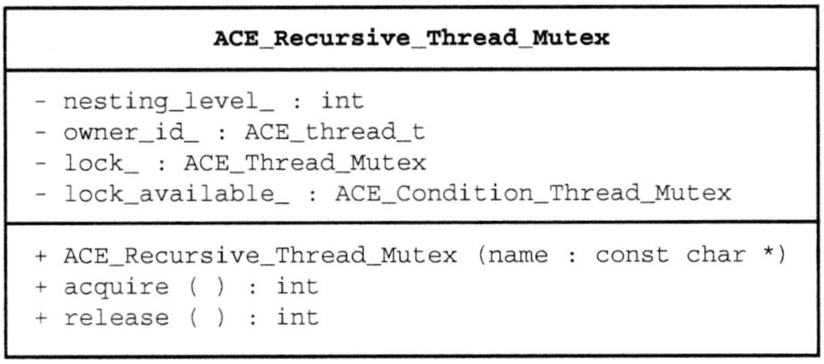

```
┌─────────────────────────────────────────────────────────┐
│              ACE_Recursive_Thread_Mutex                   │
├─────────────────────────────────────────────────────────┤
│  - nesting_level_ : int                                   │
│  - owner_id_ : ACE_thread_t                               │
│  - lock_ : ACE_Thread_Mutex                               │
│  - lock_available_ : ACE_Condition_Thread_Mutex           │
├─────────────────────────────────────────────────────────┤
│  + ACE_Recursive_Thread_Mutex (name : const char *)       │
│  + acquire ( ) : int                                      │
│  + release ( ) : int                                      │
└─────────────────────────────────────────────────────────┘
```

Figure 10.4: **The** ACE_Recursive_Thread_Mutex **Class Diagram**

The wait() method returns −1 with errno set to ETIME so that ACE_Null_ Condition works correctly when used in conjunction with the Strategized Locking pattern for classes like the Message_Queue shown in Section 10.5.

Example

By default, a UI threads mutex implementation is nonrecursive; that is, a thread that owns a mutex can't reacquire the same mutex without deadlocking on itself.[2] Although nonrecursive mutexes are efficient, they are too restrictive in certain circumstances. For example, recursive mutexes are particularly useful for callback-driven C++ frameworks, where the framework event loop performs a *callback* to user-defined code. Since the user-defined code may subsequently reenter framework code via a method entry point, recursive mutexes help prevent deadlock from occurring on mutexes held by the same thread within the framework during the callback.

To address these types of scenarios, ACE provides support for process-scoped recursive mutexes via the ACE_Recursive_Thread_Mutex class. The interface for this class is shown in Figure 10.4. The public interface of this class conforms to the ACE_LOCK* pseudo-class in Figure 10.1 on page 209. The following code illustrates how an ACE_Condition_Thread_ Mutex can be used to implement recursive mutex semantics on platforms that don't support them natively.

The nesting_level_ keeps track of the number of times a thread with owner_id_ has acquired the recursive mutex. The lock_ serializes access

---

[2]Note that Pthreads and Win32 provide recursive mutexes natively.

to the `nesting_level_` and `owner_id_`. The `lock_available_` condition variable is used to suspend nonowner threads that are waiting for the nesting level to drop to 0 and the mutex to be released. The `ACE_Recursive_Thread_Mutex` constructor initializes these data members:

```
ACE_Recursive_Thread_Mutex::ACE_Recursive_Thread_Mutex
  (const char *name, void *arg)
  : nesting_level_ (0), owner_id_ (0), lock_ (name, arg),
    // Initialize the condition variable.
    lock_available_ (lock_, name, arg) { }
```

We next show how to acquire a recursive mutex.

```
 1 int ACE_Recursive_Thread_Mutex::acquire ()
 2 {
 3   ACE_thread_t t_id = ACE_OS::thr_self ();
 4
 5   ACE_GUARD_RETURN (ACE_Thread_Mutex, guard, lock_, -1);
 6
 7   if (nesting_level_ == 0) {
 8     owner_id_ = t_id;
 9     nesting_level_ = 1;
10   }
11   else if (t_id == owner_id_)
12     nesting_level_++;
13   else {
14     while (nesting_level_ > 0)
15       lock_available_.wait ();
16
17     owner_id_ = t_id;
18     nesting_level_ = 1;
19   }
20   return 0;
21 }
```

Lines 3–5 We start by determining which thread we're called from and then acquire the `lock_` mutex using the Scoped Locking idiom.

Lines 7–12 If there's no contention, assume mutex ownership immediately. Otherwise, if we own the mutex already, just increment nesting level and proceed to avoid self-deadlock.

Lines 13–20 If the mutex is owned by another thread, we use the condition variable `lock_available_` to wait for the nesting level to drop to zero. When the `wait()` method is invoked on `lock_available_` it atomically releases the `lock_` mutex and puts the calling thread to sleep. When the nesting level finally drops to zero, we can acquire the `lock_` and assume ownership of the recursive mutex. The destructor of `guard` releases the `lock_` via the Scoped Locking idiom.

We show the `ACE_Recursive_Thread_Mutex::release()` method next:

```
int ACE_Recursive_Thread_Mutex::release ()
{
  // Automatically acquire mutex.
  ACE_GUARD_RETURN (ACE_Thread_Mutex, guard, lock_, -1);

  nesting_level_--;
  if (nesting_level_ == 0) {
    lock_available_.signal (); // Inform waiters the lock is free.
    owner_id_ = 0;
  }
  return 0; // Destructor of <guard> releases the <lock_>.
}
```

When the `signal()` method is invoked on `lock_available_`, it wakes up one of the threads waiting for the condition to be signaled.

10.7 Summary

OS platforms offer a variety of synchronization mechanisms for developers of networked applications to use when designing concurrent applications. In addition to the accidental complexities related to portability and API usage shown in previous chapters, synchronization mechanisms present another challenge: they aren't all available on today's operating systems. In this chapter, we showed how to resolve complexities, design synchronization classes that help developers make fewer mistakes, and use existing synchronization mechanisms to emulate missing ones. The result is a set of ACE synchronization wrapper facades that application developers can apply portably and robustly to satisfy many synchronization needs.

The ACE synchronization interfaces adapt the syntactically incompatible native OS synchronization mechanisms to appear uniform from the perspective of other C++ classes. These wrapper facades allow you to synchronize both processes and threads in networked applications. This chapter described the most commonly used ACE object-oriented synchronization wrapper facades. The ACE Web site (`http://ace.ece.uci.edu`) describes other synchronization wrapper facades that ACE provides.

Design Principles for ACE C++ Wrapper Facades

SYNOPSIS

This appendix is a follow-on to our discussions regarding the accidental complexities associated with using native OS APIs and how ACE resolves them using the Wrapper Facade pattern. We summarize the design principles that underlie the ACE IPC and concurrency wrapper facade classes so that you can follow and adapt them to your own projects. Hopefully, you can apply them to design and develop future classes for inclusion in ACE!

A.1 Overview

In this appendix, we describe the following principles applied throughout the design of the ACE wrapper facades:

- Use wrapper facades to enhance type safety.
- Simplify for the common case.
- Use hierarchies to enhance design clarity and extensibility.
- Hide platform differences whenever possible.
- Optimize for efficiency.

We document these principles here in abbreviated pattern form so you can understand the forces that shape ACE and apply them to your own frameworks and applications. The context for all these principles is developing wrapper facades for system-level IPC and concurrency mechanisms.

Portability and efficiency are chief concerns in ACE, so we make tradeoffs that may not be necessary or appropriate in higher-level object-oriented application frameworks.

A.2   Use Wrapper Facades to Enhance Type Safety

Higher-level programming languages, such as C++ and Java, provide enhanced type safety, which ensures that operations can't be applied to objects that don't support them. Ideally, type errors should be caught at compile time. However, OS libraries, such as those that implement the C run time, Sockets, or Pthreads, seldom expose internal data structures since that would

- Compromise efforts to provide upward compatibility
- Make multiple programming language support hard on some platforms
- Allow access to private details that should not be used by applications

OS APIs therefore often expose a C-like interface, using low-level, opaque representations of their internal data structures, for example, I/O handles and socket handles. These opaque types make it hard for compilers to detect type errors. Consequently, these errors can be detected only at run time, which increases development and debugging effort, complicates error handling, and reduces application robustness. This section describes a design principle that enhances type safety at compile time, as well as a principle that provides an *escape hatch* for cases in which strict type safety is overly restrictive.

A.2.1   Design C++ Classes That Force Correct Usage

Problem: Many limitations with the Socket API discussed in Section 2.3 stem from the following problems caused by its lack of type safety:

1. **Nonportable**—The type names and underlying representations of I/O handles vary across platforms, making them nonportable. For example, socket handles are integers on UNIX platforms and pointers on Win32.

2. **Easily misused**—Low-level representations permit I/O handles to be misused in ways that can be detected only at run time. For example, the Socket API can easily be applied incorrectly by invoking the

`accept ()` function on a data-mode socket handle that's intended to transfer data via `recv()` and `send()`.

Solution ⇒ Design C++ classes that force correct usage. Weakly typed I/O handles can be encapsulated in C++ classes that export strongly typed methods for that class's users. When application code uses these new classes, C++ compilers can ensure that only legal methods are invoked.

The following C++ code illustrates the application of this principle to the `echo_server ()` function on page 37 in Section 2.3.1:

```cpp
int echo_server (const ACE_INET_Addr &addr)
{
  ACE_SOCK_Acceptor acceptor;    // Connection factory.
  ACE_SOCK_Stream peer_stream;   // Data transfer object.
  ACE_INET_Addr peer_addr;       // Peer address object.

  // Initialize the passive acceptor and accept a new connection.
  if (acceptor.open (addr) != -1
      && acceptor.accept (peer_stream, &peer_addr) != -1) {
    char buf [BUFSIZ];

    for (size_t n; (n = peer_stream.recv (buf, sizeof buf)) > 0;)
      // send_n() handles "short writes."
      if (peer_stream.send_n (buf, n) != n)
        // Error handling omitted...
  }
}
```

This revision solves many problems with the Socket API and the use of C. For example, the `ACE_SOCK_Acceptor` class only exposes methods suitable for passively establishing connections. Since these wrapper facade classes are strongly typed, invalid operations are detected at compile time rather than at run time. It's therefore not possible to invoke `recv()`/`send()` on an `ACE_SOCK_Acceptor` or `accept ()` on an `ACE_SOCK_Stream` since these methods aren't part of those wrapper facade interfaces.

A.2.2 Allow Controlled Violations of Type Safety

Problem: As shown above, wrapper facades can shield networked applications from error-prone or platform-specific implementation details, such as whether a socket handle is represented as an integer or a pointer. Situations arise, however, in which this additional abstraction and type safety actually prevent developers from using a wrapper facade in useful ways not anticipated by its original designer. This frustrating experience can discourage developers from leveraging the other important benefits of wrapper facades.

Solution ⇒ Allow controlled violations via "escape hatches." The intent of this principle is to make it easy to use wrapper facades correctly, hard to use them incorrectly, but not impossible to use them in ways that class designers did not anticipate originally. This principle is exemplified by the `get_handle()` and `set_handle()` methods in `ACE_IPC_SAP`, which is the root base class of the ACE IPC wrapper facades described in Section 3.3 on page 52. Exposing these two methods to get or set an I/O handle allows applications to circumvent ACE IPC wrapper facade type checking when applications must use handle-based system functions.

For example, it may be necessary to obtain a socket handle for use with the `ACE_Handle_Set` class and `select()` function, as shown below:

```
ACE_SOCK_Acceptor acceptor;
ACE_Handle_Set ready_handles;
// ...

if (ready_handles.is_set (acceptor.get_handle ())
  ACE::select ((int)acceptor.get_handle () + 1, ready_handles ());
```

Naturally, these escape hatch mechanisms should be used sparingly since they decrease portability and increase the potential for errors, thereby defeating key benefits of the Wrapper Facade pattern. Situations where it's necessary to mix object-oriented and non-object-oriented abstractions, such as within the implementation of certain layers of ACE itself, should ideally be within class implementations and seldom exposed to class users. If the need for escape hatches arises often for class users, it's best to re-examine the class interface design for opportunities to refactor or redesign in order to restore type safety.

A.3   Simplify for the Common Case

API developers are responsible for devising mechanisms that enable application developers to use any functionality that the API supports. Modern operating systems, file systems, protocol stacks, and threading facilities offer a wide range of capabilities. Today's APIs are therefore often large and complex, offering a myriad of functions that may require numerous arguments to select the desired behavior.

Fortunately, the Pareto Principle, also known as the "80:20" rule, applies to software APIs; that is, most of what's commonly needed can be accomplished with a small subset of the available functionality [PS90]. Moreover, the same sets of functions are often used in the same sequence to accomplish the same or similar goals. Well-designed software toolkits take advantage of this principle by identifying and simplifying for these common use cases. The ACE wrapper facades simplify for common cases in the following ways.

A.3.1 Combine Multiple Functions into a Single Method

Problem: C-level OS system function APIs often contain a number of functions that exist to support relatively uncommon use cases. As discussed in Section 2.3.2, for example, the Socket API supports many protocol families, such as TCP/IP, IPX/SPX, X.25, ISO OSI, and UNIX-domain sockets. To support this range of protocol families, the original Socket API designers defined separate C functions in the Socket API that

1. Create a socket handle
2. Bind a socket handle to a communication endpoint
3. Mark a communication endpoint as being a "passive-mode" factory
4. Accept a connection and return a data-mode handle

Therefore, creating and initializing a passive-mode Internet-domain socket requires multiple calls, as shown below:

```
sockaddr_in addr;
int addr_len = sizeof addr;
int n_handle, s_handle = socket (PF_INET, SOCK_STREAM, 0);

memset (&addr, 0, sizeof addr);
addr.sin_family = AF_INET;
addr.sin_port = htons (port);
addr.sin_addr.s_addr = INADDR_ANY;

bind (s_handle, &addr, addr_len);
listen (s_handle);
// ...
n_handle = accept (s_handle, &addr, &addr_len);
```

Many TCP/IP servers have a sequence of either these functions or a corresponding set that connect a socket actively. There are minor variations for how port numbers are selected, but it's basically the same code rewritten for every new TCP/IP-based application. As shown in Section 2.3.1, this repetition is a major source of potential programming errors and increased debugging time that all projects can do without. Making this set of operations reuseable in a simple and type-safe manner saves time and trouble for every networked application.

Solution ⇒ **Combine multiple functions into a single method.** This simplification alleviates the need for each project to (re)write tedious and error-prone code, such as the passive-mode connection initialization code shown above. The benefits of this approach increase with the number of lines of code that are combined. The specific calls needn't be made, which reduces the potential for errors in parameter usage. The main advantage of this approach, however, is the encapsulated knowledge of the set of functions to be called and the order to call them, which avoids a major source of potential errors.

For example, the ACE_SOCK_Acceptor is a factory for passive connection establishment. Its open() method calls the socket(), bind(), and listen() functions to create a passive-mode communication endpoint. To achieve the functionality presented earlier therefore, applications can simply write the following:

```
ACE_SOCK_Acceptor acceptor;
ACE_SOCK_Stream stream;

acceptor.open (ACE_INET_Addr (port));
acceptor.accept (stream);
// ...
```

Likewise, the constructor of ACE_INET_Addr minimizes common programming errors associated with using the C-based family of struct sockaddr data structures directly. For example, it clears the sockaddr_in address structure (inet_addr_) automatically and converts the port number to network byte order, as follows:

```
ACE_INET_Addr::ACE_INET_Addr (u_short port, long ip_addr) {
  memset (&this->inet_addr_, 0, sizeof this->inet_addr_);
  this->inet_addr_.sin_family = AF_INET;
  this->inet_addr_.sin_port = htons (port);
  memcpy (&this->inet_addr_.sin_addr, &ip_addr, sizeof ip_addr);
}
```

In general, this approach yields code that's more concise, less tedious, and less error prone since it applies the Wrapper Facade pattern to avoid type-safety problems.

A.3.2 Combine Functions Under a Unified Wrapper Facade

Problem: Today's computing platforms often supply some common types of functionality, but provide access to them quite differently. There may simply be different function names that do essentially the same thing. There may also be different functions altogether, which must be called in different orders on different platforms. This shifting set of core APIs and semantics makes it hard to port applications to new platforms.

Multithreading is a good example of how APIs and semantics change across platforms. The steps to create a thread with different attributes varies widely across POSIX threads (Pthreads), UNIX International (UI) threads, Win32 threads, and real-time operating systems. The following list describes some of the key differences:

- **Function names**—The function to spawn threads is named `pthread_create()` in Pthreads, `thr_create()` in UI threads, and `Create-Thread()` in Win32.
- **Return values**—Some threading APIs return a thread ID (or handle) on success, whereas others return 0. For errors, some return a distinct value (with the error code stored elsewhere) and others return an error code directly.
- **Number of functions**—To specify thread attributes, such as stack size or priority, all of the attributes are passed to `CreateThread()` on Win32 or `thr_create()` on UI threads. In Pthreads, however, separate functions are used to create, modify, and later destroy thread attributes data structures, which are then passed to the `pthread_create()` function.
- **Order of function calls**—When multiple function calls are required, they're sometimes required to be in different orders. For example, the Pthreads draft 4 API requires a thread to be marked joinable after it's created, while other Pthreads implementations require it before.

Solution ⇒ **Combine functions under a unified wrapper facade** to properly manage the changes required when porting to different platforms. To deal with the multiple platform requirements of thread creation, for instance, the `ACE_Thread_Manager::spawn()` method accepts all its needed information via arguments (see Section A.3.3 for an important principle regarding arguments) and calls all of the OS system functions in the proper order. The different return value conventions of the platforms are accounted for and unified into one return convention used throughout ACE, that is, 0 on success, −1 on failure with the failure reason stored in `errno`. This solution allows all thread creation in ACE itself, and in user applications, to be accomplished with a single method call across all platforms.

Your challenge when designing unifying functions is to choose the granularity of the interface to expose, and which low-level functions to combine. Keep these points in mind when deciding:

- **Portability**—The wrapper facade method should strive to offer the same semantics across all platforms. This isn't always possible; for example, not all OS platforms allow creation of system-scope threads, as discussed in Section 5.4. In many cases, however, the method can mask these differences by emulating unsupported features or ignoring requested features or attributes that aren't essential. See Section A.5 for more guidance on this point.

- **Ease of use**—The caller should be able to identify how to use your wrapper facade method, what preparations need to be made before calling, such as creating attributes, and what are the return values and their meanings. Having a small number of methods is often easier to use than a larger number of related methods. In addition, beware of side effects, such as internal memory allocation, that callers must remember to handle.

A.3.3   Reorder Parameters and Supply Default Values

Problem: OS libraries contain system functions that must address a wide variety of anticipated uses, and allow access to all of a system's functionality. These functions therefore often have many arguments that are seldom used, but whose default values must be supplied explicitly. Moreover, the order of parameters in a function prototype doesn't always match the frequency with which applications pass nondefault values to the function, which increases the likelihood of coding errors. OS libraries are also often implemented in C so they can be called from a variety of languages, which prevents the use of language features and design abstractions that could help to alleviate these problems.

For example, the UI threads `thr_create()` function takes six parameters:

1. Stack pointer
2. Stack size
3. Entry point function
4. `void *` argument for the entry point function
5. Flags used to create the thread
6. Identifier of the created thread

Since most applications want default stack semantics, parameters 1 and 2 are usually 0. Yet, developers must remember to pass in the 0 values, which is tedious and error prone. It's also common for concurrent applications to spawn threads with "joinable" semantics, which means that another thread will rendezvous with and reap the thread's status when it exits. So parameter 5 has a common value, but it does change depending on the use case. Parameters 3 and 4 are the most commonly changed values. Parameter 6 is set by `thr_create()`, so it must be supplied by the caller.

Solution ⇒ **Reorder parameters and supply default values** in order to simplify for the most common cases. When designing wrapper facade classes, you can take advantage of two important factors:

- You know the common use cases and can design your interface to make the common cases easy for application developers to use.
- You can specify and use an object-oriented implementation language, such as C++, and take advantage of its features and the higher-level abstractions enabled by object-oriented design.

From the problem illustrated above, you can reorder the parameters to put commonly used parameters first and seldomly used parameters at the end, where you can give them default values.

For example, the `ACE_Thread_Manager::spawn()` parameters are ordered so that the most frequently changing parameters, such as the thread function and its `void *` argument, appear first. Default values are then given for the other parameters; for example, the default thread synchronization behavior is THR_JOINABLE. As a result, most applications can just pass the minimum amount of information necessary for the common case.

C++ default parameters can be used for other purposes, as well. For instance, the `connect()` method in the `ACE_SOCK_Connector` class has the following signature:

```
int ACE_SOCK_Connector::connect
  (ACE_SOCK_Stream &new_stream,
   const ACE_SOCK_Addr &remote_sap,
   ACE_Time_Value *timeout = 0,
   const ACE_Addr &local_sap = ACE_Addr::sap_any,
   int reuse_addr = 0,
   int flags = 0,
   int perms = 0,
   int protocol_family = PF_INET,
   int protocol = 0);
```

In contrast, the `ACE_TLI_Connector`'s `connect()` method has a slightly different signature:

```
int ACE_TLI_Connector::connect
  (ACE_TLI_Stream &new_stream,
   const ACE_Addr &remote_sap,
   ACE_Time_Value *timeout = 0,
   const ACE_Addr &local_sap = ACE_Addr::sap_any,
   int reuse_addr = 0,
   int flags = O_RDWR,
   int perms = 0,
   const char device[] = ACE_TLI_TCP_DEVICE,
   struct t_info *info = 0,
   int rw_flag = 1,
   struct netbuf *udata = 0,
   struct netbuf *opt = 0);
```

In practice, only the first several parameters of `connect()` vary from call to call. To simplify programming, therefore, default values are used in the `connect()` methods of these classes so that developers needn't provide them every time. As a result, the common case for both classes are almost identical. For example, `ACE_SOCK_Connector` looks like this:

```
ACE_SOCK_Stream stream;
ACE_SOCK_Connector connector;

// Compiler supplies default values.
connector.connect (stream, ACE_INET_Addr (port, host));
// ...
```

and `ACE_TLI_Connector` looks like this:

```
ACE_TLI_Stream stream;
ACE_TLI_Connector connector;

// Compiler supplies default values.
connector.connect (stream, ACE_INET_Addr (port, host));
// ...
```

The common signature provided by default parameters can be used in conjunction with the parameterized types discussed in [SH] to enhance *generative programming* [CE00] and handle variability using parameterized types, as described in Section A.5.3.

A.3.4 Associate Cohesive Objects Explicitly

Problem: Due to the general-purpose nature of OS-level libraries, there are often dependencies between multiple functions and data structures. Since these dependencies are implicit, however, they are hard to identify and enforce automatically. Section 2.3.1 illustrates this using the relationship between the `socket()`, `bind()`, `listen()`, and `accept()` functions. This problem is exacerbated when multiple data objects are sometimes used together, and other times used alone.

For example, when using threading facilities, a mutex is a common synchronization mechanism. A mutex is also used together with a condition variable; that is, a condition variable and a mutex are usually associated for the condition variable's lifetime. The Pthreads API is error prone in this regard because it doesn't make this association explicit. The signatures of the `pthread_cond_*()` functions take a `pthread_mutex_t *`. The syntax alone therefore doesn't denote the tight coupling between a `pthread_cond_t` and a specific `pthread_mutex_t`. Moreover, the Pthread condition variable API is tedious to use because the mutex must be passed as a parameter every time the `pthread_cond_wait()` function is called.

Solution ⇒ **Associate cohesive objects explicitly** to minimize the details that application developers must remember. Your job as a wrapper facade designer is to make the class user's job easy to do correctly and make it inconvenient (or impossible) to do it wrong. Designing one class that encapsulates multiple, related objects is one technique for accomplishing this goal because it codifies the association between cohesive objects.

This principle goes a step further than the use of wrapper facades to improve type safety described in Section A.2. The goal there was to apply the C++ type system to ensure strong type-checking. The goal here is to use C++ features to enforce dependencies between strongly typed objects. For example, to enforce the association between a condition variable and its mutex from the example above, the `ACE_Condition_Thread_Mutex` class described in Section 10.6 on page 229 contains both a condition variable and a mutex reference:

```
class ACE_Condition_Thread_Mutex {
  // ....
private:
  ACE_cond_t cond_; // Condition variable instance.
  ACE_Thread_Mutex &mutex_; // Reference to a mutex lock.
};
```

The constructor of this class requires a reference to an `ACE_Thread_Mutex` object, forcing the user to associate the mutex correctly, as shown below:

```
ACE_Condition_Thread_Mutex::ACE_Condition_Thread_Mutex
  (const ACE_Thread_Mutex &m): mutex_ (m) { /* ... */ }
```

Any other attempted use will be caught by the C++ compiler and rejected.

A.4   Use Hierarchies to Enhance Design Clarity and Extensibility

Inheritance is a defining property of object-oriented design techniques and programming languages [Mey97]. Although experience shows that deep inheritance hierarchies can be unwieldy [GHJV95], there are benefits of using inheritance judiciously to model software abstractions in a hierarchical manner, as described below.

A.4.1   Replace One-Dimensional APIs with Hierarchies

Problem: The complexity of the Socket API stems in part from its overly broad and one-dimensional design [Mar64]. For instance, all the functions appear at a single level of abstraction, as shown in Figure A.1. This one-dimensional design increases the effort needed to learn and use the Socket API correctly. To write a networked application, for example, programmers must understand most of the Socket API, even if they use only part of it. Moreover, functionality is decentralized, which duplicates code.

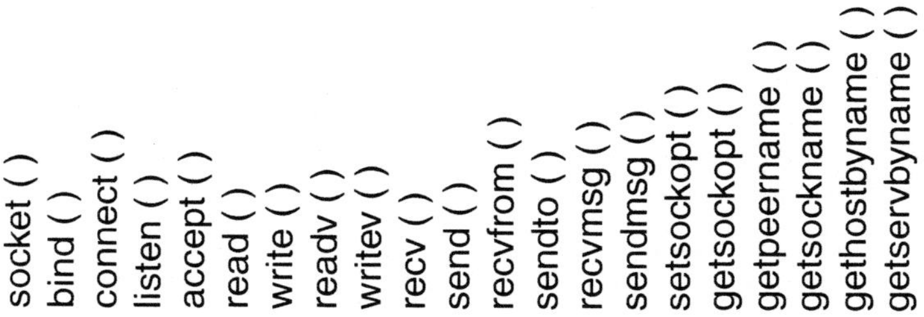

Figure A.1: **Functions in the Socket API**

Solution ⇒ **Replace one-dimensional APIs with hierarchies** to maximize reuse and code sharing. This principle involves using hierarchically related classes to restructure existing one-dimensional APIs. For instance, the ACE Socket wrapper facades were designed by clustering the Socket API functions shown in Figure A.1 into a hierarchy of classes shown in Figure 3.1 on page 47. Inheritance increases code reuse and improves modularity in ACE as follows:

- **Base classes express similarities.** Hierarchical designs avoid unnecessary duplication of code since base classes express common mechanisms provided at the root of the inheritance hierarchy. For example, the ACE IPC wrapper facades share mechanisms toward the root of the inheritance hierarchy, for example, in the ACE_IPC_SAP and ACE_SOCK base classes. These mechanisms include methods for opening/closing and setting/retrieving the underlying I/O handles, as well as certain option management functions common to all the derived wrapper facade classes.

- **Derived classes express differences.** Subclasses located toward the leaves of the inheritance hierarchy implement specialized methods that are customized for the type of communication provided. For example, subclasses of ACE_SOCK provide stream versus datagram communication and local versus remote communication.

A.4.2   Replace Pseudo-Inheritance with C++ Inheritance

Problem: Many C-level system programming APIs are error-prone due to insufficient hierarchical abstraction. For example, the Socket API network addressing mechanisms use C structures and typecasts, which provide an

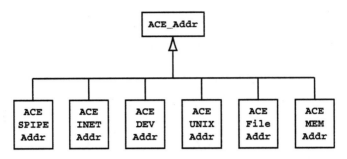

Figure A.2: **The ACE IPC Addressing Hierarchy**

awkward form of "inheritance" for Internet-domain and UNIX-domain addresses. The most general socket addressing structure is `sockaddr`, which defines a pseudo "base class" for defining address information. Its first field indicates the desired address family and its second field is a quasi-opaque byte array. Specific address family structures then define addressing information by overlaying the byte array. This pseudo-inheritance design yields many subtle bugs, as described in Section 2.3.1 and Section 3.2. In particular, the use of typecasts—combined with the weakly typed handle-based Socket API—makes it hard for compilers to detect programmer mistakes at compile time.

Solution ⇒ **Replace pseudo-inheritance with C++ inheritance.**   Rather than forcing application developers to wrestle with casts and type overlays, this principle leverages object-oriented programming language features in C++. For example, ACE defines the `ACE_Addr` class hierarchy described in Section 3.2 to provide type-safe wrapper facades for diverse network addressing formats, such as the Internet- and UNIX-domain addresses, STREAM pipes, files, and devices shown in Figure A.2. Each subclass hides address family-specific details behind a common API.

A.5   Hide Platform Differences Whenever Possible

Multiplatform software development presents many challenges to class designers because functionality can differ widely across platforms. These differences often take one of the following forms:

- **Missing and impossible**—Some platforms simply don't supply a capability that others do; for example, some platforms do not have a zombie concept (from Chapter 8) so there is no way and no need to offer a way to avoid them.

- **Missing but can be emulated**—Some platforms don't provide a capability that others do, but they do supply enough other functionality to emulate the missing capability; for example, the condition variable and readers/writer locks described in Chapter 10 are emulated on certain OS platforms.

- **Missing but an equally good feature is available**—Some platforms do not provide a capability, such as the Sockets API, but do provide an equivalent capability, such as TLI. In other situations, both features may be available, but the platform's implementation of one is more favorable than the other. For example, one may have better performance or fewer defects.

This section describes how to deal with these situations to arrive at a set of C++ classes that allow development of easily portable networked applications.

A.5.1 Allow Source to Build Whatever Is Beneficial

Problem: Platform feature sets sometimes diverge in ways that wrapper facades can't hide. For example, a wrapper facade can't magically invent kernel-thread semantics if it simply doesn't exist in the platform's feature set. The class designer now has a problem: Should a class be designed that lacks a method, or set of methods, corresponding to the missing capability?

Software that's ported to enough platforms will eventually encounter one in which an important feature isn't supported. The first reaction to this problem may be to avoid offering a class or a class method, corresponding to that capability, forcing the compiler to detect the problem at compile time. This choice is appropriate when the missing feature is of central importance to the application. For example, the ability to create a new process is a central feature to many networked applications. If a platform doesn't offer multiprocessing, it's often advantageous to know that at compile time. There are may cases, however, in which an application should be allowed to run and react to any potential issues at run time, where alternate approaches can be attempted.

Solution ⇒ **Allow source to build whatever's beneficial.** There are situations in which it's better to allow source code to compile correctly, even when the functionality it's trying to access isn't present and can't be emulated. This may be due to:

- **The ability to detect the issue at run time and allow the application to select an alternate plan of action.** This case often arises in class library design because designers can't predict all the situations in which the class may be used. In such cases, it may be better to implement a method that returns a "not implemented" indication to the caller. Thus, the caller has the freedom to choose another technique or capability, report the error and try to contine, or terminate. ACE defines a macro called ACE_NOTSUP_RETURN that serves this purpose.

- **Ignoring the missing feature yields the same effect as having it.** For this case, consider a UNIX application that uses the ACE_ Process_Options::avoid_zombies() method to avoid dealing with zombie processes (see page 168). If the application is ported to Win32, there's no such concept as a zombie process. In this case, it's perfectly acceptable to call the avoid_zombies() method and have it indicate success because the original intent of the method has been accomplished by doing nothing.

A.5.2 Emulate Missing Capabilities

Problem: Due to the wide range of capabilities and standards implemented in today's computing platforms, there's often divergence in feature sets. When porting to a new platform, this divergence yields an area of missing functionality that a project has come to rely on from previous platforms. A careful analysis of the concepts behind the features, however, often reveals alternate capabilities that can be combined to emulate the missing functionality.

Contrary to popular belief, standards are not a panacea for portable software. There are a great many standards, and platforms implement different sets of standards, often changing between OS releases. Even within a standard some features are often optional. For example, the semaphore and real-time scheduling class capabilities are optional parts of Pthreads.

When software has been developed for one platform, or set of platforms, an effort to port it to a new platform often reveals that capabilities used by the software aren't available on the new platform. This can cause a *ripple effect* throughout the project as changes are made to work around the missing feature. If a careful analysis of the new platform's feature set is made, however, it may reveal a set of features that, when combined, can be used to emulate the missing capability. If a project uses C++ wrapper facade classes intelligently, therefore, it may be able to avoid a series of expensive design and code changes.

Solution ⇒ **Emulate missing capabilities.** Classes designed according to the Wrapper Facade pattern can encapsulate a platform's native capabilities in convenient and type-safe ways. They can also contain native code that uses a platform's existing features to emulate some capability not provided otherwise. For example, the following C++ code illustrates how the ACE condition variable and mutex classes can be used to implement a process-scoped semaphore wrapper facade for OS platforms that don't implement it natively.

```
class ACE_Thread_Semaphore
{
private:
  ACE_Thread_Mutex mutex_; // Serialize access.
  // Wait for <count_> to become non-zero.
  ACE_Condition_Thread_Mutex count_nonzero_;
  u_long count_; // Keep track of the semaphore count.
  u_long waiters_; // Keeps track of the number of waiters.
public:
  ACE_Thread_Semaphore (u_int count = 1)
    : count_nonzero_ (mutex_), // Associate mutex and condition.
      count_ (count),
      waiters_ (0) {}
```

Note how the initializer for `count_nonzero_` binds the `mutex_` object to itself, in accordance with the principle of associating cohesive objects explicitly, described in Section A.3.4 on page 245.

The `acquire()` method blocks the calling thread until the semaphore count becomes greater than 0, as shown below.

```
int acquire () {
  ACE_GUARD_RETURN (ACE_Thread_Mutex, guard, mutex_, -1);
  int result = 0;

  // Count # of waiters so we can signal them in <release()>.
  waiters_++;

  // Put calling thread to sleep waiting on semaphore.
  while (count_ == 0 && result == 0)
    // Release/reacquire <mutex_>
    result = count_nonzero_.wait ();
```

```
    --waiters_;
    if (result == 0) --count_;
    return result;
  }
```

For completeness, we implement the `ACE_Thread_Semaphore`'s `release()` method below, which increments the semaphore count, potentially unblocking a thread that's waiting on the `count_nonzero_` condition variable.

```
  int release () {
    ACE_GUARD_RETURN (ACE_Thread_Mutex, guard, mutex_, -1);

    // Notify waiters that the semaphore has been released.
    if (waiters_ > 0) count_nonzero_.signal ();

    ++count_;
    return 0;
  }
  // ... Other methods omitted ...
};
```

Note how the `ACE_Thread_Semaphore` class's `acquire()` and `release()` methods both use the `ACE_GUARD_RETURN` macro (described in Sidebar 22 on page 216), which encapsulates the Scoped Locking idiom [SSRB00] to ensure the `mutex_` is locked and unlocked automatically. This design is yet another example of the principle of simplifying for the common case (described in Section A.3 on page 238).

A.5.3 Handle Variability via Parameterized Types

Problem: Networked applications and middleware often must run on a range of platforms that vary greatly in the availability and efficiency of OS capabilities. For example, certain OS platforms may possess different underlying networking APIs, such as Sockets but not TLI or vice versa. Likewise, different OS platforms may implement these APIs more or less efficiently. When writing reusable software in such heterogeneous platforms, the following forces must be resolved:

- Different applications may require different configurations of middleware strategies, such as different synchronization or IPC mechanisms. Adding new or improved strategies should be straightforward. Ideally, each application function or class should be limited to a single copy to avoid version skew.

- The mechanism selected for variation should not unduly affect run-time performance. In particular, inheritance and dynamic binding can incur additional run-time overhead due to the indirection of virtual methods [HLS97].

Solution ⇒ **Handle variability via parameterized types** rather than inheritance and dynamic binding. Parameterized types decouple applications from reliance on specific strategies, such as synchronization or IPC APIs, without incurring run-time overhead. Although parameterized types can incur compile- and link-time overhead, they generally compile into efficient code [Bja00].

For example, encapsulating the Socket API with C++ classes (rather than stand-alone C functions) helps improve portability by allowing the wholesale replacement of network programming mechanisms via parameterized types. The following code illustrates this principle by applying generative [CE00] and generic [Ale01] programming techniques to modify the echo_server() so that it's a C++ function template.

```
template <class ACCEPTOR>
int echo_server (const typename ACCEPTOR::PEER_ADDR &addr)
{
  // Connection factory.
  ACCEPTOR acceptor;
  // Data transfer object.
  typename ACCEPTOR::PEER_STREAM peer_stream;
  // Peer address object.
  typename ACCEPTOR::PEER_ADDR peer_addr;
  int result = 0;

  // Initialize passive mode server and accept new connection.
  if (acceptor.open (addr) != -1
      && acceptor.accept (peer_stream, &peer_addr) != -1) {
    char buf[BUFSIZ];

    for (size_t n; (n = peer_stream.recv (buf, sizeof buf)) > 0;)
      if (peer_stream.send_n (buf, n) != n) {
        result = -1;
        break;
      }

    peer_stream.close ();
  }
  return result;
}
```

By using ACE and C++ templates, applications can be written to be parameterized transparently with either C++ Socket or TLI wrapper facades, depending on the properties of the underlying OS platform:

```
// Conditionally select IPC mechanism.
#if defined (USE_SOCKETS)
typedef ACE_SOCK_Acceptor ACCEPTOR;
#elif defined (USE_TLI)
typedef ACE_TLI_Acceptor ACCEPTOR;
#endif /* USE_SOCKETS. */

int driver_function (u_short port_num)
{
  // ...

  // Invoke the <echo_server()> with appropriate network
  // programming APIs. Note use of the traits type for <addr>.
  ACCEPTOR::PEER_ADDR addr (port_num);
  echo_server<ACCEPTOR> (addr);
}
```

This technique works for the following reasons:

- The ACE C++ Socket and TLI wrapper facade classes expose an object-oriented interface with a common signature. In cases where interfaces aren't originally designed to be consistent, the Adapter pattern [GHJV95] can be applied to make them consistent, as described in Section A.3.3.

- C++ templates support signature-based type conformance that does not require type parameters to encompass all potential functionality. Instead, templates parameterize application code that is designed to invoke only a subset of methods that are common to the various network programming methods, such as open(), close(), send(), and recv().

In general, parameterized types are less intrusive and more extensible than alternatives, such as implementing multiple versions of the echo_server() function or littering conditional compilation directives throughout application source code.

A.6 Optimize for Efficiency

The design principles used for higher-level applications and GUI frameworks aren't necessarily appropriate for lower-levels of network programming toolkits. In particular, performance considerations often preclude the use of certain languages features, idioms, and patterns, as we describe in this section.

A.6.1 Design Wrapper Facades for Efficiency

Problem: Despite years of successful deployment, a belief persists in some application domains that object-oriented techniques and C++ are not suitable for performance-sensitive systems. For example, the dynamic binding and native exception handling features of object-oriented programming languages can be problematic in real-time embedded applications that require predictable run-time behavior, low latency, and small footprint. However, many real-time application domains, such as aerospace, call processing, process control, and distributed interactive simulation, can benefit from flexible and portable host infrastructure middleware. It's therefore essential that object-oriented software intended for these domains be designed carefully to avoid language features and patterns that add gratuitous overhead.

Solution ⇒ **Design wrapper facades for efficiency.** ACE uses the following techniques to ensure that its wrapper facades are efficient:

- Many ACE wrapper facades are concrete types; that is, their methods are nonvirtual. This design eliminates the overhead of dispatching dynamically bound methods, increases opportunities for method inlining, and enables objects to be placed in shared memory where appropriate.

- All the ACE IPC wrapper facades contain explicit `open()` and `close()` methods and their destructors don't close handles. This design prevents subtle errors caused if I/O handles are closed prematurely when transferred by value from one object to another. ACE's wrapper facades purposely avoid the use of the Bridge pattern [GHJV95] since that would incur dynamic memory allocation and reduce efficiency, rather than improve it. Instead, the principle we apply in ACE is to not perform certain types of implicit operations towards the root of class hierarchies. Rather, higher layer abstracts provide these capabilities when needed. For example, the Logging_Server class on page 81 in Section 4.4.1 closes the acceptor socket handle in its destructor, which is the common use case at that level of abstraction.

A.6.2   Inline Performance-Critical Methods

Problem: Wrapper facades enhance the portability and type safety of native C-level function APIs by providing an additional level of abstraction. If these wrapper facades aren't implemented efficiently, however, many networked application developers won't use them in lieu of existing low-level C networking APIs. Networked applications are often time-sensitive, and their developers must be vigilant about reducing latency and improving responsiveness because the network itself already exacerbates these problems. Since OS platform calls are often in time-critical parts of the execution path, developers of networked applications tend to be leery of any overhead that may decrease performance.

Solution ⇒ **Inline performance-critical methods** to minimize or eliminate any performance overhead resulting from increased type safety. ACE uses C++ inlining extensively to eliminate method call overhead stemming from the additional abstraction in its OS adaptation layer and C++ wrapper facades. Methods in the critical performance path, such as the recv() and send() methods of ACE_SOCK_Stream, are specified as C++ inline functions. Inlining is time and space efficient since these methods are short (e.g., 1 to 2 lines per method). In addition, virtual methods are used sparingly in the performance-critical parts of ACE since many C++ compiler optimizers don't fully eliminate virtual method overhead [HLS97].

A.6.3   Avoid Exception Handling in System-Level Toolkits

Problem: Experienced C++ programmers will notice that the class definitions throughout the book and in ACE don't contain exception specifications. This may seem a shortcoming at first glance since handling error indications in a call chain can be hard, and is a prime motivation for C++'s exception handling mechanisms. There are two problems, however, with using native C++ exception handling in system-level toolkits:

1. **Portability**—ACE began in 1991, well before exceptions were a part of the C++ standard. Even today, compilers are not uniform in their

support of exceptions, nor can all end users migrate to new compilers due to legacy dependencies. Since ACE must run on a wide range of compilers and platforms, any dependencies on native exceptions would preclude its portable use in some environments.

2. **Performance**—The time and space overhead incurred by many compilers is unacceptable for certain types of applications. For example, the additional memory space and execution time incurred by native exception handling is prohibitive for real-time applications in embedded systems. Even if a platform supports native exception handling, therefore, real-time and embedded applications on that platform may be unable to use it.

Solution ⇒ Avoid exception handling in system-level toolkits. ACE doesn't throw exceptions for the reasons outlined above. Internally, it uses the Thread-Specific Storage pattern [SSRB00] to convey error status information between caller and callee. This pattern allows sequential operations within a thread to access common data atomically without incurring locking overhead for each access. By placing error information into thread-specific storage, each thread can reliably set and test the status of operations within that thread without using additional locks or complex synchronization protocols.

For systems that want to use exceptions in their application software, ACE can be compiled with native C++ exception support. For platforms that use `make` to build ACE, simply add `exceptions=1` to the command line or to the `platform_macros.GNU` file.

A.7 Summary

This appendix presented design principles followed throughout ACE to achieve its goals of providing the benefits of host infrastructure middleware discussed in Section 0.3.1. Some of these principles are well known in the generative programming community [CE00], but aren't widely known to network programmers. Other principles are described more abstractly in the Wrapper Facade pattern description in [SSRB00]. Due to the well-considered and time-proven design fundamentals embodied in ACE, it's a flexible, powerful, and portable toolkit that's helped thousands of projects avoid the pitfalls associated with the accidental complexities discussed in this book.

The Past, Present, and Future of ACE

Synopsis

This appendix presents a brief history of ACE that explains its inception and open-source evolution over the past decade. We then outline the standards-based middleware based on—and bundled with—ACE. We close by discussing where we see ACE heading in the future.

B.1 The Evolution of ACE

Eric Raymond, a pioneer of the open-source movement [O'R98], is fond of saying that "Every good work of software starts by scratching a developer's personal itch" [Ray01]. While this isn't always the case, it certainly applies to ACE. This section describes the evolution of ACE—from its origins as a tool to simplify the life of a single researcher to one of the most portable and widely used C++ network programming toolkits in the world.

B.1.1 The Formative Itch

In 1990, Doug Schmidt took a break from his doctorate studies at the University of California, Irvine (UCI) to work at a Silicon Valley start-up company called Independence Technologies Inc. (ITI), which was ultimately bought by BEA Systems, Inc. ITI specialized in UNIX-based online transaction processing (OLTP), which was a novelty in 1990. It was at ITI that

Doug was exposed to Richard Stevens's classic book *UNIX Network Programming*, which Doug absorbed and applied to help develop an OLTP middleware platform written in C and C++.

In 1991 Doug returned to UCI to finish his dissertation on concurrent networking protocol processing [SS95]. His doctorate project focused on the design and optimization of *A Dynamically Assembled Protocol Transformation, Integration, and eValuation Environment* (ADAPTIVE) [SBS93]. ADAPTIVE provided customizable lightweight and adaptive protocol machines that helped improve end-to-end application performance and reduce transport system overhead [SS93].

In the early 1990s there were two vexing sources of accidental complexity associated with writing systems software such as ADAPTIVE:

1. The protocol code in ADAPTIVE was written using object-oriented design techniques and C++. It was necessary to revert to C function APIs and algorithmic design, however, when accessing OS resources, such as processes, threads, locks, sockets, shared memory, DLLs, and files.

2. The same "boilerplate" code had to be written numerous times to handle common network programming tasks, such as connection establishment, synchronous event demultiplexing and dispatching, synchronization, and concurrency architectures.

The ADAPTIVE Communication Environment (ACE) was created to resolve these two frustrations. The first publicly available release of ACE in 1992 ran on SunOS 4.x and 5.x. Its roughly 10,000 lines of code combined C++ features, advanced OS mechanisms, and patterns to provide an extensible and efficient object-oriented networking software development toolkit.

Had Doug not released ACE using an open-source distribution model, it would likely have faded away after he finished his doctorate. Fortunately, he'd been contributing to the free software community for many years, having written the GNU GPERF perfect hash function generator [Sch90] and parts of the GNU LIBG++ library along with Doug Lea [Lea88]. He was therefore familiar with the benefits of building a community [SP01] around open-source processes and tools. A key strength of open-source development models is their ability to scale to large user communities, where application developers and end users can assist with many quality assurance, documentation, and support activities.

B.1.2   The Turning Point

By 1994, ACE had matured to the point where it was being used in several dozen commercial projects, including network management at Ericsson [SS94] and Iridium [Sch00]. At that point, Doug became an Assistant Professor at Washington University, St. Louis. This transition coincided with a surge of commercial interest in using middleware to help improve networked application software portability and flexibility.

ACE was well positioned to surf the early wave of interest in middleware. As a result, Doug and his research group at Washington University received funding from many visionary sponsors, including ATDesk, BBN, Boeing, Cisco, DARPA, Ericsson, Hughes, Icomverse, Iridium, Kodak, Krones, Lockheed Martin, Lucent, Motorola, Nokia, Nortel, NSF, Raytheon, SAIC, Siemens MED, Siemens SCR, Siemens ZT, Sprint, and Telcordia. These sponsors recognized that it was too costly and time consuming for them to independently rediscover and reinvent *ad hoc* solutions to their core networked application software challenges. Fortunately, the participants on the ACE project had identified, documented, and reified key patterns and frameworks to address these challenges, which Doug's sponsors then applied to reduce many tedious and expensive aspects of developing and maintaining their networked applications.

Over the next six years, around U.S.$7 million of sponsor funding enabled Doug to hire dozens of graduate students and full-time staff. Many of these people have worked for years in the Distributed Object Computing (DOC) Groups at Washington University in St. Louis, and now at UCI, where Doug has returned as a tenured Associate Professor in the Electrical and Computer Engineering department. Together, the DOC groups have:

1. Greatly expanded the capabilities of ACE, which is about 25 times its original size and contains hundreds more classes and frameworks.

2. Ported ACE to dozens of new OS/compiler platforms, which are summarized in Sidebar 1 on page 14.

3. Written scores of magazine articles and technical papers that describe the patterns and performance of the wrapper facades and frameworks in the ACE toolkit. The ability to download these papers from `http://www.cs.wustl.edu/~schmidt/publications.html` enabled worldwide developers to assess the scope and quality of ACE to determine how it could best meet their needs.

The members of the DOC Group and the ACE user community have been instrumental in transitioning ACE from the personal hobby of a single researcher into one of the world's most widely used C++ frameworks for concurrent object-oriented network programming across a wide range of hardware and software platforms.

B.1.3 Crossing the Chasm

While Doug and his group at Washington University were working on ACE version 3.x in 1996, Steve Huston was doing consulting and networked application development. In one project he needed C++ networking software to meet an aggressive development schedule. A Web search yielded ACE. Unfortunately, ACE wasn't ported to the project's platform (Unixware). The project was doomed without the capabilities ACE provided, however, so Steve began the port to Unixware. The time to port ACE to a new platform, learn enough about ACE to do the job, and then develop the system was less than it would have taken Steve to write the necessary networking software from scratch. The new system performed efficiently and the result was the first of many ACE success stories [Gro].

Realizing the gains achievable with ACE, Steve kept an eye on the DOC Group and the ACE mailing list. Although ACE improved continually, it was still used mostly by researchers and industrial R&D groups. While ACE was too practical to be left solely in the hands of researchers, Steve recognized that high-quality support was needed in order for ACE to cross the chasm [Moo91] to support mainstream commercial software developers. The wheels started turning late in 1996 and by mid-1997 Steve had renamed his company Riverace Corporation (http://www.riverace.com) and focused it on support and product services that make ACE easier to learn and apply.

Today, Riverace provides support and consulting services that help companies make the best use of ACE in their development projects. The company continues to improve the quality of ACE as an open-source product, providing a level of commercial support that's helping to expand ACE's use into enterprise software development worldwide. ACE now has the "look and feel" of commercial software, and all of its benefits come without any run-time or developer licensing fees. Sidebar 24 outlines the open-source license used for ACE.

Sidebar 24: The ACE Open-Source License

The ACE open-source license is similar to the so-called *BSD UNIX* open-source license. Users are free to use, modify, copy, and distribute, perpetually and irrevocably, the ACE source code and object code produced from the source, as well as copy and distribute modified versions of this software. In particular, ACE can be used in proprietary software and users are under no obligation to redistribute any source code that's built with or derived from ACE. Complete copyright and licensing information for ACE is available in the file $ACE_ROOT/COPYING in the ACE release.

B.1.4 Middleware Standards

Toward the latter half of the 1990s, information technology was clearly becoming commoditized; that is, key hardware and software artifacts were getting faster, cheaper, and better at an increasingly predictable pace. For the past decade we've all benefited from the commoditization of hardware, such as CPUs and storage devices, and networking elements, such as IP routers. More recently, many software layers and components are becoming commoditized due to the maturation of the following standards:

- **Programming languages,** such as Java and C++
- **Operating environments,** such as POSIX and Java virtual machines and
- **Middleware**, such as CORBA, Enterprise Java Beans, and the .NET Web services [SS01].

A consequence of the commoditization of these software artifacts is that industries long protected by high barriers to entry, such as telecom and aerospace, are more vulnerable to disruptive technologies [Chr97] and global competition, which can drive prices to marginal cost.

Since Doug felt that the long-term success of the software industry depends on the adoption of useful open standards, he began two spin-off projects that focused on transitioning the ACE research into open middleware standards. This section describes the results of these spin-off efforts, which yielded the two standards-based middleware toolkits—TAO and JAWS—shown in Figure B.1. TAO and JAWS were developed using the

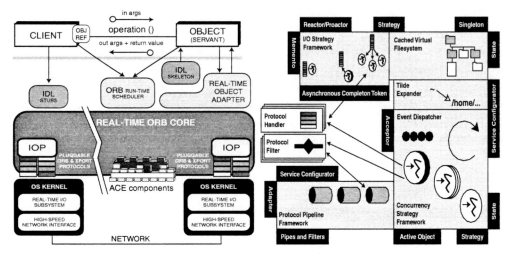

(1) THE ACE ORB (TAO)   (2) The JAWS Web Server Framework

Figure B.1: **Standards-Compliant Middleware Based on ACE**

wrapper facades and frameworks provided by ACE, as described below.

The ACE ORB (TAO)

TAO is a high-performance, real-time implementation of the CORBA specification [SLM98]. It contains the network interface, OS, networking protocol, and CORBA middleware capabilities shown in Figure B.1 (1). Many
of the patterns used in TAO are described in [SC00]. Like ACE, TAO is
open-source software, which is freely available for download at the URL
`http://ace.ece.uci.edu/TAO`.

The DOC Group's work on TAO has played an important role in several
standardization efforts:

- It influenced the OMG's real-time CORBA specification [Obj01], par-
  ticularly its explicit binding and portable synchronizer features.
- It has been included as one of two ORBs selected for DISA's Joint
  Tactical Architecture (JTA) in the DII COE.
- It has been used as the basis for the DMSO HLA/RTI distributed
  interactive simulations standard [OSLN99].

Today, TAO is used in hundreds of research and commercial projects
in the aerospace, telecommunication, simulation, health care, scientific

computing, and financial services domains around the world. It has the distinction of being the first CORBA ORB flown successfully in a fighter aircraft [Lac98]. TAO is supported by OCI (`http://www.theaceorb.com`) using an open-source license and business model that's similar to River-ace's.

The JAWS Adaptive Web Server (JAWS)

JAWS is a high-performance, adaptive Web server [HS99] built using the ACE frameworks. It implements the HTTP 1.0 specification. Figure B.1 (2) illustrates the major structural components and patterns in JAWS. JAWS is structured as a framework of frameworks. The overall JAWS framework contains the following components and frameworks:

- **Concurrency strategies,** which implement concurrency mechanisms such as thread per request and thread pool, that can be selected adaptively at run time or preselected at initialization time;
- **I/O strategies,** which implement various I/O mechanisms, such as asynchronous, synchronous, and reactive I/O;
- **Event dispatcher,** which coordinates the handling of events between JAWS's I/O and concurrency strategies;
- **Protocol handlers,** which implement the parsing and handling of HTTP requests;
- **Protocol pipeline,** which allows filter operations to be incorporated easily with the data being processed by protocol handlers; and
- **Cached virtual filesystem,** which improves Web server performance by reducing the overhead of filesystem accesses via caching strategies, such as *least recently used (LRU)* and *least frequently used (LFU)*.

Each of these frameworks is structured as a set of collaborating objects implemented by combining and extending components in ACE. The patterns constituting JAWS are described in [SSRB00]. Like ACE and TAO, JAWS is used in many commercial projects. It's also open-source software—distributed with the ACE release in the $ACE_ROOT/apps/ directory.

ACE has been fundamental to the success of TAO and JAWS. Moreover, the flow of technology has been synergistic. For example, the process of implementing and refactoring [FBB+99] TAO and JAWS has yielded many new classes, as well as refined and optimized many classes and frameworks in ACE.

B.1.5   The Impact of Open Source

There are thousands of developers and end users in the ACE open-source community. Without their support it's unlikely that ACE would have been as successful as it has for the following reasons:

Lack of sufficient capital investment.   Over 100 person-years of effort have been expended to develop ACE+TAO. Assuming that each person-year costs a conventional company around U.S.$200 thousand in salary and benefits, this effort would have required around U.S.$20 million in funding using a conventional closed-source development model. As mentioned on page 261, it cost the DOC groups' sponsors only one-third of this amount to develop ACE+TAO. Much of the difference was made up by contributions of time and effort by the ACE+TAO open-source community.

Lack of short-term return on investment.   It took several years for ACE to mature to a point where it could be used for production systems. For example, many ACE framework required multiple iterations to determine the appropriate APIs, patterns, and relationships. Few companies or venture capitalists would be willing to invest in a middleware project for this long, particularly when the end result was given away for free!

Lack of time, interest, and available platforms.   Developing highly portable middleware requires a substantial amount of effort on relatively "mundane" tasks, such as ensuring that the software builds and runs cleanly on dozens of compilers and OS platforms. Even if a core group of developers had sufficient time and interest (which is unlikely in chronically underfunded advanced R&D environments), it would be prohibitively expensive to obtain all the necessary hardware/software platforms necessary to create and maintain all these ports. Fortunately, the open-source model allowed the DOC groups to leverage the vast human and computing resources available on the Web to ensure that many mundane tasks were completed in a timely and economical manner [SP01].

Lack of broad technical expertise.   ACE has benefited greatly from software contributions and guidance from middleware experts throughout the world. Doug had been involved in the GNU C and C++ projects during the latter years of the 1980s along with free software pioneers, such as Richard Stallman, Doug Lea, and Michael Tiemann. When he started developing ACE he therefore understood the value of creating a community of technical experts to augment and support the capabilities of a software toolkit.

As soon as the first working build of ACE was complete in 1991 it was available for anonymous ftp—HTTP and the Web as we know it today didn't exist at that point. This immediately spawned a small user community to help fix bugs and port ACE to new platforms, thereby reinforcing the value of free software—the term "open source" did not exist at that point either!

B.2 The Road Ahead

We're focusing our future efforts on ACE as follows:

Improved documentation. ACE's lack of comprehensive and easy-to-use documentation has impeded its mainstream success somewhat. A large, multifaceted effort to remedy this problem is underway and will continue to be a focus in the future. In 2000, Carlos O'Ryan and Darrell Brunsch spearheaded an effort at UCI to convert ACE's reference material generation to Doxygen [Dim01]. Doxygen provides better expression of ACE's usage and the resulting reference material is much easier to use. The improved reference material and the upcoming publication of *The ACE Programmer's Guide* [HJS] and *C++ Network Programming, Volume 2: Systematic Reuse with ACE and Frameworks* [SH] will help many more C++ developers make the most of ACE's power and flexibility.

New and updated platforms. We will continue to improve and extend ACE to support new releases of its existing operating systems. New platforms will be explored, driven primarily by interest and demand from the ACE user community and Riverace customers. ACE's C++ feature usage will also expand. ACE works with most C++ compilers, some from the days of Cfront. As time goes on and more compilers adhere to the C++ standard, ACE's "window of compiler support" will slide, instead of being enlarged. This evolution will allow ACE to leverage modern C++ standard features, such as native exceptions, partial template specialization, template member functions, and the Standard C++ Library.

Increased robustness. ACE has an extensive set of regression tests that run on dozens of platforms continuously each day. These tests automatically detect compilation errors, configuration errors, run-time errors, and memory errors. At any point in time, you can keep track of the status of ACE by examining the output of these regression tests at http:

`//ace.ece.uci.edu/scoreboard/`. Since ACE is a large piece of software, we'll keep expanding its regression testing capabilities to ensure that its quality and robustness continue to improve.

Reduced memory footprint. The core ACE library's size ranges from 700KB to 1.5MB on common OS platforms, and is significantly larger when built with full debugging information. In some environments, particularly memory-constrained embedded systems [NW01], the memory footprint of ACE can be a hindrance. We have therefore embarked on an effort that enables subsets of ACE to be built so applications only incur the memory overhead for parts they need, without incurring overhead for parts they don't. For more information on the ACE subsetting effort see `$ACE_ROOT/docs/ACE-subsets.html` in the ACE software release.

Let us know if you're interested in getting involved in these projects!

B.3   Concluding Remarks

Over the past decade, we've worked on many aspects of networked application R&D, ranging from blue-sky academic research to hands-on product development and consulting. In our experience, the most effective way to bring the power of advanced software R&D techniques to mainstream commercial software developers is to

1. Develop high-quality reusable software based on cutting-edge systems research.
2. Work with early adopters to deploy it in real-world applications.
3. Provide commercial support and services to help transition and assimilate the new techniques to mainstream software developers.

Significant penetration into commercial markets rarely occurs until researchers demonstrate the benefits of their techniques in real-world operational systems. Completely decoupling technology from research, however, can curb the leading-edge R&D efforts required to improve and extend new technology. Close cooperation between research and commercial groups help maintain forward development and smooth migration into the mainstream. Combined commercial/academic efforts, such as Riverace and the DOC Group, require patience and teamwork to maintain the best of both worlds. The results can be quite rewarding for all parts of the team, as well as for the user community that benefits from their collaborations.

Glossary

Abstract Class A class that does not implement all the methods defined in its interface. An abstract class defines a common interface for its subclasses.

Acceptor-Connector Pattern A design pattern that decouples the connection and initialization of cooperating peer services in a networked system from the processing they perform once connected and initialized.

Accidental Complexity Complexity that arises as a side-effect of limitations with tools and techniques, such as type-unsafe APIs and procedural design, used to develop software within an application domain.

Active Connection Establishment The connection role played by a peer application that initiates a connection to a remote peer (compare with *Passive Connection Establishment*).

Active Object An object that implements the Active Object pattern (compare with *Passive Object*).

Active Object Pattern A design pattern that decouples method execution from method invocation in order to enhance concurrency and simplify synchronized access to objects that reside in their own threads of control.

Algorithmic Decomposition A design paradigm in which programs are decomposed by functionality.

API Application programming interface. The external interface of a software platform, such as an operating system, that is used by systems or applications built on top of it.

Aspects   A property of a program, such as memory management, synchronization, or fault tolerance, that cross-cuts module boundaries.

Asynchronous I/O   A mechanism for sending or receiving data in which an I/O operation is initiated but the caller does not block waiting for the operation to complete.

Bandwidth   The capacity of a communication medium, such as a network or *bus*.

Barrier Synchronization   A thread synchronization mechanism that allows a designated group of threads to synchronize their progress when each attains a certain state, such as completion of some collective operation or task. A barrier represents a specific point in the execution path. Each thread that reaches the barrier point waits for the other threads to also reach that point. When all threads in the set reach the barrier, the barrier is "dropped" and all threads simultaneously continue execution.

Broadcast   A broadcast is a special form of *multicast*, where messages are transmitted from a sender to all receivers in a particular domain.

Bus   A high-speed communication channel that links computing devices, such as CPUs, disks, and network interfaces.

Busy Wait   A technique used by a thread to wait for a lock by executing a tight loop and polling to see if the lock is available on each iteration, in contrast to waiting for the lock to be released by sleeping and allowing other threads to run.

Callback   An object registered with a dispatcher, which calls back to a method on the object when a particular event occurs.

Client   In our descriptions, client denotes a role, component, or subsystem that invokes or uses the functionality offered by other components.

Collocation   The activities associated with placing an object into the same process or host with the clients that access it. Collocation is often applied to improve locality of reference (compare with *Distribution*).

Common Data Representation (CDR)   The standard format defined by CORBA to marshal and demarshal data. It uses a bicanonical "receiver makes right" representation that only incurs overhead if the byte order of the sender differs from the byte order of the receiver.

Common Middleware Services   This layer of middleware defines domain-independent services, such as event notifications, logging, multimedia streaming, persistence, security, global time synchronization, real-time scheduling and distributed resource management, fault tolerance, concurrency control, and recoverable transactions, that allocate, schedule, and coordinate various resources throughout a distributed system.

Component   An encapsulated part of a software system that implements a specific service or set of services. A component has one or more interfaces that provide access to its services. Components serve as building blocks for the structure of a system. On a programming language level, components may be represented as modules, classes, objects, or a set of related functions. A component that does not implement all the elements of its interface is called an abstract component.

Component Configurator Pattern   A design pattern that allows an application to link and unlink its component implementations at run time without having to modify, recompile, or relink the application statically.

Concrete Class   A class from which objects can be instantiated. In contrast to abstract classes, all methods are implemented in a concrete class. The term is used to distinguish concrete subclasses from their abstract superclass.

Concurrency   The ability of an object, component, or system to execute operations that are "logically simultaneous" (compare with *Parallelism*).

Condition Variable   A condition variable is a synchronization mechanism used by collaborating threads to suspend themselves temporarily until condition expressions involving data shared between the threads attain desired states. A condition variable is always used in conjunction with a mutex, which the thread must acquire before evaluating the condition expression. If the condition expression is false the thread atomically suspends itself on the condition variable and releases the mutex, so that other threads can change the shared data. When a cooperating thread changes this data, it can notify the condition variable, which atomically resumes a thread that had previously suspended on the condition variable and acquires its mutex again.

Connection   A full association that is used by peers to exchange data between endpoints of a network application.

Contention Scope   The domain in which a thread competes for resources (such as CPU time). See *Process Scope* and *System Scope*.

Cooperative Cancelation A thread cancelation mechanism implemented in ACE whereby the canceling thread requests one or more threads to cancel themselves. The threads are expected to honor the request at a convenient point, but are not forced to.

CORBA The Common Object Request Broker Architecture (CORBA), a distributed object computing middleware standard defined by the Object Management Group (OMG).

Critical Section Code that should not execute concurrently in an object or subsystem can be synchronized by a critical section. A critical section is a sequence of instructions that obeys the following invariant: while one thread or process is executing in the critical section, no other thread or process can execute in the critical section.

Daemon A server process that runs continuously in the background performing various services on behalf of clients.

Data and Instruction Caches Special high-speed memory collocated with a CPU that can improve overall system performance.

Data-Mode Socket See Socket.

Datagram A self-contained, independent message that carries sufficient information to be routed from a source host to a destination host without relying on earlier exchanges between the source and destination host or the network.

Deadlock A deadlock is a concurrency hazard that occurs when multiple threads attempt to acquire multiple locks and become blocked indefinitely in a circular wait state.

Deferred Cancelation A thread cancelation mechanism whereby the cancelation is deferred until the to-be cancelled thread asks for any pending cancelation to be carried out.

Demarshaling The conversion of a *marshaled* message to a host-specific format from a host-independent format.

Demultiplexing A mechanism that routes incoming data from an input port to its intended receivers. There's a 1:N relationship between input port and receivers. Demultiplexing is commonly applied to incoming events and data streams. The reverse operation is known as multiplexing.

Design Pattern A design pattern provides a scheme for refining components of a software system or the relationships between them. It describes a commonly-recurring structure of communicating components that solves a general design problem within a particular context.

Distribution   The activities associated with placing an object into a different process or host than the clients that access it. Distribution is often applied to improve fault tolerance or to access remote resources (compare with *Collocation*).

Distribution Middleware   This layer of middleware automates common network programming tasks, such as connection and memory management, marshaling and demarshaling, end-point and request demultiplexing, synchronization, and multithreading, so that developers can program distributed applications much like *stand-alone applications*, that is, by invoking operations on target objects without concern for their location, language, OS, or hardware.

Domain   Denotes concepts, knowledge and other items that are related to a particular problem area. Often used in "application domain" to denote the problem area addressed by an application. On the Internet, a domain is a logical addressing entity, such as uci.edu or riverace.com.

Domain Analysis   An inductive, feedback-driven process that examines an application domain systematically to identify its core challenges and design dimensions in order to map them onto effective solution techniques.

Domain-Crossing Penalty   A performance cost incurred when system function calls cross from user-space to kernel-space. In addition to any interruption involved in changing to a privileged access mode, I/O calls must often copy data to and from user-space memory, adding to the delay.

Domain-specific Middleware Services   This layer of middleware defines services tailored to the requirements of particular domains, such as telecommunications or e-commerce. Domain-specific middleware services target specific vertical markets rather than the more broadly reusable services provided by underlying middleware layers.

Double-Checked Locking Optimization Pattern   A design pattern that reduces contention and synchronization overhead whenever critical sections of code must acquire locks in a thread-safe manner just once during program execution.

Dynamic Binding   A mechanism that defers the association of an operation name (a message) to the corresponding code (a method) until run time. Used to implement polymorphism in object-oriented languages.

Endpoint   The termination point of a connection.

Escape Hatch A provision to allow use of a system feature in ways unforeseen by its designers.

Event A message that conveys the occurrence of a significant activity, together with any data associated with the activity.

Event Loop A program structure that continuously waits for and processes events.

Exception Safe A component is exception safe if an exception raised in the component or propagated from a component called by the component does not cause resource leaks or an unstable state.

Factory A method or function that creates and assembles the resources needed to instantiate and initialize an object or component instance.

Flow Control A networking protocol mechanism that prevents a fast sender from overrunning the buffering and computing resources of a slow receiver.

Framework See *Object-Oriented Framework*.

Gather-Write An output operation that transmits the contents of multiple non-contiguous data buffers in a single operation.

Generative Programming A programming technique focusing on designing and implementing software components that can be combined to generate specialized and highly optimized systems that fulfill specific requirements.

Generic Programming A programming technique that unites design patterns and C++ parameterized types to enable developers to achieve expressive, flexible, efficient, and highly reusable code.

Half-Sync/Half-Async Pattern An architectural pattern that decouples asynchronous and synchronous processing in concurrent systems, to simplify programming without reducing performance unduly. This pattern introduces two intercommunicating layers, one for asynchronous and one for synchronous service processing. A queueing layer mediates communication between services in the asynchronous and synchronous layers.

Handle A handle identifies resources that are managed by an operating system kernel. These resources commonly include, among others, network connections, open files, timers, and synchronization objects.

Host An addressable computer attached to a network.

Host Infrastructure Middleware	This layer of middleware encapsulates concurrency and IPC mechanisms available on hosts to create OO network programming capabilities that eliminate many tedious, error-prone, and non-portable aspects associated with developing networked applications via native OS APIs, such as Sockets or Pthreads.
Hot Spot	A (usually small) section of code that is executed frequently.
Idiom	An idiom is a low-level pattern specific to a programming language. An idiom describes how to implement particular aspects of components or the relationships between them using the features of the given language.
Inherent Complexity	Complexity that arises from fundamental properties of a domain that complicate application development (see Accidental Complexity).
Inheritance	A feature of object-oriented languages that allows new classes to be derived from existing ones. Inheritance defines implementation reuse, a subtype relationship, or both. Depending on the programming language, single or multiple inheritance is possible.
Inlining	A compile-time optimization technique that replaces a call to a function or method with the actual code body of that function or method. Inlining long function/method bodies can lead to code "bloat," with negative effects on storage consumption and paging.
Interface	A publicly accessible portion of a class, component, or subsystem.
Internet	A worldwide "network of networks" that is based on the Internet Protocol (IP). Widely considered to be the most important human invention since fire and MTV.
Internet Protocol (IP)	A network layer protocol that performs "best-effort" segmentation, reassembly, and routing of packets.
Interprocess Communication (IPC)	Communication between processes residing in separate address spaces. Examples of IPC mechanisms include shared memory, UNIX pipes, message queues, and socket communication.
Intranet	A network of computers within a company or other organization. Such a network may be secured from outside access and provide a platform for company-wide information exchange, cooperative work, and work flow, using Internet technologies for communication.
Jitter	The standard deviation of the latency for a series of operations.

Latency The delay experienced by operations.

Layer A level of abstraction that defines a particular set of services in a hierarchy. Layer$_n$ is a consumer of services at layer$_{n-1}$ and a supplier of services to layer$_{n+1}$.

Leader/ Followers Pattern An architectural pattern that provides an efficient concurrency model where multiple threads take turns sharing a set of event sources in order to detect, demultiplex, dispatch, and process service requests that occur on the event sources.

Least Frequently Used (LFU) A caching strategy in which the entry that was least frequently used is evicted first.

Least Recently Used (LRU) A caching strategy in which the entry that was least recently used is evicted first.

Linearization The process of *marshaling* richly typed data, such as arrays, lists, or graphs, into a linear memory buffer.

Lock A mechanism used to implement some type of a *critical section*. A lock that can be acquired and released serially, such as a static mutex, may be added to a class. If multiple threads attempt to acquire the lock simultaneously, only one thread will succeed and the others will block until the lock is available. Other locking mechanisms, such as semaphores or readers/writer locks, define different synchronization semantics.

Lock-Step A protocol design paradigm that requires a request to be replied to before a subsequent request is issued.

Marshaling The conversion of a set of data from a host-specific format into a host-independent format.

Memory Management Unit (MMU) An MMU protects separate process address spaces from accidental or malicious corruption by other active processes in the system.

Message Messages are used to communicate between objects, threads, or processes. In an object-oriented system the term message is used to describe the selection and activation of an operation or the method of an object. This type of message is synchronous, which means that the sender waits until the receiver finishes the activated operation. Threads and processes often communicate asynchronously, in which the sender continues its execution without waiting for the receiver to reply.

Message Passing An IPC mechanism used to exchange messages between threads or processes (compare with *Shared Memory*).

Middleware A set of layers and components that provides reusable common services and network programming mechanisms. Middleware resides on top of an operating system and its protocol stacks but below the structure and functionality of any particular application.

Monitor Object Pattern A design pattern that synchronizes the execution of concurrent methods to ensure that only one method at a time runs within an object. It also allows an object's methods to schedule their execution sequences cooperatively.

Multicast A networking protocol that allows a sender to transmit messages efficiently to multiple receivers (compare with *Unicast*).

Mutex A mutex is a "mutual exclusion" locking mechanism that ensures only one thread at a time is active concurrently within a critical section in order to prevent race conditions.

Networked Application Architecture An architecture that facilitates the use of software components and resources that can be placed throughout a distributed system and used to execute networked applications.

Nonrecursive Mutex A mutex that must be released before it can be re-acquired by any thread. Compare with *Recursive Mutex*.

Object-Oriented Framework An integrated set of classes that collaborate to provide a reusable software architecture for a family of related applications. In an object-oriented environment a framework consists of abstract and concrete classes. Instantiation of such a framework consists of composing and subclassing from existing classes.

Object Request Broker A middleware layer that allows clients to invoke methods on distributed objects without concern for object location, programming language, operating system platform, networking protocols, or hardware.

One-Way Method Invocation A call to a method that passes parameters to a server object but does not receive any results from the server (compare with *Two-Way Method Invocation*).

Out-of-Band Data Data that is delivered outside of the normal byte stream traffic; also known as urgent data.

Parallelism The ability of an object, component, or system to execute operations that are "physically simultaneous" (compare with *Concurrency*).

Parameterized Type A programming language feature that allows classes to be parameterized by various other types (compare with *Template*).

Passive Connection Establishment
The connection role played by a peer application that accepts a connection from a remote peer (compare with *Active Connection Establishment*).

Passive-Mode Socket
See Socket.

Passive Object
An object that borrows the thread of its caller to execute its methods (compare with *Active Object*).

Pattern
A pattern describes a particular recurring design problem that arises in specific design contexts and presents a well-proven solution for the problem. The solution is specified by describing its constituent participants, their responsibilities and relationships, and the ways in which they collaborate.

Pattern Language
A family of interrelated patterns that define a process for resolving software development problems systematically.

Peer-to-Peer
In a distributed system peers are processes that communicate with each other. In contrast to components in client-server architectures, peers may act as clients, as servers, or as both, and may change these roles dynamically.

Pipes and Filters Pattern
An architectural pattern that provides a structure for systems that process a stream of data.

Platform
The combination of hardware and/or software that a system uses for its implementation. Software platforms include operating systems, libraries, and frameworks. A platform implements a virtual machine with applications running on top of it.

Port Number
A 16-bit number used to identify an endpoint of communication in the TCP protocol.

Priority Inversion
A scheduling hazard that occurs when a lower-priority thread or request blocks the execution of a higher-priority thread or request.

Proactor Pattern
An architectural pattern that allows event-driven applications to efficiently demultiplex and dispatch service requests triggered by the completion of asynchronous operations, to achieve the performance benefits of concurrency without incurring certain of its liabilities.

Process A process provides resources, such as virtual memory, and protection capabilities, such as user/group identifiers and a hardware-protected address space, that can be used by one or more threads in the process. Compared with a thread, however, a process maintains more state information, requires more overhead to spawn, synchronize, and schedule, and often communicates with other processes via message passing or shared memory.

Process-Scope contention A concurrency policy whereby the scope of threading or synchronization contention occurs within a process on a host (compare with *System-Scope Contention*).

Protocol A set of rules that describe how messages are exchanged between communicating peers, as well as the syntax and semantics of these messages.

Protocol Stack A group of hierarchically layered protocols.

Quality of Service (QoS) A collection of policies and mechanisms designed to control and enhance communication properties, such as bandwidth, latency, and jitter.

Race Condition A race condition is a concurrency hazard that can occur when multiple threads simultaneously execute within a critical section that is not properly serialized.

Reactor Pattern An architectural pattern that allows event-driven applications to demultiplex and dispatch service requests that are delivered to an application from one or more clients.

Readers/Writer Lock A lock that allows multiple threads to access a resource concurrently, but allows only one thread at a time to modify the resource and further prevents concurrent access and modifications.

Recursive Mutex A lock that can be reacquired by the thread that owns the mutex without incurring self-deadlock on the thread. Compare with *Nonrecursive Mutex*.

Refactoring An incremental activity that abstracts general-purpose behavior from existing software to enhance the structure and reusability of components and frameworks.

Reify The act of creating a concrete instance of an abstraction. For example, a concrete reactor implementation reifies the Reactor pattern and an object reifies a class.

Ripple Effect The phenomenon of having to making changes necessitated by a previous change's side effects. Picture the ripples emanating from a rock dropped into a calm lake.

Scatter-Read An input operation that stores data into multiple caller-supplied buffers instead of a single contiguous buffer.

Scheduler A mechanism that determines the order in which threads or events are executed.

Scoped Locking Idiom A C++ idiom that ensures a lock is acquired when control enters a scope and released automatically when control leaves the scope, regardless of the return path from the scope.

Semaphore A locking mechanism that maintains a count. As long as the count is greater than zero a thread can acquire the semaphore without blocking. After the count becomes zero, however, threads block on the semaphore until its count becomes greater than zero as a result of another thread releasing the semaphore, which increments the count.

Serialization A mechanism for ensuring that only one thread at a time executes within a critical section in order to prevent race conditions.

Service In the context of network programming, a service can either be (1) a well-defined capability offered by a server, such as the ECHO service provided by the Inetd super-server, (2) a collection of capabilities offered by a server daemon, such as the INETD super-server itself, or (3) a collection of server processes that cooperate to achieve a common task, such as a collection of RWHO daemons in a local area network (LAN) subnet that periodically broadcast and receive status information reporting user activities to other hosts.

Shared Library A library that can be shared by multiple processes and linked into and out of a process address space dynamically in order to improve application flexibility and extensibility at run time (also known as a *Dynamically Linked Library*, or DLL).

Shared Memory An operating system mechanism that allows multiple processes on a computer to share a common memory segment (compare with *Message Passing*).

Sleep-Lock A synchronization implementation that waits for a lock to be released by sleeping and allowing other threads to run (compare with *Spin-Lock*).

Smart Pointer A smart pointer is a C++ object that looks and acts like a built-in pointer but can achieve effects, such as caching, persistence, or thread-specific storage access, that built-in pointers don't support.

Socket A family of terms related to network programming. A socket is an endpoint of communication that identifies a particular network address and port number. The Socket API is a set of function calls supported by most operating systems and used by network applications to establish connections and communicate via socket endpoints. A data-mode socket can be used to exchanged data between connected peers. A passive-mode socket is a factory that returns a handle to a connected data-mode socket.

Spin-Lock A synchronization implementation that waits for a lock by executing a tight loop and polling to see if the lock is available on each iteration (compare with *Sleep-Lock*).

Stand-Alone Application Architecture An architecture that requires all of the application's components and resources to be in one computer that does not rely on another to execute the application.

Starvation A scheduling hazard that occurs when one or more threads are continually preempted by higher-priority threads and never execute.

Strategized Locking Pattern A design pattern that parameterizes synchronization mechanisms that protect a component's critical sections from concurrent access.

Synchronization Mechanism A locking mechanism that coordinates the order in which threads execute.

Synchronous I/O A mechanism for sending or receiving data in which an I/O operation is initiated and the caller blocks waiting for the operation to complete.

System A collection of software and/or hardware performing one or several services. A system can be a platform, an application, or both.

System-Scope contention A concurrency policy whereby the scope of threading or synchronization contention occurs between processes on a host (compare with *Process-Scope Contention*).

Template A C++ programming language feature that enables classes and functions to be parameterized by various types, constants, or pointers to functions. A template is often called a generic or parameterized type.

Thread An independent sequence of instructions that executes within an address space that can be shared with other threads. Each thread has its own run-time stack and registers, which enables it to perform synchronous I/O without blocking other threads that are executing concurrently. Compared to processes, threads maintain minimal state information, require relatively little overhead to spawn, synchronize and schedule, and usually communicate with other threads via objects in their process's memory space, rather than shared memory.

Thread-Per-Connection A concurrency model that associates a separate thread with each network connection. This model handles each client that connects with a server in a separate thread for the duration of the connection. It is useful for servers that must support long-duration sessions with multiple clients. It is not useful for clients, such as HTTP 1.0 Web browsers, that associate a single request with each connection, which is effectively a *thread per request* model.

Thread-Per-Request A concurrency model that spawns a new thread for each request. This model is useful for servers that must handle long-duration request events from multiple clients, such as database queries. It is less useful for short-duration requests, due to the overhead of creating a new thread for each request. It can also consume a large number of operating system resources if many clients send requests simultaneously.

Thread Pool A concurrency model that allocates a set of threads that can perform requests simultaneously. This model is a variant of *thread per request* that amortizes thread creation costs by prespawning a pool of threads. It is useful for servers that want to limit the number of operating system resources they consume. Client requests can be executed concurrently until the number of simultaneous requests exceeds the number of threads in the pool. At this point, additional requests must be queued until a thread becomes available.

Thread-Safe Safe from any undesired side effects (*race conditions*, data collisions, etc.) caused by multiple threads executing the same section of code concurrently.

Thread-Safe Interface Pattern A design pattern that minimizes locking overhead and ensures that intracomponent method calls do not incur "self-deadlock" by trying to reacquire a lock that is held by the component already.

Thread-Specific Storage (TSS) Pattern	A design pattern that allows multiple threads to use one "logically global" access point to retrieve an object that is local to a thread, without incurring locking overhead on each object access.
Traits	A type that conveys information used by another class or algorithm to determine policies or implementation details at compile time.
Transmission Control Protocol (TCP)	A connection-oriented transport protocol that exchanges byte streams of data reliably, in order, and unduplicated between a local and remote endpoint.
Transport Layer	The layer in a protocol stack that is responsible for end to end data transfer and connection management.
Transport Layer Interface (TLI)	TLI is a set of function calls provided in System V UNIX and used by network applications to establish connections and communicate via connected transport endpoints.
Type Safe	A property enforced by a programming language's type system to ensure that only valid operations can be invoked upon instances of types.
Unicast	A networking protocol that allows a sender to transmit messages to a single receiver (compare with *Multicast*).
Unicode	A standard for character representation that includes characters for most written languages as well as representations for punctuation, mathematical notations, and other symbols.
Unreliable Transport Protocol	A transport protocol that makes no guarantee concerning transmitted data's disposition; it may never arrive, arrive out of order, or arrive multiple times.
User Datagram Protocol (UDP)	An unreliable, connectionless transport protocol that exchanges datagram messages between local and remote endpoints.
Virtual Machine	An abstraction layer that offers a set of services to higher-level applications or other virtual machines.
Virtual Memory	An operating system mechanism that permits developers to program applications whose address space is larger than the amount of physical memory on the computer.
Weakly Typed	A datum whose declared data type does not fully reflect its intended or purported use.
Wrapper Facade	One or more classes that encapsulate functions and data within a type safe OO interface.

Zombie A process that's exited, but which still occupies a process table slot. A zombie remains in this state until a parent process obtains its exit status.

Bibliography

[ABLL92]   Thomas E. Anderson, Brian N. Bershad, Edward D. Lazowska, and
            Henry M. Levy. Scheduler Activation: Effective Kernel Support for
            the User-Level Management of Parallelism. *ACM Transactions on
            Computer Systems*, pages 53–79, February 1992.

[AGH00]   Ken Arnold, James Gosling, and David Holmes. *The Java
            Programming Language*. Addison-Wesley, Boston, 2000.

[Ale01]   Andrei Alexandrescu. *Modern C++ Design: Generic Programming and
            Design Patterns Applied*. Addison-Wesley, Boston, 2001.

[AOS⁺00]   Alexander B. Arulanthu, Carlos O'Ryan, Douglas C. Schmidt,
            Michael Kircher, and Jeff Parsons. The Design and Performance of a
            Scalable ORB Architecture for CORBA Asynchronous Messaging. In
            Proceedings of the Middleware 2000 Conference. ACM/IFIP, April
            2000.

[AOSK00]   Alexander B. Arulanthu, Carlos O'Ryan, Douglas C. Schmidt, and
            Michael Kircher. Applying C++, Patterns, and Components to
            Develop an IDL Compiler for CORBA AMI Callbacks. *C++ Report*,
            12(3), March 2000.

[Aus98]   Matt Austern. *Generic Programming and the STL: Using and
            Extending the C++ Standard*. Addison-Wesley, Reading,
            Massachusetts, 1998.

[BA90]   M. Ben-Ari. *Principles of Concurrent and Distributed Programming*.
            Prentice Hall International Series in Computer Science, 1990.

[BC94]   Arindam Banerji and David L. Cohn. Shared Objects and vtbl
            Placement – Revisited. *Journal of C Language and Translation*,
            6(1):44–60, September 1994.

[Bec00]   Kent Beck. *Extreme Programming Explained: Embrace Change.*
            Addison-Wesley, Boston, 2000.

[Bja00]   Bjarne Stroustrup. *The C++ Programming Language, 3rd Edition.*
            Addison-Wesley, Boston, 2000.

[Bla91]   U. Black. *OSI: A Model for Computer Communications Standards.*
            Prentice-Hall, Englewood Cliffs, New Jersey, 1991.

[BMR+96]   Frank Buschmann, Regine Meunier, Hans Rohnert, Peter
            Sommerlad, and Michael Stal. *Pattern-Oriented Software
            Architecture – A System of Patterns.* Wiley and Sons, New York, 1996.

[Boo94]   Grady Booch. *Object Oriented Analysis and Design with Applications
            (2nd Edition).* Benjamin/Cummings, Redwood City, California, 1994.

[Box97]   Donald Box. *Essential COM.* Addison-Wesley, Reading,
            Massachusetts, 1997.

[Bro87]   Frederick P. Brooks. No Silver Bullet: Essence and Accidents of
            Software Engineering. *IEEE Computer*, 20(4):10–19, April 1987.

[But97]   David R. Butenhof. *Programming with POSIX Threads.*
            Addison-Wesley, Reading, Massachusetts, 1997.

[CB01]   G. Coulson and S. Baichoo. Implementing the CORBA GIOP in a
            High-Performance Object Request Broker Environment. *ACM
            Distributed Computing Journal*, 14(2), April 2001.

[CE00]   Krzysztof Czarnecki and Ulrich Eisenecker. *Generative Programming:
            Methods, Tools, and Applications.* Addison-Wesley, Boston, 2000.

[Chr97]   Clayton Christensen. *The Innovator's Dilemma: When New
            Technologies Cause Great Firms to Fail.* Harvard Business School
            Press, Cambridge, Massachusetts, 1997.

[CS92]   Douglas E. Comer and David L. Stevens. *Internetworking with
            TCP/IP Vol III: Client – Server Programming and Applications.*
            Prentice Hall, Englewood Cliffs, NJ, 1992.

[DC90]   Stephen E. Deering and David R. Cheriton. Multicast routing in
            datagram internetworks and extended LANs. *ACM Transactions on
            Computer Systems*, 8(2):85–110, May 1990.

[Dim01]   Dimitri van Heesch. Doxygen. http://www.doxygen.org, 2001.

[EKB+92]   J.R. Eykholt, S.R. Kleiman, S. Barton, R. Faulkner, A Shivalingiah,
            M. Smith, D. Stein, J. Voll, M. Weeks, and D. Williams. Beyond
            Multiprocessing... Multithreading the SunOS Kernel. In *Proceedings
            of the Summer USENIX Conference*, San Antonio, Texas, June 1992.

[FBB+99]   Martin Fowler, Kent Beck, John Brant, William Opdyke, and Don
             Roberts. *Refactoring - Improving the Design of Existing Code.*
             Addison-Wesley, Reading, Massachusetts, 1999.

[FJS99a]   Mohamed Fayad, Ralph Johnson, and Douglas C. Schmidt, editors.
             *Building Application Frameworks: Object-Oriented Foundations of
             Framework Design.* Wiley & Sons, New York, 1999.

[FJS99b]   Mohamed Fayad, Ralph Johnson, and Douglas C. Schmidt, editors.
             *Implementing Application Frameworks: Object-Oriented Frameworks
             at Work.* Wiley & Sons, New York, 1999.

[Fow97]   Martin Fowler. *Analysis Patterns.* Addison-Wesley, Reading,
             Massachusetts, 1997.

[FS97]   Mohamed E. Fayad and Douglas C. Schmidt. Object-Oriented
             Application Frameworks. *Communications of the ACM*, 40(10),
             October 1997.

[Gal95]   Bill Gallmeister. *POSIX.4 Programming for the Real World.* O'Reilly,
             Sebastopol, California, 1995.

[GHJV95]   Erich Gamma, Richard Helm, Ralph Johnson, and John Vlissides.
             Design Patterns: Elements of Reusable Object-Oriented Software.
             Addison-Wesley, Reading, Massachusetts, 1995.

[Gro]   DOC Group. ACE Success Stories.
             http://www.cs.wustl.edu/~schmidt/ACE-users.html.

[GS99]   Aniruddha Gokhale and Douglas C. Schmidt. Optimizing a CORBA
             IIOP Protocol Engine for Minimal Footprint Multimedia Systems.
             *Journal on Selected Areas in Communications special issue on Service
             Enabling Platforms for Networked Multimedia Systems*, 17(9),
             September 1999.

[HJS]   Stephen D. Huston, James C.E. Johnson, and Umar Syyid. *The ACE
             Programmer's Guide.* Addison-Wesley, Boston (forthcoming).

[HLS97]   Timothy H. Harrison, David L. Levine, and Douglas C. Schmidt. The
             Design and Performance of a Real-time CORBA Event Service. In
             Proceedings of OOPSLA '97, pages 184–199, Atlanta, GA, October
             1997. ACM.

[HP91]   Norman C. Hutchinson and Larry L. Peterson. The *x*-kernel: An
             Architecture for Implementing Network Protocols. *IEEE Transactions
             on Software Engineering*, 17(1):64–76, January 1991.

[HS99]   James Hu and Douglas C. Schmidt. JAWS: A Framework for High
              Performance Web Servers. In Mohamed Fayad and Ralph Johnson,
              editors, *Domain-Specific Application Frameworks: Frameworks
              Experience by Industry*. Wiley & Sons, New York, 1999.

[HV99]   Michi Henning and Steve Vinoski. *Advanced CORBA Programming
              With C++*. Addison-Wesley, Reading, Massachusetts, 1999.

[IEE96]   IEEE. *Threads Extension for Portable Operating Systems (Draft 10)*,
              February 1996.

[JBR99]   Ivar Jacobson, Grady Booch, and James Rumbaugh. *Unified
              Software Development Process*. Addison-Wesley Object Technology
              Series. Addison-Wesley, Reading, Massachusetts, 1999.

[JM98]   Bruce Jacob and Trevor Mudge. Virtual Memory: Issues of
              Implementation. *IEEE Computer*, 31(6):33–43, June 1998.

[JO99]   Anthony Jones and Jim Ohlund. *Network Programming for Microsoft
              Windows*. MS Press, 1999.

[Joh97]   Ralph Johnson. Frameworks = Patterns + Components.
              Communications of the ACM, 40(10), October 1997.

[Jor91]   David Jordan. Instantiation of C++ Objects in Shared Memory.
              Journal of Object-Oriented Programming, March-April 1991.

[Jos99]   Nicolai Josuttis. *The C++ Standard Library: A Tutorial and
              Reference*. Addison-Wesley, Reading, Massachusetts, 1999.

[Kha92]   Khanna, S., *et al.* Realtime Scheduling in SunOS 5.0. In
              Proceedings of the USENIX Winter Conference, pages 375–390.
              USENIX Association, 1992.

[Kic97]   Gregor Kiczales. Aspect-Oriented Programming. In *Proceedings of
              the 11th European Conference on Object-Oriented Programming*, June
              1997.

[Koe88]   Andrew Koenig. *C Traps and Pitfalls*. Addison-Wesley, 1988.

[Kof93]   Thomas Kofler. Robust iterators for ET++. *Structured Programming*,
              14(2):62–85, 1993.

[KSS96]   Steve Kleiman, Devang Shah, and Bart Smaalders. *Programming
              with Threads*. Prentice Hall, Upper Saddle River, NJ, 1996.

[Lac98]   Ralph Lachenmaier. Open Systems Architecture Puts Six Bombs on
              Target. http://www.cs.wustl.edu/~schmidt/TAO-boeing.html,
              December 1998.

[Lea88]   Doug Lea. libg++, the GNU C++ Library. In *Proceedings of the 1ˢᵗ C++ Conference*, pages 243–256, Denver, CO, October 1988. USENIX.

[Lea99]   Doug Lea. *Concurrent Java: Design Principles and Patterns, Second Edition.* Addison-Wesley, Reading, Massachusetts, 1999.

[Lew95]   Bil Lewis. *Threads Primer: A Guide to Multithreaded Programming.* Prentice-Hall, Englewood Cliffs, NJ, 1995.

[LGS00]   David L. Levine, Christopher D. Gill, and Douglas C. Schmidt. Object Lifetime Manager – A Complementary Pattern for Controlling Object Creation and Destruction. *C++ Report*, 12(1), January 2000.

[Mar64]   Herbert Marcuse. *One Dimensional Man: Studies in Ideology of Advanced Industrial Society.* Beacon Press, Boston, 1964.

[MBKQ96]   Marshall Kirk McKusick, Keith Bostic, Michael J. Karels, and John S. Quarterman. *The Design and Implementation of the 4.4BSD Operating System.* Addison Wesley, Reading, Massachusetts, 1996.

[Mey96]   Scott Meyers. *More Effective C++.* Addison-Wesley, Reading, Massachusetts, 1996.

[Mey97]   Bertrand Meyer. *Object-Oriented Software Construction, Second Edition.* Prentice Hall, Englewood Cliffs, NJ, 1997.

[Moo91]   Geoffrey Moore. *Crossing the Chasm: Marketing and Selling High-Tech Products to Mainstream Customers.* HarperCollins, New York, 1991.

[MSKS00]   Sumedh Mungee, Nagarajan Surendran, Yamuna Krishnamurthy, and Douglas C. Schmidt. The Design and Performance of a CORBA Audio/Video Streaming Service. In Mahbubur Syed, editor, *Design and Management of Multimedia Information Systems: Opportunities and Challenges.* Idea Group Publishing, Hershey, PA, 2000.

[NGSY00]   Balachandran Natarajan, Aniruddha Gokhale, Douglas C. Schmidt, and Shalini Yajnik. Applying Patterns to Improve the Performance of Fault-Tolerant CORBA. In *Proceedings of the 7ᵗʰ International Conference on High Performance Computing (HiPC 2000)*, Bangalore, India, December 2000. ACM/IEEE.

[NL91]   Bill Nitzberg and Virginia Lo. Distributed Shared Memory: A Survey of Issues and Algorithms. *IEEE Computer*, pages 52–60, August 1991.

[NW01]   James Noble and Charles Weir. *Small Memory Software: Patterns for Systems with Limited Memory.* Addison-Wesley, Boston, 2001.

[Obj01]   Object Management Group. *The Common Object Request Broker: Architecture and Specification*, 2.5 edition, September 2001.

[O'R98]   Tim O'Reilly. The Open-Source Revolution. *Release 1.0*, November 1998. http://www.oreilly.com/catalog/opensources/.

[OSLN99] Carlos O'Ryan, Douglas C. Schmidt, David Levine, and Russell Noseworthy. Applying a Scalable CORBA Events Service to Large-scale Distributed Interactive Simulations. In *Proceedings of the 5th Workshop on Object-oriented Real-time Dependable Systems*, Montery, CA, November 1999. IEEE.

[Par72]   David L. Parnas. On the Criteria To Be Used in Decomposing Systems into Modules. *Communications of the ACM*, 15(12), December 1972.

[POS95]   Information Technology – Portable Operating System Interface (POSIX) – Part 1: System Application: Program Interface (API) [C Language], 1995.

[POS^{+}00] Irfan Pyarali, Carlos O'Ryan, Douglas C. Schmidt, Nanbor Wang, Vishal Kachroo, and Aniruddha Gokhale. Using Principle Patterns to Optimize Real-time ORBs. *Concurrency Magazine*, 8(1), 2000.

[PS90]   Adam Porter and Richard Selby. Empirically Guided Software Development Using Metric-Based Classification Trees. *IEEE Software*, March 1990.

[PTM97]   Jelica Protic, Milo Tomaevic, and Veljko Milutinovic. *Distributed Shared Memory Concepts and Systems*. IEEE Computer Society Press, 1997.

[Rag93]   Steve Rago. *UNIX System V Network Programming*. Addison-Wesley, Reading, Massachusetts, 1993.

[Ray01]   Eric Raymond. *The Cathedral and the Bazaar: Musings on Linux and Open Source by an Accidental Revolutionary*. O'Reilly, February 2001. http://www.oreilly.com/catalog/cathbazpaper/.

[Ric97]   Jeffrey Richter. *Advanced Windows, Third Edition*. Microsoft Press, Redmond, WA, 1997.

[RJB98]   James Rumbaugh, Ivar Jacobson, and Grady Booch. *The Unified Modeling Language Reference Manual*. Addison-Wesley Object Technology Series. Addison-Wesley, Reading, Massachusetts, 1998.

[SBS93]   Douglas C. Schmidt, Donald F. Box, and Tatsuya Suda. ADAPTIVE: A Dynamically Assembled Protocol Transformation, Integration, and eValuation Environment. *Journal of Concurrency: Practice and Experience*, 5(4):269–286, June 1993.

[SC00]   Douglas C. Schmidt and Chris Cleeland. Applying a Pattern
           Language to Develop Extensible ORB Middleware. In Linda Rising,
           editor, *Design Patterns in Communications*. Cambridge University
           Press, 2000.

[Sch90]   Douglas C. Schmidt. GPERF: A Perfect Hash Function Generator. In
           Proceedings of the 2nd C++ Conference, pages 87–102, San Francisco,
           California, April 1990. USENIX.

[Sch94]   Curt Schimmel. *UNIX Systems for Modern Architectures: Symmetric
           Multiprocessing and Caching for Kernel Programmers*.
           Addison-Wesley, Reading, Massachusetts, 1994.

[Sch00]   Douglas C. Schmidt. Applying a Pattern Language to Develop
           Application-level Gateways. In Linda Rising, editor, *Design Patterns
           in Communications*. Cambridge University Press, 2000.

[SH]   Douglas C. Schmidt and Stephen D. Huston. *C++ Network
           Programming, Volume 2: Systematic Reuse with ACE and
           Frameworks*. Addison-Wesley, Boston (forthcoming).

[SKKK00]   Douglas C. Schmidt, Vishal Kachroo, Yamuna Krishnamurthy, and
           Fred Kuhns. Applying QoS-enabled Distributed Object Computing
           Middleware to Next-generation Distributed Applications. *IEEE
           Communications Magazine*, 38(10):112–123, October 2000.

[SLM98]   Douglas C. Schmidt, David L. Levine, and Sumedh Mungee. The
           Design and Performance of Real-Time Object Request Brokers.
           Computer Communications, 21(4):294–324, April 1998.

[SMFGG01] Douglas C. Schmidt, Sumedh Mungee, Sergio Flores-Gaitan, and
           Aniruddha Gokhale. Software Architectures for Reducing Priority
           Inversion and Non-determinism in Real-time Object Request
           Brokers. *Journal of Real-time Systems, special issue on Real-time
           Computing in the Age of the Web and the Internet*, 21(2), 2001.

[Sol98]   David A. Solomon. *Inside Windows NT, 2nd Ed.* Microsoft Press,
           Redmond, Washington, 2nd edition, 1998.

[SP01]   Douglas C. Schmidt and Adam Porter. Leveraging Open-Source
           Communities to Improve the Quality and Performance of
           Open-Source Software. In *First Workshop on Open-Source Software
           Engineering, 23rd International Conference on Software Engineering*,
           May 2001.

[SS93]   Douglas C. Schmidt and Tatsuya Suda. Transport System
           Architecture Services for High-Performance Communications
           Systems. *IEEE Journal on Selected Areas in Communication*,
           11(4):489–506, May 1993.

[SS94]   Douglas C. Schmidt and Tatsuya Suda. An Object-Oriented
            Framework for Dynamically Configuring Extensible Distributed
            Communication Systems. *IEE/BCS Distributed Systems Engineering
            Journal (Special Issue on Configurable Distributed Systems)*,
            2:280–293, December 1994.

[SS95]   Douglas C. Schmidt and Tatsuya Suda. Measuring the Performance
            of Parallel Message-based Process Architectures. In *Proceedings of
            the Conference on Computer Communications (INFOCOM)*, pages
            624–633, Boston, April 1995. IEEE.

[SS01]   Richard E. Schantz and Douglas C. Schmidt. Middleware for
            Distributed Systems: Evolving the Common Structure for
            Network-centric Applications. In John Marciniak and George
            Telecki, editors, *Encyclopedia of Software Engineering*. Wiley & Sons,
            New York, 2001.

[SSRB00]   Douglas C. Schmidt, Michael Stal, Hans Rohnert, and Frank
            Buschmann. *Pattern-Oriented Software Architecture: Patterns for
            Concurrent and Networked Objects, Volume 2*. Wiley & Sons, New
            York, 2000.

[Ste92]   W. Richard Stevens. *Advanced Programming in the UNIX
            Environment*. Addison-Wesley, Reading, Massachusetts, 1992.

[Ste93]   W. Richard Stevens. *TCP/IP Illustrated, Volume 1*. Addison-Wesley,
            Reading, Massachusetts, 1993.

[Ste96]   W. Richard Stevens. *TCP/IP Illustrated, Volume 3*. Addison-Wesley,
            Reading, Massachusetts, 1996.

[Ste98]   W. Richard Stevens. *UNIX Network Programming, Volume 1:
            Networking APIs: Sockets and XTI, Second Edition*. Prentice-Hall,
            Englewood Cliffs, NJ, 1998.

[Ste99]   W. Richard Stevens. *UNIX Network Programming, Volume 2:
            Interprocess Communications, Second Edition*. Prentice-Hall,
            Englewood Cliffs, NJ, 1999.

[Sun98]   Sun Microsystems, Inc. *Java Remote Method Invocation Specification
            (RMI)*, October 1998.

[Szy98]   Clemens Szyperski. *Component Software — Beyond Object-Oriented
            Programming*. Addison-Wesley, Reading, Massachusetts, 1998.

[Tan96]   Andrew S. Tanenbaum. *Computer Networks*. Prentice-Hall, Upper
            Saddle River, New Jersey, 3rd edition, 1996.

[wKS00]   Martin Fowler with Kendall Scott. *UML Distilled - A Brief Guide to the Standard Object Modeling Language (2nd Edition)*. Addison-Wesley, Boston, 2000.

[Woo97]   Bobby Woolf. The Null Object Pattern. In Robert Martin, Frank Buschmann, and Dirk Riehle, editors, *Pattern Languages of Program Design*. Addison-Wesley, Reading, Massachusetts, 1997.

Index

The C++ In-Depth Series

Bjarne Stroustrup, Series Editor

Modern C++ Design
Generic Programming and Design
Patterns Applied
By Andrei Alexandrescu
0201704315
Paperback
352 pages
© 2001

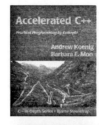

Accelerated C++
Practical Programming by Example
By Andrew Koenig and
Barbara E. Moo
020170353X
Paperback
352 pages
© 2000

Essential C++
By Stanley B. Lippman
0201485184
Paperback
304 pages
© 2000

C++ Network Programming, Volume 1
Mastering Complexity with ACE and
Patterns
By Douglas C. Schmidt and
Stephen D. Huston
0201604647
Paperback
336 pages
© 2002

The Boost Graph Library
User Guide and Reference Manual
By Jeremy G. Siek, Lie-Quan Lee, and
Andrew Lumsdaine
0201729148
Paperback
352 pages
© 2002

Exceptional C++
47 Engineering Puzzles, Programming
Problems, and Solutions
By Herb Sutter
0201615622
Paperback
240 pages
© 2000

More Exceptional C++
40 New Engineering Puzzles,
Programming Problems, and Solutions
By Herb Sutter
020170434X
Paperback
304 pages
© 2002

C++ Network Programming, Volume 2
Systematic Reuse with ACE and
Frameworks
By Douglas C. Schmidt and
Stephen D. Huston
0201795256
Paperback
384 pages
© 2003

Applied C++
Practical Techniques for
Building Better Software
By Philip Romanik and Amy Muntz
0321108949
Paperback
352 pages
© 2003

Exceptional C++ Style
40 New Engineering Puzzles, Programming
Problems, and Solutions
By Herb Sutter
0201760428
Paperback
352 pages
© 2005

Also Available

The C++ Programming Language, Special Edition
By Bjarne Stroustrup
0201700735
Hardcover | 1,040 pages | © 2000

Written by the creator of C++, this is the most widely read and most trusted book on C++.

Register
Your Book

at www.awprofessional.com/register

You may be eligible to receive:

- Advance notice of forthcoming editions of the book
- Related book recommendations
- Chapter excerpts and supplements of forthcoming titles
- Information about special contests and promotions throughout the year
- Notices and reminders about author appearances, tradeshows, and online chats with special guests

Contact us

If you are interested in writing a book or reviewing manuscripts prior to publication, please write to us at:

Editorial Department
Addison-Wesley Professional
75 Arlington Street, Suite 300
Boston, MA 02116 USA
Email: AWPro@aw.com

Visit us on the Web: http://www.awprofessional.com